Aharon Oppenheimer
Rabbi Judah ha-Nasi

Aharon Oppenheimer

Rabbi Judah ha-Nasi

Statesman, Reformer,
and Redactor of the Mishnah

Mohr Siebeck

Aharon Oppenheimer, born 1940; 1993–2000 editor of "Zion – a quarterly for research in Jewish history"; 1996–2010 Sir Isaac Wolfson Professor of Jewish Studies at Tel Aviv University; currently Professor emeritus of Jewish History at Tel Aviv University.

The original work was published by the Zalman Shazar Center as part of the Biographical Series: Outstanding Minds and Creative Personalities in Jewish History.

ISBN 978-3-16-150685-7

Die Deutsche Nationalbibliothek lists this publication in the Deutsche Nationalbibliographie; detailed bibliographic data are available on the Internet at *http://dnb.dnb.de*.

© 2017 by Mohr Siebeck Tübingen, Germany. www.mohr.de

The book was typeset by Martin Fischer in Tübingen, printed by Gulde Druck in Tübingen and bound by Buchbinderei Nädele in Nehren.

Printed in Germany.

To my children, Yael and Tzachi
and my grand children
Yoav, Michael and Amitai

Preface

Rabbi Judah haNasi headed the independent Jewish leadership institutions at the turn of the second and third centuries CE. He conducted the affairs of the patriarchate with a high hand, was renowned for his learning and behaved like a kind of anointed king. He was also incredibly rich, a consummate politician, and close to the Roman authorities. He made *taqqanot*/corrective rulings, in the light of circumstances, and tried to cancel mitzvot/commandments, which entailed hardship for the Jews of his time, such as the regulations about *shemitah*/not using the land in the sabbatical year, and he was ahead of his times in his humane and liberal decisions. Rabbi Judah haNasi completed the redaction of the Mishnah, giving the Jewish people the work that is second in importance only to the Torah; although by so doing he put a brake on the development of the oral law. This book will attempt to present his character and his life, and examine the significance of his work in his generation and in succeeding ones.

This book first appeared in Hebrew in 2007 in a popular edition without footnotes or indices, as part of a series of monographs on famous Jewish writers and thinkers published by the Zalman Shazar Centre for Jewish History. I would like to thank the executive director Zvi Yekutiel, who agreed to the publication of the book as a scientific edition in English, as well as the editors of the Hebrew se-

ries, Professor Aviezer Ravitski, followed by Professor Anita
Shapira. I am indebted to the publishers Mohr Siebeck in
Tübingen who invited me to publish the present English
edition. I thank the editorial assistants Dr Claus-Jürgen
Thornton and Mr Klaus Hermannstädter. I thank Dr
Susan Weingarten, who translated and edited the book.
I am extremely grateful to Maʿayan Avineri-Rebhun, the
director of publishing at the Shazar Centre, and to Reu-
ven Sofer, who drew the maps with an experienced hand.
I thank Dr Ronit Porat who prepared the index quickly,
accurately and with erudition. And last but not least, my
wife Nili, who ensures that nothing leaves my desk without her expert scrutiny and helpful advice – blessed shall
she be above women.

Tel Aviv University, March 2017   Aharon Oppenheimer

Table of Contents

Abbreviations

ANRW II	*Aufstieg und Niedergang der römischen Welt,* II: *Principat* (eds. H. Temporini & W. Haase; Berlin & New York, 1974 ff.)
Asufot	*Asufot: Annual for Jewish Studies*
BT	Babylonian Talmud
CAH	*The Cambridge Ancient History* (Cambridge, 1.1924 ff.)
Cathedra	*Cathedra: A Quarterly for the History of Eretz Israel and Its Yishuv*
CCSL	Corpus Christianorum. Series Latina
CII	J.-B. Frey, *Corpus Inscriptionum Iudaicarum* (2 vols.; Rome, 1936–52)
GLAJJ	M. Stern, *Greek and Latin Authors on Jews and Judaism,* 3 vols. (Jerusalem, 1974–84)
HUCA	*Hebrew Union College Annual*
JJS	*Journal of Jewish Studies*
JQR	*Jewish Quarterly Review*
JSJ	*Journal for the Study of Judaism in the Persian, Hellenistic and Roman Period*
JT	Jerusalem Talmud
LEŠONENU	*LEŠONENU: A Journal for the Study of the Hebrew Language and Cognate Subjects*
M	Mishnah
MGWJ	*Monatsschrift für Geschichte und Wissenschaft des Judentums*
MWJ	*Magazin für die Wissenschaft des Judentums*
PAAJR	*Proceedings of the American Academy for Jewish Research*
PG	J. P. Migne, *Patrologiae Cursus Completus, series Graeca*

PL	J. P. Migne, *Patrologiae Cursus Completus, series Latina*
REJ	*Revue des études juives*
SHA	Scriptores Historiae Augustae
Sidra	*Sidra: A Journal for the Study of Rabbinic Literature*
Tarbiz	*Tarbiz: A Quarterly for Jewish Studies*
Tos.	Tosefta
Zion	*Zion: A Quarterly for Research in Jewish History* (The Historical Society of Israel)

Introduction

Rabbi Judah haNasi's patriarchate, when he headed the independent Jewish leadership institutions (around 175–220 CE), was a golden age for Jewish life in Palestine. All the time he was patriarch there were good relations with the Roman authorities, the economic situation was excellent, and Jewish society was cohesive. The leadership institutions set the pattern of life in the Land of Israel, and even had a certain degree of hegemony over the Diaspora. Together with these more material achievements, there was a new momentum in intellectual creativity, centering on the final redaction of the Mishnah. Rabbi Judah haNasi was the driving force in all these processes: he succeeded in his approaches to the Roman authorities and they accepted him; and he stabilised the economy and contributed to its normalisation by a series of rulings. It was he who consolidated Jewish society and brought it under his control – by approaching both the Jewish city elites as well as the ʿammei haʾaretz who were ignorant of Torah and who had been rejected by the leadership institutions before his time. His greatest project, which has ensured him a lasting memorial in the consciousness of generations of Jews, is the final redaction of the Mishnah. The Mishnah of Rabbi Judah haNasi formed the basis for the Jerusalem Talmud, i.e. the Talmud of the Land of Israel, as well as the Babylonian Talmud, which has beeen the source of Halakha throughout the generations up to our own time. But the political, economic and social aspects of his leadership are scarcely less important than this project, both for his own generation, and for those to come.

In the Talmudic sources, Rabbi Judah haNasi is called simply 'Rabbi,' or 'our Holy Rabbi.' The title 'Rabbi' denotes him as *the* rabbi and patriarch, a sage and leader for whom it is unnecessary to mention his name and office in order to know who is being spoken of. We should note, however, that in Palestinian sources the title 'Rabbi' without any extras was also applied on a handful of occasions to other leaders of the patriarchal dynasty close to Rabbi's time, after the title had been applied to him. Rabbi is one of the very few people in Jewish history who have received the appellation *qadosh*/holy, which is in fact the title of God himself – the Holy One blessed be He – and is used to denote a man of the highest level, someone who is a crown of perfection and purity, clean of secular matters and especially close to God, sometimes even to the extent that he is said to be an example of *qiddush hashem*/the sanctification of the divine name. The Jerusalem Talmud relates this title to Rabbi's extreme modesty: 'Why was he called "our Holy Rabbi"? Because he never looked at his circumcision all his life.'[1] In other words, his title 'Holy' derives from the fact that he never looked at his genitals.

The main source for the study of the times of Rabbi Judah haNasi is the Talmudic literature: the Mishnah,

---

[1] JT Megillah i, 72b, col. 754 and parallels.

Tosefta, Midrashei Halakha, Jerusalem (Palestinian) Talmud, Babylonian Talmud, Midrashei Aggadah, etc. In this literature there is a spectrum of innumerable *halak-hot*/religious regulations, *'aggadot*/narratives, and sayings attributed to Rabbi, as well as many statements of the rabbis about him. It is the task of the historian to sort out the authentic basis from the rest of this material about him, to look at both the man and his work. The writings of Roman authors and historians can help only a little here. This was good time for the Jewish people, when there were no revolts against the Romans, so that these writers had little interest in Rabbi in particular, or in the Jews of the Palestine of his time in general. Thus the main benefit for the history of the Jews that can be gained from these classical works is a contribution to understanding the general historical context. But even in this respect we have relatively few sources providing information about the Severan period (named after the dynasty of Roman emperors who ruled between 193–235 CE, and called after their founder, Septimius Severus), during which most of Rabbi's activities took place. Most of the evidence of the Church Fathers, the great teachers and writers of ancient Christianity, belongs to the period after Rabbi, and their contribution to research into his character and activities must therefore be limited, especially since they are often apologetic in their relations with Judaism, so that it is even more difficult to extract authentic information from them. However, archaeological finds, such as inscriptions from synagogues, tombstones, and coins; roads and milestones; remains of buildings; and pottery do cast some light on individual matters related to the history of Rabbi Judah haNasi and his period.

The main difficulty in relying on the Talmudic literature in order to extract authentic information from it about Rabbi's times is rooted in the general problematics of the use of Talmudic literature as a historical source. By the very nature of the Talmudic literature, historical data appears there only accidentally. This literature did not have any historiographical aims, but concentrated on religious regulations (Halakha) and didactic theology (Aggadah), intended to draw people to the Torah and its study. The associative and anecdotal character of the Talmudic literature also means that we cannot expect a clear and wide-ranging picture of the historical situation, and certainly not a scientific historical approach, aimed at preserving information for generations to come on 'what really happened.' The Talmudic literature contains pieces of evidence contemporary with Rabbi side by side with anachronistic evidence about him, together with sources which try to solve problems connected with his character and activities historically and philosophically. All this evidence was subject to the work of a later editor, for whom Rabbi's times were already a hazy and distant memory. Even when a statement is attributed to a certain rabbi, there is no certainty that it was really said by him, for the editors allowed themselves a certain measure of freedom and attributed sayings to rabbis who never said them. Thus it is not possible to rely on the names of rabbis as the ultimate tool for dating a statement, which limits the possibility of writing a biography of Rabbi according to the statements attributed to him in the Talmudic literature.

There is a school of scholars which claims that in analysing the activities of the rabbis in the Talmudic literature
precedence is to be given to the literary approach. In this
view, the Talmudic story does not describe a series of historical events, but preserves anecdotes related to isolated
cases. It does not contain coherent connected history, but
descriptions of limited events comprehensible only in their
own context. Moreover, there are different traditions about
some of the events, sometimes contradictory ones, as a result of the fact that those who recorded the traditions gave
a free hand to their imagination to re-create what they had
learned from others. The historian must relate to these
deeds of the rabbis as literature. It is because of this they
have no value for historical research, which by its very nature is supposed to be exact and depend on facts.

Yet another approach, which has developed over the
last few decades, particularly in the United States and in
Europe, sharply criticises the system commonly used in
Israel for extracting historical significance from the Talmudic sources. This approach claims that in order for it to
be possible to rely on the Talmudic literature as a source
for historical research, we must discuss every one of the
pieces of evidence mentioned in it by itself, to go down to
the tiniest detail and to analyse whether it is of historical
significance. On the face of it, this approach is remarkable
for its scientific exactness, and it can be used to shatter
the speculations which characterised the research which
preceded it, which tended to rely on the Talmudic literature as a historical source, or to find in it historic kernels.
However, its weakness lies in the fact that it shuts its eyes

to the picture which can be obtained from looking at the sources as a single whole, a whole which produces a critical mass of material. Thus at the end of the day, this approach tends to produce speculations no less far-fetched and no more well-founded than those they criticise.

At the beginning of this century, Seth Schwartz, an American Jewish scholar of Late Antiquity, put forward a proposal which cancels out almost completely any possibility of relying on the Talmudic literature as a historical source. In his opinion, the rabbis who produced the Talmudic literature were a small and marginal group, without any influence at all on Jewish society at the time of the Mishnah and Talmud. The members of this group engaged in debates only with each other, while the great mass of Jews who lived in Palestine at the time were *de facto* almost pagans. Thus in his view, the rabbis did not represent the people, or its leadership, and the Talmudic literature has nothing to do with reality. Instead of reconstructing Jewish history by examining and analysing the Talmudic sources, as is usual in historical research, Schwartz chooses to build a model based on one or two speculations, each of which he bases on two or three sources. Since his research methods are inductive and not deductive, the reconstruction of Jewish history using his methodology is even more flawed than the methods he sets out to attack.[2]

The search for historical significance and the historical nuclei of sources in the Talmudic literature is widely ac-

---

[2] S. Schwartz, *Imperialism and Jewish Society 200 B.C.E. to 640 C.E.* (Princeton, 2001).

cepted among scholars of the period of the Mishnah and the Talmud, both inside and outside Israel. This method of research has the advantage that it relies on a huge corpus of sources which can be relied on, more or less consistently. When this firm foundation is rejected, more or less reasonably, the alternative will always be in the realms of speculation. In Schwartz' opinion, Jews are a coherent society only if they are ultra-orthodox. But this is not the case, for leaders like Rabbi Judah haNasi gave Jews the opportunity to lead their lives in the spirit of the time without their Judaism suffering. Rabbi's power was nourished not only by his dominant status among the rabbis, but also by his relations with the Romans on the one hand, and the Jewish city elite on the other. His power and status as seen in the sources reflect a realistic and rational situation, and are not the result of the imagination of later rabbis. Even if Schwartz is correct in his theory that a large part of the people had pagan tendencies, the decline in the attractiveness of paganism as a religious belief in the world around them allowed the rabbis to be lenient in matters that were once thought of as *'avodah zarah*/pagan cult, and in this way they stayed in touch with the whole of Jewish society. For example, the patriarchs themselves are mentioned in an inscription included in the mosaic floor of the synagogue at Ḥammat Tiberias, which is dated to the fourth century CE, the period when Rabbi's descendents were active. In the centre of this mosaic is a zodiac and at its centre is Helios, the god of the sun in Greek mythology. A similar mosaic has also been uncovered in a synagogue from the beginning of the fifth century at Zippori/Sepphoris, where Rabbi Judah haNasi lived for some of his life. These finds, as well as various sayings and Halakhot of the rabbis, are evidence that during the second to the fifth centuries the pagan elements in these and other mosaics lost their original pagan meaning, and were included even in synagogues as artistic elements which were accepted at the time. This is hinted at in the Jerusalem Talmud, where it says that Rabbi Yoḥanan, Rabbi's pupil, did not object to people drawing on walls. In an addition to this passage found in the Cairo Genizah, Rabbi Abun did not object to people who made pictures in mosaic.[3] In other words, even if the reality was sometimes somewhat distant from the Halakha, it was not completely cut off from it, and we can certainly not speak of the rabbis as being cut off from the people: the rabbis did not fail to see the needs of the people, nor did the people fail to relate to the words of the rabbis. As in our own time, so in antiquity: not all the people observed all the 613 mitzvot, but in antiquity, unlike our own times, religion was the background of the life of the people, just as nationality is today, and the Jews of Palestine had no leaders other than the rabbis.

Today there is a further approach which denies the leadership of the rabbis of the Mishnah and the Talmud, but if we accept this then we will lose any remnant of historical authenticy in their words.

There is, in fact, an advantage to studying Rabbi's character and work using the Talmudic literature, as opposed to the study of many other historical subjects in this lit-

---

[3] JT Avodah Zarah iii, 42d, col. 1396.

erature. Rabbi himself redacted the Mishnah, and this marked the end of the period of the Tannaim in general, while apparently within a generation (up to the middle of the third century) the Tosefta and the Tannaitic Midrashim were also finally redacted. Thus the evidence in all the sources mentioned is contemporary with Rabbi. The historian is therefore left only to sort out whether these pieces of evidence have historical significance or whether they do not, and are merely to be considered as legendary. This advantage exists to a certain extent also in relation to the Baraitot in the Talmuds, but in spite of the fact that these contain the words of Tannaim, it is possible that these show the hand of a later editor. In contrast, we have to relate to the historical veracity of the Amoraic evidence with far more scepticism the more it relates to the Jews and Palestine in the time of the Tannaim, including Rabbi Judah haNasi. This is even more true of the evidence of the Babylonian Talmud, not to mention the Midrashim, and the anthologies of Midrashim from still later periods. The root of the problematics inherent in using the Babylonian Talmud in order to reconstruct Jewish history in the days of Rabbi is not just that it was written a long time after the events described in it, and far away from the scene of those events, but also that it tends to give a legendary aura to the traditions, as well as literary additions and decorations. There is greater use of fine language and imagination in the Babylonian Talmud than in the Jerusalem Talmud, and in this light there can be no doubt that we should generally prefer the evidence of the Jerusalem Talmud to that of the Babylonian Talmud for historical research in all respects, especially in all that relates to the history of the Jews in their land.

However, this is not axiomatic. Not all the evidence about Palestine in the Babylonian Talmud is necessarily unreliable, nor are its parallels in the Jerusalem Talmud always more reliable. Sometimes it is even the Babylonian Talmud which preserves a tradition which is older and more reliable. Some evidence for this can be seen from the fact that sometimes the same tradition is preserved in both Talmuds, and the text of the two versions is very similar in context and language. If so, then it is possible that some traditions about Palestine were only preserved in the Babylonian Talmud, and there is a possibility that this is historically reliable. There are also cases where there is other evidence from outside the Talmudic literature, which supports the historical reliability of evidence about Palestine, even though this is only extant in the Babylonian Talmud.

When we have a case of evidence that has a definitively political or realistic colouring, there is no reason to doubt its trustworthiness. It is possible to presume that this tradition contains a kernel of history, and to use it to reconstruct the period of Rabbi Judah haNasi, even if it appears only in the Babylonian Talmud or the later Talmudic literature. Even if we include in this evidence motifs which look unreal on the face of it, as happens with many of the events described in the Talmudic literature, the presence of these imaginary elements does not necessarily reduce the historical reliability of other motifs with a realistic colouring included in the same episode or passage. We can certainly learn about the character of Rabbi, his activities and

his time from one part of the Talmudic description, and see
the other part as simply a legendary layer. For example, the
Babylonian Talmud tells us that Rabbi Pinḥas b. Yair, the
ḥasid, the most outstanding of Rabbi's opponents, brought
down fire from heaven in order to keep himself away from
Rabbi's messengers who were coming to make peace with
him. The attribution of this 'miracle' to Rabbi Pinḥas ben
Yair should not cancel out the historical reliability of the
rest of the elements in the description of the episode, such
as Rabbi's desire to renew good relations with Rabbi Pinḥas
b. Yair. In another case, the Babylonian Talmud describes
a tunnel which led from the house of the Roman emperor
'Antoninus' (probably Caracalla) to the house of Rabbi
Judah haNasi (see below, pp. 51–52). Seeing this element
as legendary does not prevent us from acknowledging the
motif underlying this description, which is evidence of
the existence of real connections and mutual recognition
between Rabbi and the Roman authorities.

The best situation for the scholar is when it is possible
to extract historical meaning from Talmudic sources, by
confirming them via independent external sources. As
noted, Roman men of letters and historians do not mention Rabbi Judah haNasi in their writings at all. It seems
that in spite of the special close relations between Rabbi
and the Roman authorities which are recorded in the Talmudic sources, these were not enough to arouse the interest
of Roman historians in the Jewish leader of *Syria-Palaestina*
(the name given by the Romans to the former *provincia
Iudaea,* the Land of Israel, after the suppression of the Bar
Kokhva revolt) which was relatively far from Rome, and

was also not one of the more important Roman provinces. We must stress again that in these sources there is also very little information about the Severan period in general. Thus our knowledge of this period is much less than that which we can obtain about other periods of Roman history. For example, the Roman historian Cassius Dio (about 160–230 CE), who also held important administrative posts, summed up the history of Rome from its beginnings to the year 229 CE in his *Roman History*. But even in this work, which contains the most important and detailed description of all the sources we have about the Bar Kokhva revolt, he provides merely a very sketchy description of the Severan period in which he lived. Herodian (ca. 180–250), a younger contemporary of Cassius Dio, does not relate at all in his *History of the Period after Marcus Aurelius* to *provincia Syria-Palaestina* or to other small provinces. On the other hand, evidence relating to Jews at the time of Rabbi in the *Historia Augusta,* a collection of biographies of Roman emperors and pretenders to the imperial throne from Hadrian to Numerianus (117–284), is extremely problematic, as the historical reliability of this source is lower than that of any other ancient historical writings. However, there is more help available in the evidence of the Roman historians about the Severan urbanisation policies, which also included Palestine, and in the Roman legislation relating to the status of Jews in the cities. This evidence dovetails with the evidence of the Talmudic literature on the *taqqanot*/corrective rulings, made by Rabbi in order to encourage Jewish settlement of Jews in those cities of Palestine with a non-Jewish majority, as well as the evidence on Rabbi's policies related to the distribution of the burden of the taxes which the Romans imposed on those Jews who were members of the city leadership institutions (which afterwards imposed taxes on the rest of the inhabitants of the city).

In the writings of the Church Fathers there are scattered pieces of evidence about Rabbi Judah haNasi. Usually there is no reason to doubt their historical veracity, and they may also dovetail with evidence from the Talmudic literature. The outstanding example of this is the evidence contemporary with Rabbi, that the Roman authorities recognised his authority to deal with capital cases *de facto,* and he was allowed to give death sentences, which was not usual in the provinces, as we shall see below (pp. 61–66).

Of all the archaeological finds dated to the time of the activity of Rabbi Judah haNasi, there is particular significance to the finds unearthed at Beit She'arim and at Zippori/Sepphoris, two places where Rabbi lived during his adult life, and where he acted as *nasi'* and led the Beit haVa'ad (as the leadership of the rabbis is called in the Jerusalem Talmud: it is only in the Babylonian Talmud farther away from the events in time and place that this institution is called the Sanhedrin). In both these places, extensive archaeological excavations have been conducted, and there is still room for more. The excavations have not discovered remains which can be definitively connected to Rabbi himself, and it is doubtful if we can reasonably expect any such remains, but the finds revealed in general which are dated to the years when he was active, can cast light on the context of daily life in which Rabbi worked, as well as on different traditions which are connected to him in the Talmudic literature. For example, Rabbi's burial in Beit She'arim, described in the Talmudic literature, was presumably the main reason for Beit She'arim to become a necropolis, a city of the dead, the most ornate burial ground which has been discovered in Palestine to date, where the Jewish dead were brought for burial from home and even from abroad. However, the particular place of burial of Rabbi himself in the necropolis has not yet been discovered, as we shall see below (pp. 230–231). In a Greek inscription from Qiṣion in eastern Upper Galilee (near present-day Rosh Pina) dated to 197 CE, perhaps from the local synagogue, we can see the gratitude of the Jews towards the Severan emperors. This inscription connects nicely with the spirit of the Talmudic evidence about the close relations between Rabbi and 'Antoninus.' One of the coins discovered in Diocaesarea (the Roman name for Zippori / Sepphoris from the time it became a *polis*, apparently under Hadrian) bears the head of the Emperor Caracalla (Marcus Aurelius Antoninus [198–217]) who is generally identified with the 'Antoninus' who was Rabbi's friend. On the other side of the coin there is a Greek inscription: 'Diocaesarea the holy, autonomous city of refuge, friend and ally of the holy Senate and people of Rome.' The numismatician Ya'akov Meshorer thought mistakenly that this inscription related to the self-governing leadership institutions of the Jews, i.e. Rabbi Judah haNasi and the Beit haVa'ad and recorded their friendship with the Roman senate. However, this is speculation which derives from an inexact translation of the Greek inscription. But the inscription still informs us of the good relations between the Roman authorities and the city leadership of Diocaesarea, where a majority of inhabitants were Jews, and where, as we have noted, the Jewish leadership institutions headed by Rabbi were sited at this time.

It is also appropriate to our study to analyse the impression made by the figure of Rabbi Judah haNasi on the generations which succeeded him. Even if a particular episode in the Babylonian Talmud does not appear to be authentic, very often it still reflects the attitude of the Babylonian Amoraim to Rabbi, how he was perceived in their eyes, and how they wanted future generations to see him.

This book cannot be a biography in the ordinary sense of the word. Every biography has to have two parts: one which describes the course of the life of its subject, and one which describes the work. It is quite clear that the part which describes the course of the life of Rabbi Judah haNasi cannot be like biographies of people from modern times. Rabbi's life one thousand eight hundred years ago is veiled in the mists of time. We do not know his exact date of birth, the year he succeeded to the patriarchy, or the year he died. We know nothing substantial about the way he looked – was he tall or short? fat or thin? handsome or ugly? We have no clear knowledge about his behaviour – was he charming or supercilious? How did he relate to his family? Did he have brothers and sisters? And so on. It is true that there is some information on these questions in the Talmudic sources (for example, they tell us he was tall) but usually this is to be found in the part which appears to us legendary, and which was written many years after he died. However, discussion of the course of any life in a biography, however fascinating, must be secondary to the activity of its subject. This is all the more relevant in a biography like this of Rabbi, in the light of the gaps in the sources. Thus the discussion of the course of Rabbi's life in this book is extremely limited, and it is confined to the first and last chapters. The rest of the chapters provide an analysis of Rabbi's work, and an assessment of his contribution and his influence both in his own generation and in those which followed him. These chapters concentrate on the lengthy period of Rabbi's patriarchate only, and are intended to clarify the working expressions of his leadership in all fields: in his policy; in the economic reforms he instituted; in social life; in the field of religious life, including, of course, his great creation, the Mishnah.

To sum up, this book deals with a list of questions, such as what led to the establishment of close relations and mutual admiration between Rabbi Judah haNasi and the Roman authorities? What was the nature of the links between Rabbi and the rabbis of his time? What was the connection between his economic status and his economic and social outlook? What incited him to rule reformatory *taqqanot?* Which of his *taqqanot* continued the ways of his predecessors, and which of them took a new direction against all the accepted ideas of his time? What were the principles he used in organising the Mishnah? The difficulty in giving incontrovertible answers to most of these questions is rooted in the methodological problems in the use of the sources about Rabbi which are found in the Talmudic literature: in which sources can we find authentic evidence about him or identify any sort of historic kernel? Where can we dovetail evidence from the Talmudic literature with evidence from Roman authors, the Church Fathers, or archaeological finds?

Chapter 1

Rabbi Judah haNasi
and His Place in Public Life

1. The Dates of Rabbi

When did Rabbi Judah haNasi live? A Palestinian midrashic tradition tells us: 'The day Rabbi ʿAqiva died, our Rabbi was born.'[1] Rabbi ʿAqiva was one of the *harugei malkhut*/ the martyrs killed by the Roman authorities during the *gezerot shemad*/ the repressive legislation, which the Romans instituted following the Bar Kokhva revolt, which were in full force between 135/136–138 CE. Rabbi Judah haNasi appears to have succeeded to the patriarchate between the years 170–180 CE, and died in extreme old age around the year 220. According to the Midrash just mentioned, Rabbi Judah haNasi was born on the day Rabbi ʿAqiva was martyred. This is possible chronologically, but it is completely clear that the main intent of the Midrash was to point out that the moment one leader, a leading rabbi and saviour of the people died, then immediately another leader, a leading rabbi and saviour of the people was born, so that the Jewish people is never without a leader.

At any rate, it is significant that Rabbi Judah haNasi was born at or near to the time of the repressive Roman legislation, and was young in the Ushah period, the pe-

---

[1] Genesis Rabbah 58,2 (eds. Theodor & Albeck, p. 619).

riod which was so called after the village of that name in lower Galilee where the leadership institutions recovered from the repressive legislation, following the death of the emperor Hadrian. There are a few traditions which associate Rabbi Judah haNasi in his youth with Ushah: for example, there is evidence in the sources that as a young boy he read *Megillat Esther,* the Scroll of Esther, in front of Rabbi Judah bar Ilaᶜi in Ushah.[2] Rabbi Judah haNasi was educated in the *batei midrash* / study houses, of various important rabbis of the generation, including: Rabbi Meir, Rabbi Shimᶜon b. Yoḥai, Rabbi Judah bar Ilaᶜi, Rabbi Elᶜazar b. Shammuᶜa, Rabbi Yaᶜaqov bar Qursi and Rabbi Joshua b. Qorḥa.[3] In this way, Rabbi Judah haNasi became acquainted with different halakhic schools, absorbed their attitudes, and learned to appreciate them. This certainly contributed a great deal to Rabbi's abilities to carry out his work of redacting the Mishnah, for it meant that he was endowed with the approach and understanding needed to edit the different versions of the Mishnah written by the most important rabbis of Ushah. His varied halakhic education also meant that he related with respect to ideas which were different from his own, whether they were proposed by the rabbis of his own generation, or the rabbis who preceded him (see pp. 206–208 below).

---

[2] Tos. Megillah ii, 8 (ed. Lieberman, p. 350); cf JT Megillah ii, 3b, col. 760; BT Megillah 20a.

[3] On the traditions dealing with Rabbi's studies in the different Batei Midrash, see O. Meir, *Rabbi Yehudah haNasi* (Tel Aviv, 1999, Heb.), pp. 42–44.

As a student of various teachers in the Ushah period, Rabbi Judah haNasi was apparently usually much appreciated, but this was not always the case, as we see from the following incident described in the Jerusalem Talmud:

Rabbi said: I asked and did not find the statement of ben Shammu'a on an androgynous person, and they ganged up [against me] around him.[4]

In other words, Rabbi wanted to learn from Rabbi El'azar b. Shammu'a how he explained the Halakhot relating to an androgynous person, and the other pupils banded together to prevent him learning from him.

We do not know exactly in which year Rabbi became patriarch. However, since it is clear that he came to the height of his power as a leader in the time of the Severan emperors, whose dynasty began in the year 193, the question of exactly in which year he succeeded to the patriarchate is not very important. The year Rabbi died is also uncertain. In general, it was not usual to note details like this in the Talmudic literature about Jewish leaders of the time. There is almost no rabbi about whom we can say exactly when he was born and in which year he died. As for Rabbi Judah haNasi, all that is known is that in the year 219 he was still patriarch. According to the evidence of Rav Sherira Gaon in his letter, in this year Rabbi's pupil Rav returned to Babylonia, and the Talmud gives evidence that it was Rabbi Judah haNasi who gave Rav *semikhah/*

---

[4] JT Yevamot viii, 9d, col. 872; cf more detailed versions in BT Yevamot 84a.

ordination, just before he left Palestine.[5] It is true that the letter of Rav Sherira Gaon was only written in 986/987, but it is considered as a sort of historiographic study in the history of the Mishnah and the Talmud, for it is reasonable to suppose that it relies on earlier sources and traditions which have not reached us.[6] A similar date for the return of Rav to Babylonia is noted in the book *Seder tanna'im ve-amora'im,* which was written in the second half of the ninth century, and is considered the first attempt to write a historical and methodological introduction to the Mishnah and the Talmud.[7]

According to Shemuel Safrai, it is possible that Rabbi Judah haNasi was still alive even later than 219. A Talmudic tradition tells us that after the Romans imposed *aurum coronarium*/ crown tax, on the inhabitants of Tiberias, the Jews of the city turned to Rabbi and demanded that the rabbis should share the burden of the Roman tax with them. But Rabbi Judah haNasi ruled that the rabbis should be exempted from it.[8] In the end, the tax was cancelled. In a papyrus discovered in Egypt, dated to the year 222, the

---

[5] Iggeret Rav Sherira Gaon, ed. Lewin, p. 78; BT Sanhedrin 5a.

[6] On the way the letter was written, see, M. Schlüter, *Auf welche Weise wurde die Mishna geschrieben? Das Antwortschreiben des Rav Sherira Gaon; mit einem Faksimile der Handschrift Berlin Qu. 685 (Or. 160) und des Erstdrucks Konstantinopel 1566* (Tübingen, 1993); I. M. Gafni, 'On Talmudic Historiography in the Epistle of Rav Sherira Ga'on: Between Tradition and Creativity' (Heb.), *Zion* 73 (2008), pp. 271–296; R. Brody, 'The Epistle of Sherira Gaon,' *Rabbinic Texts and the History of Late-Roman Palestine* (eds. M. Goodman & P. Alexander; Oxford/ New York, 2010), pp. 253–264.

[7] Chapter 2 (ed. Grossberg, p. 100).

[8] BT Bava Batra 8a (on this tradition, see below, pp. 75–80).

first year of the reign of Severus Alexander, we see that this Roman emperor exempted local people from the payment of *aurum coronarium* on the occasion of his ascent to the imperial throne.[9] Safrai dovetailed the Talmudic evidence about Tiberias with the archaeological find from Egypt, and claimed that the statement in the Talmud that the tax was cancelled relates to Severus Alexander's exempting the Jews of Palestine from the tax. Thus this would be evidence, in his opinion, that Rabbi Judah haNasi was still patriarch in the year 222.[10] However it is as well to note that this episode as recounted in the Babylonian Talmud includes many legendary elements, and it is doubtful whether we can relate to this cancellation of the tax as an authentic event. It is also difficult to know whether Severus Alexander's cancellation of the tax was the only occasion of the cancellation of this tax in the time of Rabbi Judah haNasi. Whatever the case, since there are only three years between the return of Rav to Babylonia and the year of the imperial edict, it would seem more reasonable to keep to the evidence of Rav Sherira Gaon and to accept that Rabbi Judah haNasi was alive and in office in the year 219 at least, even if not at the later date. In any event, neither of the two pieces of evidence supplies us with incontrovertible evidence about the date of Rabbi's death.

---

[9] Papyrus Fayûm 20, from 24 June 222. See B. P. Grenfell et al., *Fayûm Towns and Their Papyri* (London, 1900), pp. 116–123.

[10] S. Safrai, 'The *Nesi'ut* in the Second and Third Centuries and Its Chronological Problems' (Heb.), *Proceedings of the Sixth World Congress of Jewish Studies,* vol. II (ed. A. Shinan; Jerusalem, 1975), pp. 51–57 (= idem, *In Times of Temple and Mishnah* [Jerusalem, 1994, Heb.], pp. 620–626).

2. Statesman and Reformer

The days of Rabbi Judah haNasi's patriarchate (about 175–220 CE) were a golden age for the Jewish people in their land, at least in comparison with the rest of the period between the destruction of the Second Temple in 70 CE, and the Muslim conquest in 640. The historian can never finally decide the question of what part was played by a leader in shaping history, and what part was played by circumstances, but with Rabbi Judah haNasi we may be certain that he contributed significantly to the survival of the Jews in their land and to the course of their history. This was due in particular to two qualities he was blessed with: his ability as a statesman and politician, and his vision as a reformer. Rabbi Judah haNasi was an outstandingly adept politician and every process he initiated shows his calculation and enterprise. He co-operated with the Roman authorities, and they for their part strengthened his status, both with lands which they gave him as a gift or on loan, and with special conditions which they granted him, such as the *de facto* recognition of his authority to try capital cases, an authority which was not given to leaders in other provinces. Indeed, the political climate of his time was so good that Rabbi even wanted to cancel the fast of *tishᶜa be-ʾav*/ the Ninth of Av, although the Temple had not been rebuilt, but he was forced to withdraw this revolutionary reform because the other rabbis did not agree with him.

Rabbi Judah haNasi was close to those Jews who held office on the city councils, and they – once they saw his wealth and his status in the eyes of the authorities – accepted his leadership and his judgements. He was high-handed in his leadership of the world of the rabbis, and his patriarchate had some of the characteristics of monarchy or even messianism. His responses to the demonstrations of opposition towards himself which arose among the rabbis made clever and manipulative use of the principle of the stick and the carrot: – rejection on the one hand, and encouragement on the other. Rabbi Judah haNasi brought in daring reforms in the fields of religion, economics and society, all in order to achieve normalisation of Jewish everyday life. Thus, for example, in the economic field he wanted to cancel *shemitah*/ the ban on working the land in the seventh, sabbatical year, even though this is an explicit *mitzvah*/ a commandment from the Torah. He instituted a policy of liberalisation in the purchase of lands which the Romans had confiscated from Jews, and gave economic incentives to Jewish settlers in cities where the majority of the population was pagan. In the social sphere, he took up initiatives to strengthen the unity of the people and back up his own status, by associating with the rich as well as the '*ammei ha*'*aretz*/ the people ignorant of Torah. At the same time, he protected the exceptional rights of the rabbis, such as, for example, exemption from paying certain taxes. In spite of his high status and his prowess as a reformer, he knew when to backtrack on exceptionally daring reforms when the other rabbis objected to them. Thus, for example, he gave up his intention to cancel *shemitah* entirely following the negative reaction of Rabbi Pinḥas b. Yair, who was the head of the *ḥasidim*/ pietists and had the charisma of a popular leader.

The most significant pieces of evidence for examining the reforms of Rabbi Judah haNasi are his *taqqanot*. A *taqqanah* is a Halakha which replaces an earlier Halakha, in order to suit the new situation which has been created as a result of changing circumstances. The *taqqanah* creates something which did not exist previously, thus correcting a problem which has arisen or introducing a correction to an existing way of behaving. It should be stressed that the *taqqanot* of Rabbi Judah haNasi did not only relate to the sphere of religion, but also to political conditions and to social and economic life. Changes in circumstances in these fields led to rulings of *taqqanot* instituted to straighten out things which had gone awry: the Aramaic verb *t-q-n* is a translation of the Hebrew *y-sh-r/* to correct or straighten. The repeated trend which is uppermost in Rabbi Judah haNasi's collection of *taqqanot* is the aspiration to normalise Jewish everyday life at all levels. Some elements of Rabbi Judah haNasi's *taqqanot* are continuations of *taqqanot* which were ruled in generations which preceded him, but other parts are completely new and revolutionary in relation to all that was customary before his patriarchate.

A further impulse for the actions of Rabbi Judah haNasi was his aspiration to centralisation. He wanted to concentrate the authority of the leadership in his own hands, and in order to do so he took over the right to grant *semikhah,* in other words, the right to ordain a man to the office and title of a rabbi, and to allow him to join the Beit haVaʿad (literally the 'committee house,' the name given to the rabbinical institution of self-government). A rabbi with *semikhah* was allowed to teach the Halakhot of what is forbidden and permitted, for example in the laws of what is or is not kosher, and to judge cases relating to money regulations and transgressions which demand fines, etc. It is clear that concentrating *semikhah* in the hands of Rabbi Judah haNasi meant that those who wanted *semikhah,* and those who prepared people for *semikhah* were politically dependent on him. Rabbi did not rest there, but even kept an eye on rabbinical pupils during the time they were prepared for *semikhah,* as well as doing away with the right of rabbis to teach out of doors, so that his control would not thereby be weakened. Pupils who were about to get *semikhah* were no longer allowed to serve as trainees, or to begin to operate in some of the areas which were given to those with *semikhah,* such as teaching the Halakhot of what is forbidden and what is permitted. Rabbi Judah haNasi was the only leader in all the period of the Mishnah and the Talmud who controlled the granting of *semikhah* exclusively and totally, and no one except for him was allowed to act or even to give an opinion in this central field, as we shall see in more detail below.

3. Redactor of the Mishnah

A Talmudic statement says: 'From the days of Moses up to Rabbi, we never found Torah and greatness in one place.'[11] Beyond the expression of appreciation for the persona of

---

[11] M Peah i, 1.

Rabbi Judah haNasi, the two people mentioned in this statement are joined together in the rabbinic consciousness not only because of their achievements in leading the people each in his own generation, but also because of the legacy which they bequeathed to the generations following them. In the eyes of the rabbis, the most important things in this legacy were the two basic books of Judaism: the Torah, which was given through Moses and the book second to it in importance, the Mishnah of Rabbi Judah haNasi.

The rabbis developed two systems in the methods of teaching and handing on the Halakha. The first system juxtaposed every Halakha from the oral law next to the verse it matched, and taught the Halakhot through *midrash*/exegesis, as an integral part of teaching Scripture. The other system collected all the Halakhot together and arranged them in groups according to subject: Halakhot relating to the Sabbath, to *shemitah,* to damages etc – and taught the Halakhot by repetition of these subject groups. In the Ushah generation, before Rabbi Judah haNasi, opinions were already divided on this question, as we see in the following Baraita:

What is *mishnah?* Rabbi Meir says: *Halakhot;* Rabbi Judah [bar Ila'i] says: *Midrash.*[12]

Rabbi Judah haNasi redacted the Mishnah according to the system attributed to Rabbi Meir.

Rabbi Judah haNasi organised the Mishnah systematically. However, he was not the first to deal with editing

---

[12] BT Qiddushin 49a.

and organising the Mishnah. The beginning of this editorial work took place in the days of Rabban Yoḥanan b.
Zakkai, and Rabbi ʿAqiva did a great deal of it too. Rabbi
ʿAqiva also founded a kind of school of editing the Mishnah, and each one of his most important pupils who were
active in the Ushah generation collected his own Mishnah.
Rabbi Judah haNasi, who was the pupil of these rabbis, organised the final order of the Mishnah from the different
collections of the Ushah generation, giving preference to
the Mishnah of Rabbi Meir as the most faithful representative of the Mishnah of Rabbi ʿAqiva. In-depth philolog-
ical analysis can identify in the Mishnah we now have the
different Mishnahs of the rabbis of the Ushah generation.

Rabbi Judah haNasi's important work was the final redaction of the Mishnah, and his achievement is in its acceptance as *the* collection, or, as the Talmud calls it, *matnitin*/our Mishnah.

The rest of the Tannaitic material which did not find its
place in the Mishnah remains as *baraitot*/external material. The Mishnah is a literary work which is typified by a
systematic structure. Disagreements on different halakhic
subjects are included in it, but it does not include all the
shaqla vetraya/back and forth arguments, which form the
background to the creation of Halakha. Halakhot in the
Mishnah, of course, relate to the laws of the Torah, but
only rarely do they cite a biblical verse. Scholarship has debated now for generations on the question of which principles Rabbi Judah haNasi used to organise the Mishnah, but
has still not come to an agreed conclusion on the subject.
The final redaction of the Mishnah brought about the cre-

ation of a single common substantial basis for the Halakha. Any new material created after its redaction went into the Talmuds, and was treated as exegesis of the Mishnah. The final redaction also gave rise to the transition from the period of the Tannaim, the rabbis of the Mishnah, to the period of the Amoraim, the rabbis of the Talmud, and as a result of the publication of the Mishnah an Amora cannot disagree with the opinion of a Tanna. Thus the final redaction of the Mishnah was not only a breakthrough, but also put a brake on any possibility for developing the oral law.

There can be no doubt that it was the exceptional and authoritative personality of Rabbi Judah haNasi, and his outstanding personal endowments, in combination with the clement political and economic conditions of his time which brought about the acceptance of the Mishnah as the work which determined matters of Halakha in the opinion of all the rabbis. (On all this see below in more detail.)

4. The Title *'nasi''*

The literal meaning of the title *nasi'* is something uplifted, exalted, higher than others, and it thus signifies the high status of the person bearing it. At different times the title has been used for people who fulfilled different leadership functions. In biblical times it was given to the heads of tribes or the heads of families, as well as to rulers of peoples or states, and it is found in works dealing with Israel in the wilderness as well as in the days of settlement in the land. The title *nasi'* appears often in the book of Ezekiel, where it is used both of the kings of Judah at the time of the prophet, and also of the ruler of the Jewish people at the End of Days. Ezekiel also uses the title to denote the kings of other peoples whose authority was restricted, as well as the rulers of distant peoples. The title *nasi'* also appears in Phoenician dedicatory inscriptions from Hellenistic times, which have been found in Athens. It is also found in Southern Arabia in a similar context. In the days of the Second Temple the title *nasi'* continued to be used by different leaders. The book of Ezra has evidence that Xerxes gave the vessels from the Temple to 'Sheshbazzar the *nasi'* of Judah' (Ezra 1.8), and Sheshbazzar brought them up to Jerusalem. It would seem that Sheshbazzar is in fact Shenazer, the son of Jehoiachin, king of Judah, and the title '*nasi'* of Judah' is there to denote his status as ruler of Judah under the Persian king. Shim'on the Hasmonean, the last surviving son of Mattathias, received the title *ethnarchos*/ethnarch, literally 'ruler of the people,' in addition to being the High Priest and commander of the army. It is quite possible that this Greek title *ethnarchos* was used instead of the Hebrew *nasi'*. The secular leader who was active together with the Priest in the Judaean Desert sect was also called *nasi'*.[13]

The first people to bear the title *nasi'* continuously were the *zugot*/the pairs of rabbis, and they were also the first leaders in the world of the rabbis for whom this title was used. Hillel, one of the last of the *zugot,* was considered the

---

[13] J. Liver, s.v. 'Nasi'' (Heb.), *Encyclopaedia Biblica,* vol. V (Jerusalem, 1968, Heb.), cols. 978–983, and bibliography *ad loc.*

ancestor of the dynasty of the *nasi'* after the destruction
of the Temple. The term *zugot* was used for the rabbis in
the chain of reception of the oral law, who were the link
connecting the Men of the Great Synagogue with the Tannaim. The first of each pair was given the title *nasi'*, while
the second was *'av beit din*/ the head of the law court. The
sources do not make clear the exact significance of these
titles, or the offices they designated. Of course it is possible that the description in the Mishnah of the *zugot* that
'the first were *nesi'im* and the second were heads of the
Beit Din'[14] is anachronistic, taken either from the self-governing leadership institutions in the Ushah period, or the
time after Rabbi Judah haNasi, when the *nasi'* and the *'av
beit din* headed the self-governing leadership institutions.

After the destruction of the Temple, the title *nasi'*
was given to Shim'on bar Kokhva, the leader of the revolt called by his name, who was not one of the rabbis.
His letters, which were found in the caves of the Judaean
Desert, describe him as *Nesi' Yisra'el,* and some of the
coins minted at the time of the revolt bear the inscription
'*Shim'on Nesi' Yisra'el.*'[15] We do not know exactly what
significance the title *nasi'* held for him. It is possible that
it signified a leader who was less than a king, but the opposite is also possible: that it signified a status which was

---

[14] M Hagigah ii, 2.

[15] On Bar Kokhva's title, see the opinion of E. Habas (Rubin), 'The
Title of Shim'on ben Kosba' (Heb.), *Jerusalem and Eretz Israel: Arie
Kindler Volume* (eds. J. Schwartz, et al.; Jerusalem, 2000), pp. 133–146
and the response of H. Shapira, '"Nasi'" and "Dynasty": A Response'
(Heb.), *Zion* 70 (2005), pp. 105–107.

greater than that of an ordinary king, like the king of the
End of Days in the book of Ezekiel. It should be noted
that Rabbi ʿAqiva proclaimed Bar Kokhva 'King Messiah,'
but this messianic status can also be interpreted in two
different ways: in the sense of a redeemer and saviour of a
divine and supernatural nature, or in a more realistic way,
in the sense of an earthly commander and leader, whose
charisma was rooted in his legendary strength. At any rate,
Bar Kokhva is the first person from the time of the Second
Temple, Mishnah or Talmud who is known for certain to
have borne the title *nasiʾ*.

The first head of the rabbinic leadership after the destruction of the Temple for whom the title *nasiʾ* was in-
separable from his name was Rabbi Judah haNasi. The
title expressed the fact that he was the representative of the
people to the Roman authorities, just as he was the head
of the Beit haVaʿad, i. e. head of the leadership of the rabbis.[16] In English it is common to find this title translated
as 'prince' or 'patriarch.'

Rabbi Judah haNasi was also a member of a dynasty of
leaders. His father, Rabban Shimʿon b. Gamliel, had the

---

[16] On the title *nasiʾ* and the institution of the *nesiʾut*/patriarchate
see, E. Habas (Rubin), *The Patriarch in the Roman-Byzantine Era: The
Making of a Dynasty* (Ph.D. Thesis, Tel Aviv University, 1991, Heb.);
D. Goodblatt, *The Monarchic Principle: Studies in Jewish Self-Government in Antiquity* (Tübingen, 1994); M. Jacobs, *Die Institution des jüdischen Patriarchen* (Tübingen, 1995); C. Hezser, *The Social Structure of
the Rabbinic Movement in Roman Palestine* (Tübingen, 1997); S. Stern,
'Rabbi and the Origins of the Patriarchate,' *JJS* 54 (2003), pp. 193–215;
S. Schwartz, 'Political, Social, and Economic Life in the Land of Israel, 66–c. 235,' *The Cambridge History of Judaism*, vol. 4: *The Late Roman-Rabbinic Period* (Cambridge, 2006), pp. 23–52.

same function in the Ushah period. Rabbi Judah haNasi's grandfather, Rabban Gamliel of Yavneh, had also headed the Beit haVaʿad for some of the time when the leadership of the people was sited at Yavneh. Before Rabban Gamliel of Yavneh, the leadership of the rabbis had been headed by Rabban Yoḥanan b. Zakkai, the founder of the centre at Yavneh, who did not belong to the dynasty. After the death of Rabban Gamliel of Yavneh, which probably took place before the Quietus revolt (a rebellion in Palestine in parallel to the Diaspora revolt in the days of Trajan which took place in the years 115–117 CE), his son Rabban Shimʿon b. Gamliel did not immediately succeed him as leader. It is possible that the rabbi who filled that office was Rabbi Tarfon, who was sited in Lod/Lydda, especially as it appears from the sources that the whole Beit haVaʿad moved from Yavneh to Lod. Rabban Yoḥanan b. Zakkai and Rabbi Tarfon were priests, and they seem to have been elected to head the Beit haVaʿad because of their priestly status. Rabbi Elʿazar b. Azariah, who according to the Talmudic tradition took the place of Rabban Gamliel of Yavneh when he was temporarily removed from office, was also a priest. It would appear that in the period between the destruction of the Second Temple and the Bar Kokhva revolt, the priests still drew power from their status in the days when the Temple still stood. Aside from the question of when they began to use the title *nasi* to denote the figure who stood at the head of the leadership institution of the rabbis, it is clear that after the destruction of the Second Temple the leadership of the people consisted of a body composed of two component parts. The first of these was a clever leader of high economic status, belonging to one of the best families. (This family became at some stage the patriarchal dynasty, and claimed to be related to Hillel the Elder and, from the time of Rabbi, to the royal House of David itself.) The second component in the leadership was the group of other rabbis with *semikhah,* a body described in the Palestinian sources as Beit haVaʿad, or Beit Din, and in the Babylonian Talmud as the Sanhedrin. Between these two components, which formed one leadership body, there was continual tension. The head of the Beit haVaʿad – who eventually received the title *nasi* – aspired to a quasi-royal status, and wanted to be the only authority to determine central matters, such as the fixing of the calendar (sanctification of the New Moon and intercalation of the year), design of the prayers, and so on. In contrast, the other leading rabbis wanted to see their head as no more than *primus inter pares.*

To sum up: After the destruction of the Temple the heads of the Beit haVaʿad received the title 'Rabban' to denote their status, and the first of these to receive it was Rabban Yoḥanan b. Zakkai, even though he did not belong to the dynasty of Hillel, followed by Rabban Gamliel of Yavneh, who did belong to the dynasty. The first to be certainly called *nasi* in the period of the Second Temple, Mishnah and Talmud was the leader of the revolt, Bar Kokhva. The title 'Rabban' returned with Rabban Shimʿon b. Gamliel, who headed the leadership institutions in the Ushah period. It is possible that failure of the revolt with its catastrophic consequences was one of the reasons why the title of *nasi* was not transferred immediately from Bar

Kokhva to Rabban Shimʿon b. Gamliel. The first of those heading the Beit haVaʿad who received the title *nasi* was Rabbi Judah haNasi (and naturally there was no longer any reason to call him 'Rabban,' since this would have resulted in unnecessary duplication of titles).[17] In other words, the use of the title borne by Bar Kokhva was renewed for Rabbi, but not with the same meaning, although there are a number of similarities between the leadership of Rabbi Judah haNasi and that of Bar Kokhva. After the death of Rabbi Judah haNasi there was a division between the *nesiʾut*/the patriarchate, which continued to be used as a term of political leadership, and the Beit haVaʿad, which continued as the spiritual and religious leadership, as we shall see below.

The patriarchal dynasty continued to rule continuously for about two hundred more years after the death of Rabbi Judah haNasi, until it was abolished by the Romans. The division which took place after the death of Rabbi, between the secular political leadership and the spiritual and religious leadership, is somewhat reminiscent of the division which crystallised at the same period in Jewish Babylonia between the rule of the exilarch and the spiritual leadership of the Yeshivot.

Thus Rabbi Judah haNasi was not only the first of the heads of the Beit haVaʿad to receive the title *'nasi,'* but he was also the only one of those who held this title who was

---

[17] In spite of all this, this book will relate to the heads of the Beit haVaʿad who preceded Rabbi Judah haNasi after the destruction of the Temple at times by the title *nasi*/patriarch, or the patriarchal dynasty, in order to simplify matters.

at one and the same time leader of the people in all senses – political, spiritual and religious – and thus was far more powerful than any of the others who headed the leadership of the rabbis, either those who were entitled *rabban* before him, or those called *nasi᾿* after him. Of all the patriarchs, he was the one who came nearest to a quasi-royal status; only he headed the leadership institutions alone without other office-holders being appointed beside him; and he was the only one to grant *semikhah* to rabbis. However, all this does not mean that there was no opposition to his manner of leadership even within the Beit haVaʿad, as we shall see below. He had a certain degree of hegemony over the Diaspora, including the largest diaspora community in Babylonia. His patriarchate was recognised by the Roman authorities in a way in which they recognised no other Jewish leader, before or after him, and the different strata of Jewish society, including the city elites and the Jewish members of the *boule*/the city council, bowed to his authority.

5. Rabbi: Quasi-King, Messiah and Redeemer

There are a number of similarities between the image of Rabbi Judah haNasi and the image of Bar Kokhva, who lived half a century before him. Both of them bore the title *nasi᾿*, and both of them claimed a relationship to the royal House of David, as we shall see below. Both of them dealt in practice with matters related to renting land. Both of them were regarded almost as kings of the Jewish people.

Both of them were messiahs/anointed ones, in the realistic and rational meaning of the word: Rabbi ʿAqiva said of Bar Kokhva: 'This is the king messiah,'[18] while Rabbi Ḥiyya, the rabbi second to Rabbi Judah haNasi in importance, related to him the verse: 'The breath of our nostrils, God's anointed [= messiah]' (Lamentations 4.20).[19] Hopes of redemption were based on both of them, but they supported different methods of achieving this goal. Bar Kokhva wanted to achieve it all at once, through a powerful revolt against Roman rule, while Rabbi Judah haNasi wanted to achieve it through a step-by-step policy, all the while co-operating with the Roman authorities.[20] The verse from the book of Lamentations cited by Rabbi Ḥiyya continues: '… of whom we said, Under his shadow we shall live among the nations.' And it is indeed the case that the political status of Rabbi Judah haNasi made the burden of Roman rule much lighter, and allowed the Jews of Palestine to live under his protection in conditions of peace and prosperity. We can see that the time of Rabbi Judah haNasi was seen as the beginning of the redemption, which was to be achieved in stages, from this vivid passage:

It so happened that Rabbi Ḥiyya the Great and Rabbi Shimʿon bar Ḥalafta were walking in the valley of the Arbel early in the morning, and they saw the light of the first ray of the dawn breaking. Rabbi Ḥiyya the Great said to Rabbi Shimʿon bar Ḥalafta the Esteemed:

---

[18] JT Taʾaniyot iv, 68d, col. 733.

[19] Q.v. JT Shabbat xvi, 15c, col. 437.

[20] See, A. Oppenheimer, 'Messianismus in römischer Zeit: Zur Pluralität eines Begriffes bei Juden und Christen,' *Jahrbuch des Historischen Kollegs 1997* (ed. E. Müller-Luckner; Munich, 1998), pp. 53–74 (= idem, *Between Rome and Babylon* [Tübingen, 2005], pp. 263–282).

This is what the redemption of Israel is like: at the beginning [the light – and hence the redemption – grows] little by little, but the more it progresses, the faster it grows.[21]

These important rabbis, contemporaries of Rabbi Judah haNasi, are walking in the valley of the Arbel in lower Galilee and comparing the beginning of redemption with the dawn. Just as it is difficult to discern the dawn at the beginning, and afterwards it is difficult to keep up with its development, and at the end it succeeds with its full light and strength, so the redemption: its beginning is painful, but at the end it will flourish. It is especially meaningful that these words were said at this particular site, for the valley of the Arbel played a central part in traditions which stress the difficulties at times of crisis.[22] Rabbi Ḥiyya was not the only one to associate the days of Rabbi with redemption. Rav, who was the son of Rabbi Ḥiyya's sister, returned from Babylonia to Palestine to learn Torah from Rabbi Judah haNasi and Rabbi Ḥiyya and afterwards returned to Babylonia and founded the Yeshivah at Sura. He compared Rabbi Judah haNasi to the messiah when he said:

If he is alive he is like our holy Rabbi.[23]

---

[21] JT Berakhot i, 2c, col. 3; and cf JT Yoma iii, 40b, cols. 571–572; Song of Songs Rabbah 6,16; Esther Rabbah 10,14; Midrash Psalms 22,13 (ed. Buber, p. 187). In the statement in the Babylonian Talmud, the days of Rabbi are also seen as redemption, and are compared to those of figures such as Mordechai and Esther, Daniel and his companions, and the Hasmoneans (BT Megillah 11a).

[22] See JT Peah vii, 20a, col. 106; and cf JT Sotah i, 17b, col. 911; JT Sotah ix, 24b, col. 949; and see also JT Taaniyot iv, 69b, col. 736; cf Pesiqta deRav Kahana 14,10 (ed. Mandelbaum, pp. 233–234).

[23] BT Sanhedrin 98b.

In other words, if the messiah were living in Rav's generation, he would be identified with Rabbi Judah haNasi.

The hopes of redemption centred on Rabbi Judah haNasi, as well as his authority and power, found the peak of their expression in relating him to the royal House of David. Rabbi himself, when he held the office of patriarch, fixed the sign for the sanctification of the month as:

David, King of Israel, is alive and here.[24]

In the eyes of Rabbi Judah haNasi, the messiah – that is, he himself – was simply a sort of reincarnation of King David who had been resurrected. Thus Rabbi Judah haNasi himself ruled that the days of the messiah are three generations away from the destruction of the Temple, a calculation which fits his time.[25] The following source wants to strengthen this relationship, and make it dependent on Hillel, the ancestor of the patriarchal dynasty:

They calculated and said: To whom is Hillel related? Rabbi Levi said: They found a genealogical scroll in Jerusalem and it was written in it that Hillel is from David, Rabbi Ḥiyya the Great is from Shefatyah son of Avital, the house of Kalba Savua is from Caleb and the house of Tzizat haKeset is from Avner …[26]

At first sight it looks as if that Rabbi Levi, who came from the third generation of Palestinian Amoraim, is presenting evidence from a sort of archaeological find from Jerusalem, but a closer and more critical look at this 'genealogical

---

[24] BT Rosh haShanah 25a.
[25] BT Sanhedrin 99a according to the Munich MS: 'two to three generations.'
[26] BT Rosh HaShanah 25a.

scroll' shows that it is nothing of the kind. For how could the Jerusalemites have known of Rabbi Ḥiyya, who was a contemporary of Rabbi who lived about 130 years after the destruction of the Temple, and even more so, know how to reconstruct his relationship to Shefatyah son of Avital, one of David's sons (II Samuel 3.4)?

It is also difficult to imagine that the inhabitants of Jerusalem from the time of the war which resulted in the destruction of the Temple would have known the family tree of Caleb b. Jephuneh from the time of Joshua, or that of Avner the commander of the army of Saul. The similarity between the names Kalba and Caleb certainly was more influential than the preservation – which is in fact impossible – of the genealogy of the family of Kalba Savua over more than a thousand years. The same is true for Hillel, for it is not reasonable to suppose that he preserved a genealogy for over five hundred years from the days of Jehoiachin or Hezekiah, the last kings of the House of David. There is no evidence at all that Rabban Gamliel, the grandfather of Rabbi, or his father, Rabban Shimʿon b. Gamliel, were related to the royal House of David. It is clear that the intention in this source was to create a suitable family tree for Rabbi Judah haNasi in order to compare his status to a quasi-king and messiah.[27]

Rabbi Judah haNasi himself asked Rabbi Ḥiyya: Am I obliged for a *saʿir*/an offering of a male goat?[28] This question expected a positive answer which would give

---

[27] See J. Liver, *The House of David* (Jerusalem, 1959, Heb.), pp. 28–32, 37–39.

[28] BT Horayot 11b.

him equal status to a king. As such, he takes on the obligation – if he sins – to bring an offering of a male goat,[29] whereas an ordinary person, if he or she sinned unwittingly, is obliged to bring an offering of a female goat. At the same time as Rabbi Judah haNasi's relationship to the royal House of David was being fixed, a similar genealogy was also attributed to Rav Huna, the exilarch in Babylonia. But the relationship of the exilarch to the House of David was considered to be through the paternal line, and this took precedence over the relationship of the patriarch to David, which was through the maternal line. This is the reason for Rabbi Ḥiyya's reply:

He said to him: Your *tzarah*/ rival wife is in Babylonia.[30]

For just as the *tzarah*/ the second wife is a rival to the first, so Rabbi had a rival in Babylonia in the shape of the exilarch, and had the Temple been still standing, it would have been the exilarch who brought a male goat for his sins, for his relationship to the House of David took precedence. This result is, of course, only to be expected in a tradition cited by the Babylonian Talmud which wants to give precedence to the exilarch, but traditions cited in Palestinian sources also demonstrate that Rabbi Judah haNasi himself recognised this precedence:

Rabbi was very modest, and he used to say: Everything anyone says to me I do, except for what the ancestors of Beteyrah did to my ancestor [Hillel], when they removed themselves from the patriarchate and appointed him. If Rav Huna the exilarch comes here, I will

---

[29] M Horayot iii, 2–3.
[30] BT *loc. cit.*

set him above me, for he is from Judah and I am from Benjamin, he is from the male [line] and I am from the female [i. e. his relationship to David is from the paternal line and mine is from the maternal]. Once Rabbi Ḥiyya the Great entered and said to him: Look! Rav Huna is outside. Rabbi's face fell. He said to him: His coffin is here. He said to him [Rabbi to Rabbi Ḥiyya]: Go out and see who wants you outside. So he went out and did not find anyone. Then he knew that he was angry with him, and he did not go in to him for thirty days.[31]

There is a legendary aura surrounding this episode, but various details are taken from reality, such as the bringing of the dead from the Diaspora to be buried in the Land of Israel or temporary suspension from the leadership institution as a disciplinary method. It is interesting that the same Rabbi Ḥiyya who saw the days of Rabbi Judah haNasi as the time of redemption criticises Rabbi on other occasions. We may indeed be able to distinguish a sense of irony on the part of the teller of this episode, who describes Rabbi as 'very modest,' where his modesty is expressed in his unwillingness to give up his patriarchate to anyone other than the exilarch, whom he does not believe will come to Palestine. When he hears that he has in fact arrived, his face falls, for he thinks that someone like Rabbi Ḥiyya, who came from Babylonia, is liable to insist that he carry out his promise.

The sons of Rabbi Ḥiyya also criticised Rabbi Judah haNasi's open displays of power, and here they compare him to the exilarch:

---

[31] JT Kilayim ix, 32b, col. 174; cf JT Ketubbot xii, 35a, cols. 1009–1010; Genesis Rabbah 33,3 (eds. Theodor & Albeck, pp. 305–306); see the comments of Liver, *The House of David* (above, n. 27), pp. 41–46 on the reliability of the attribution of the exilarch to the House of David.

Judah and Hezekiah, the sons of Rabbi Ḥiyya, would sit at table before Rabbi, and never said anything. He said to them [Rabbi Judah haNasi to those waiting on him]. Give more wine to the youngsters, so they will say something. When they got drunk, they began to say: The Son of David will not come until two houses in Israel come to an end, and these are: the exilarch in Babylonia, and the patriarch in the Land of Israel, as it says: *And he shall be for a sanctuary; but for a stone of stumbling and for a rock of offence to both the houses of Israel* (Isaiah 8.14). He said to them [Rabbi Judah haNasi to the two sons of Rabbi Ḥiyya]: Are you insulting me in my presence? Rabbi Ḥiyya said to him: Rabbi, don't take this too hard: *yayin*/wine has the numerical value of seventy, and *sod*/a secret, has the value of seventy. Wine goes in, the secret comes out.[32]

The stinging polemic of the words of Judah and Hezekiah is clear, for they are saying that the messiah (the Son of David) will not come until the dynasties of the patriarch in the Land of Israel and the exilarch in Babylonia come to an end, for both these men related themselves to the royal House of David from that time. When he comes to defend his sons, Rabbi Ḥiyya says: 'When wine goes in, the secret comes out,' in other words, it is not that their drunkenness led them to lie or to talk nonsense, but to reveal a secret in public.[33] Rabbi Ḥiyya's defence does not help his sons: and they are punished by being refused *semikhah* all their lives, as we shall see further below (pp. 140–141).

However, in spite of this, it is Rabbi Ḥiyya who tells us, while attributing all the glory of kingship to Rabbi Judah

---

[32] BT Sanhedrin 38a.

[33] For a literary analysis of this subject, see M. Lavi, 'The Talmudic Narrative Mosaic: Teaching Torah, Greatness and Redemption: The Narratives of Rabbi and Rabbi Ḥiyya as Examples' (Heb.), *Jewish Studies: An Internet Journal* 8 (2009), pp. 51–98.

haNasi, that at Rabbi's funeral the priests gave up their sanctity of office, and they were allowed to join the funeral and contract impurity, in the same way as they were allowed to contract impurity at the funeral of a king. 'As Rabbi Ḥiyya said: On the day that Rabbi died, holiness was abolished'.[34]

---

[34] BT Ketubbot 103b. The version in the Munich MS has: 'the priest-hood was abolished.'

Chapter 2

Rabbi Judah haNasi's Relations
with the Roman Authorities

1. From the *gezerot shemad*/Repressive Legislation,
to Recognition of Rabbi

The Jews lived under Roman rule in the Land of Israel from the conquest by Pompey's legions in 63 BCE. During the two hundred and fifty or so years from then till the patriarchate of Rabbi Judah haNasi there were two wars in the country between Jews and Romans: the Great Revolt (or Jewish War) between the years 66–70 CE, at the end of which Jerusalem was destroyed and the Temple burnt, and the Bar Kokhva revolt between the years 132–135/136, which took place a generation or two before the patriarchate of Rabbi. This uprising was much fiercer and more extensive than the so-called Great Revolt, but the Jews finally suffered a crushing defeat at the hands of the Romans. The Bar Kokhva revolt ended with the almost total desolation of Judaea, which until then had been the Jewish centre in the Land of Israel, and the seat of the leadership institutions. Between the revolts there were smaller outbreaks of rebellion, in particular what is generally known as the War of Quietus, in parallel with the Diaspora Revolt in the days of Trajan (115/116–117 CE).

Following the Bar Kokhva revolt, the Romans used a heavy hand against the Jews. It was not enough for them that large numbers of Jews were killed and injured, that many captives were sold into slavery and much land was confiscated. In addition they also instituted the harsh repressive legislation, known in the Talmudic sources as *gezerot hashemad*. The aim of the Romans here was to prevent the Jews from recovering and planning to revolt again. This legislation included laws which banned the very existence of the leadership institutions, as well as any sort of assemblies of Jews and public study of the Torah. They also forbade the observance of many central mitzvot, such as *milah*/circumcision, *tefillin*/phylactories, *tzitzit*/ritual fringes, Mezuzah, *lulav*/one of the Four Species, *matzah*/unleavened bread and many others. Similarly, Jews appear to have been forbidden to enter Jerusalem.[1] Although some of these harsh laws ended with the death of the Emperor Hadrian in the year 138, and particularly after the accession of Antoninus Pius and his dynasty to the imperial throne, Roman policy in Palestine was still a policy of suppression. However, in the time of the Antonines the leadership institutions were restored at Ushah in Galilee, and Jewish settlement in the area of Judaea began to recover.

In the days of Rabbi a real change took place in the relations between the Jews of Palestine and the Roman authorities. There can be little doubt that this change was closely linked to Rabbi's exceptional personality and his methods of leadership, as well as the accession of the Sev-

---

[1] For a summary of the scholarly opinions on the authenticity of this ban, see, O. Irshai, 'Constantine and the Jews: The Prohibition against Entering Jerusalem – History and Hagiography' (Heb.), *Zion* 60 (1995), pp. 129–137.

eran dynasty to the imperial throne, and general Roman policy. One of the factors leading to improved relations between the Jews and the Severan emperors appears to have been due to the stance of the Jews in the struggle for the imperial throne in the East in the years 193–194, between Septimius Severus, who eventually founded the new dynasty, and Pescennius Niger, the governor of Syria. This was part of the struggle over the imperial throne between the various generals who commanded the armies on the borders of the empire. These generals did not accept the accession to the throne of Didius Iulianus after he had murdered Pertinax, who had ruled as emperor for a very short time at the beginning of the year 193. In this struggle the Samaritan inhabitants of Palestine sided with Niger. However, it was his rival, Septimius Severus, who was eventually victorious, and he demoted Neapolis/Shechem, the city of the Samaritans, from its status as *polis*. The Jews, in contrast, appear to have received a number of privileges, as we shall see below.

The general policy of the imperial house at that time was to encourage local customs and traditions, especially in the East of the Empire, the cradle of the Severan dynasty. Oriental religions and philosophers and thinkers from the East were very popular in Rome. The cultural syncretism that was part of this wide policy was aimed at coupling the Greek East to the Roman West of the Empire. This policy came to a peak in the year 212, in a law which granted Roman citizenship to almost all the inhabitants of the Empire. This was one of the acts of legislation of the emperor Caracalla. According to this law, known by the name of the *constitutio Antoniniana,*[2] Roman citizenship was granted to all the free inhabitants of the Roman Empire. It should be seen as an important stage in the development of the legal status of the inhabitants of the Empire and the basis of the unity of the Roman world.

2. Rabbi and Antoninus

In the Talmudic literature there are about a hundred different traditions which tell of the close relations between Rabbi Judah haNasi and 'Antoninus the Roman Emperor.'[3] It is true that there are traditions of 'meetings' between other rabbis and the Roman Emperor or the 'great men of Rome,' for example the conversations between Rabbi Joshua b. Ḥananiah and the Emperor Hadrian, or between Rabbi ʿAqiva and Tineius Rufus, the Roman governor of Judaea, or the talks of Rabban Gamliel of Yavneh and his colleagues with important people and members of the government in Rome, but these meetings usually include questions about the Torah, Halakha, and Aggadah. In con-

---

[2] This law is cited by Ulpian in that part of his work which is preserved in the Digesta I 5.17.

[3] S. Krauss, *Antoninus und Rabbi* (Vienna, 1910); M. D. Herr, 'The Historical Significance of the Dialogues between Jewish Sages and Roman Dignitaries,' *Scripta Hierosolymitana* 22 (1971), pp. 123–150; C. Hezser, *The Social Structure of the Rabbinic Movement in Roman Palestine* (Tübingen, 1997), pp. 441–446, index; O. Meir, *Rabbi Yehudah haNasi* (Tel Aviv, 1999, Heb.), pp. 263–299; A. M. Gray, 'The Power Conferred by Distance from Power: Redaction and Meaning in b. A. Z. 10a–11a,' *Creation and Composition* (ed. J. L. Rubenstein; Tübingen, 2005), pp. 23–99.

trast, there are different elements in the meetings of Rabbi and 'Antoninus.'

A large part of Rabbi's wealth, which helped him in achieving his high status with the Romans, as well as with the elite of Jewish city society, came to him from the Romans themselves, and in particular from Antoninus. There is no reason to doubt the sources, which we shall discuss below, which give evidence of lands which Rabbi received as a gift or in leasehold from Antoninus, although it is reasonable to suppose that where the emperor is cited as giving the gift in the sources, in fact it was the Roman governor or another high Roman official who gave it. Most of the sources about Rabbi and Antoninus, however, rarely rise above the level of legends and folk tales, which at most can only reflect generally the good relations between Rabbi and the authorities. Thus for example we find the following source:

Every day [Antoninus] used to serve Rabbi, feed him, give him drink, [and] when he wanted to go to bed he would bend down before the bed and say to him: Step up on me to your bed.[4]

Here Antoninus is presented using motifs taken from the practice of 'serving the rabbis' – the way in which pupils were supposed to serve their teachers – or from examples of honouring parents, where this virtue is also exaggerated. An even more exaggerated legendary example which is actually found in the Jerusalem Talmud, which is usually more reliable in its traditions about Palestine than the Babylonian Talmud, is the discussion in the two talmudim

---

[4] BT Avodah Zarah 10b.

on the question of whether Antoninus converted to Judaism or not.[5] However, there are a number of expressions which give evidence of a connection between Rabbi and Antoninus together with a certain recognition of Judaism, and it is more likely that these sources reflect some sort of historical reality, such as the following:

Antolinus [sic] made a lamp for the synagogue. Rabbi heard and said: Blessed be God who put it into his heart to make a lamp for the synagogue.[6]

We may compare this to a similar episode concerning a pagan, which took place in Pumbeditha in Babylonia:

She'azraq the Arab gave a lamp to the synagogue of Rav Judah.[7]

The words of Rabbi's lament after the death of Antoninus: 'The bundle has fallen apart,'[8] would also seem on the face of it to reflect a historical reality. But the Talmud attributes the same words[9] to Rav on the death of Adrechan,[10] and so in this case the words attributed to Rabbi in the Babylonian Talmud may in fact be a reflection of a Babylonian situation.

---

[5] JT Megillah i, 72b; iii, 74a, cols. 754–755, 764; BT *loc. cit.* For an analysis of the sources see, S. J. D. Cohen, 'The Conversion of Antoninus,' *The Talmud Yerushalmi in Graeco-Roman Culture,* vol. I (ed. P. Schäfer; Tübingen, 1998), pp. 141–171.

[6] JT Megillah iii, 74a, col. 764.

[7] BT Arakhin 6b.

[8] BT Avodah Zarah 10b.

[9] BT Avodah Zarah 10b–11a.

[10] This is Arteban in the Spanish MS of the Jewish Theological Seminary, New York, ed. Abramson. What is certainly meant is Arteban IV or V, the last of the kings of the Parthian dynasty who died in 224 CE.

As noted, the sources dealing with Rabbi and Antoninus mostly include 'conversations' which took place between the two men. In these conversations the emperor asks for Rabbi's advice on family matters, as well as political matters; the emperor shows interest in the mitzvot of the Jewish religion, in theology, and in eschatology but also 'discusses with Rabbi' general scientific subjects, such as ethics, metaphysics, astronomy and biology.

An example of a conversation on political matters can already be found in the Tannaitic literature, when Antoninus takes advice from Rabbi Judah haNasi on a journey he wants to make to Alexandria.[11] In the Tannaitic literature there is also an example of a conversation about beliefs and opinions. Antoninus is presented here as a philosopher, who asks Rabbi a question in principle about reward and punishment: why the body is held responsible and punished for sins which have been incited by the spirit which it is ruled by.[12]

According to the Talmudic tradition, the two men exchanged letters and gifts between themselves,[13] and Antoninus' need to take advice from Rabbi was so strong that

---

[11] Mekhilta deRabbi Ishmaʿel, vaYehi-Beshallaḥ 6 (eds. Horovitz & Rabin, p. 137).

[12] Mekhilta deRabbi Ishmaʿel, Shirah-Beshallaḥ 2 (eds. Horovitz & Rabin, p. 125), and see in the commentary the fuller versions of this parable in some of the textual versions of the Mekhilta. It is probable that the copyists of the Mekhilta confined themselves to demonstrating the main elements of the parable mentioned there, as they knew it already from the Babylonian Talmud, where there is a full version of the parable, and Antoninus' question is also presented more fully (BT Sanhedrin 91a–b).

[13] For example: JT Sheviʿit vi, 36d, col. 199.

'he had a tunnel which went from his house to the house of Rabbi.'[14] In other words, according to this source, there was a tunnel which ran from the house of Antoninus in Rome to Rabbi's house in Beit Sheʿarim / Sepphoris, which the Roman emperor used to use when he needed to meet Rabbi and consult him secretly. Anyone who discovered him visiting Rabbi through the tunnel would be killed at once. It is clear that these sources are no more than folklore, but it is possible that they derive in part from the great interest in Judaism which existed at the time in Rome, on the background of the good relations between Jews and Romans in the Severan period, and the fact that Rabbi Judah haNasi was interested in science and the arts as well as the study of the Halakha. Here it is interesting to note that the Babylonian Talmud attributes to him preference for non-Jewish wisdom over the wisdom of Jewish sages in one particular case:

Our rabbis taught: The sages of Israel say: In the day the sun goes under the firmament, and at night above the firmament. But the sages of the peoples of the world say: In the day the sun goes under the firmament, and in the night below the earth. Rabbi said: Their claim seems better than ours, for by day wells are cold, and at night they are warm.[15]

The sages of Israel and the sages of the world are concerned by the question of where the sun goes at night. According to the Jewish sages, at night the sun is above the sky, while according to the sages of the world it is below the surface of the earth. Rabbi accepts the opinion of the sages of the

---

[14] BT Avodah Zarah 10b.
[15] BT Pesaḥim 94b.

world, and backs it up with his own reasoning: the water in wells is hotter at night than it is during the day, which he sees as evidence that the sun must go beneath the earth at night, as the non-Jewish sages say, and during this passage it heats the water in the wells. This would appear to be further evidence of Rabbi Judah haNasi's close acquaintance with the learning of non-Jews.

Many scholars have laboured long over the identification of 'Antoninus,' Rabbi's friend,[16] especially since Antoninus is one of the elements in the official names of several emperors who ruled during the time of Rabbi, including Marcus Aurelius Antoninus (161–180); Marcus Aurelius Commodus Antoninus, known as Commodus (176–192); Marcus Aurelius Antoninus, known as Caracalla (198–217); and Marcus Aurelius Antoninus, known as Elagabalus (218–222). There are those who were sure that Antoninus was the name of one of the Roman governors, and not necessarily of the emperor himself. On the face of it, the candidate most likely to have had 'conversations' with Rabbi about philosophy, morality and theology was the emperor Marcus Aurelius (161–180), the enlightened philosopher emperor. But since these conversations appear to be legendary, we cannot use them to fix the identity of Antoninus without being able to point to things which he did which the Jews could have benefited from. Moreover, since we have noted that most of Rabbi's patriarchate covered the time of the Severan dynasty, it is reasonable to suppose that 'Antoninus' was one of this dy-

---

[16] See n. 3 above.

nasty, and not Marcus Aurelius, who was the adopted son
of Antoninus Pius, the founder of the Antonine dynasty
which preceded them. Most contemporary scholars agree
that what is meant is the emperor of the Severan dynasty,
Caracalla.[17] Caracalla, the son of the founder of the Severan
dynasty Septimius Severus, was born in the year 188, and
when he was eleven years old his father asked the senate
to award him the title *imperator designatus*/emperor elect.
Thus Caracalla was emperor together with his father until
the death of the latter in 211. After this he reigned for one
year together with his brother Geta (Publius Septimius
Geta) and after murdering him at the beginning of 212, he
ruled as sole emperor, until he himself was killed in 217.
Caracalla came to the East and may have visited Palestine
at least once.[18] In the biography of Caracalla in the *Historia
Augusta,* it says that when he was a seven year old child, his
father and the father of another Roman child who was his
childhood friend, beat this child with a whip because he
became Jewish. Caracalla was furious with his father and
the child's father about this beating, and refused to look
them in the face for a long time.[19]

It is true that the historical veracity of this source, written at the end of the fourth century is very dubious,[20]

---

[17] This nickname was given to him only after the year 213 when he
began to wear a long Germanic upper garment by this name.

[18] Dio lxxix 1 (ed. Boissevain, p. 403); Herodian iv 10.1.

[19] Itineraria Romana 149:5–150:154; 199:1–4; 199:11–200:203 (ed.
Cuntz, pp. 21, 27 = *GLAJJ* 2, pp. 488–490); SHA, *Antoninus Caracallus*
1,6 (ed. Hohl, vol. I, p. 183 = *GLAJJ* 2, pp. 626–627). It should be noted
that these are both very problematic sources as regards their authenticity.

[20] See, R. Syme, *Ammianus and the Historia Augusta* (Oxford, 1968).

but the friendly relations of Caracalla towards the Jews also appears in the exegesis of the church father Jerome to the verse from the book of Daniel (11.34), *Now when they shall fall they shall receive a little help,* which he says some Jews relate to Severus and his son Antoninus.[21] It should be remembered that it was at this time that Septimius Severus and Caracalla gave the Jews the right to serve in honourable functions on the city councils, as we shall see below, and this was also the time of the cultural symbiosis mentioned above. All these pieces of evidence, then, i. e. his name, the chronological match, his positive attitude to Jews, which was like the attitude of his father and indeed the whole Severan dynasty, demonstrate that Caracalla is the most likely of the Roman emperors for us to identify with Antoninus, Rabbi's conversation partner.

Jewish gratitude to Septimius Severus and his sons Caracalla and Geta, who treated them so well, can be seen in the Greek inscription discovered in Qişion in eastern upper Galilee (near present-day Rosh Pina) which is dated to the end of the second century CE, and which presumably comes from a synagogue:

For the welfare of our lords the emperors: Lucius Septimius Severus and Marcus Aurelius Antoninus [known as Caracalla] and Lucius Septimius Geta his sons, because of a vow the Jews [dedicated this inscription].[22]

---

[21] Jerome, *Com. in Dan., PL* 25, col. 570 = CCSL 75A (ed. Glorie, p. 924).

[22] *CII* 2, no. 972; L. Roth-Gerson, *The Greek Inscriptions from the Synagogues in Eretz-Israel* (Jerusalem, 1987, Heb.), pp. 125–129.

This inscription is the only one of its kind from Palestine of this time. There is an inscription in a similar style from Mughar,[23] but this does not mention the word 'Jews,' and it is dated to the time of Constantine I, in the twenties or thirties of the fourth century. There can be little doubt that the inscription from Qişion demonstrates, from a Jewish point of view, the special network of relations which developed between the Jews and their Roman rulers in the Severan period, i.e. in the days of Rabbi Judah haNasi. There are three emperors mentioned in the inscription, for, as noted, the two sons of Septimius Severus, Caracalla and Geta, were co-rulers with their father. It should be noted as well that next to this inscription there is a decoration in the form of a wreath, and in this the name of the wife of the emperor Septimius Severus is mentioned, Iulia Domna Augusta.[24]

We should note that similar inscriptions have been found in Pannonia and in Ostia.[25] In parallel to these there is also a *kenishta deAsiverus,* a synagogue of Severus,

---

[23] Present-day Mughar is a Druze settlement on the southern slopes of Mt Hazon in lower Galilee, and most scholars identifiy it with Maaraya, the seat of the priestly course of the Bilga family in Roman times. See Y. Stepansky, 'Archaeological Discoveries in Mughar' (Heb.), *Cathedra* 97 (2000), pp. 169–171.

[24] The addition of the name of the empress is usual in this sort of inscription in the provinces, and does not derive, as some scholars have suggested, from Jewish appreciation of the influence of Julia Domna.

[25] For the inscription from Pannonia see, *CII* I, p. 489, no. 677; for the inscription from Ostia, the port of Rome, see M. F. Squarciapino, 'The Synagogue at Ostia,' *Archaeology* 16 (1963), p. 203.

in Rome, which appears in Midrash Genesis Rabbati.[26]
One possible explanation for the name of this synagogue is
that it was called after the emperor. If this is so, then it is a
unique case of a synagogue called after a Roman emperor.
Since it was not usual in Rome to call buildings after the
name of a ruler, there is also the possibility that it was simply called after a man named Severus, a common name at
the time among Jews as well, who gave money to build it.
Furthermore, reliance on this late Midrash as a historical
source is extremely questionable.[27]

A certain problem in all this idyllic picture of relations
between Jews and Romans in general and between Rabbi
and Antoninus (if indeed we identify him with Caracalla)
in particular, arises from an isolated and exceptional piece
of evidence found in the *Historia Augusta* in the chapter on
Septimius Severus. There it says that the senate bestowed
Iudaicus triumphus/a triumph over the Jews, to the son of
Septimius Severus, i. e. Caracalla, because of his successes
in Syria.[28] However, there is no basis for the theory that
the Jews revolted during the days of Septimius Severus
and his son Caracalla. All the evidence indicates that the
opposite is true, and that this was a peak period of good
relationships between the Jews and Romans in general, and
between the Severans and Rabbi Judah haNasi in particu-

[26] 40,8 (ed. Albeck, p. 209). See S. Krauss, *Synagogale Altertümer* (Vienna, 1922; repr. Hildesheim, 1966), pp. 254–255, 326.

[27] This Midrash is attributed to Rabbi Moshe ha-Darshan from Nar-
bonne who was active in the first half of the eleventh century.

[28] SHA, *Septimius Severus* 16,7 (ed. Hohl, vol. I, p. 149 = *GLAJJ* 2,
pp. 623–624).

lar. It is possible that the *Historia Augusta* put in a victory over Judaea under the influence of the victory of Titus in the Great Revolt, which was known to the author of this book through the works of Tacitus, Suetonius or Eutropius.[29] At any rate, we must not take the *Historia Augusta* as a source which we can rely on alone, and we cannot draw historical conclusions from it.

3. Rabbi's Bodyguard

After his prayers, Rabbi used to add a request that God should preserve him from evil men, from evil happenings, and from other evil effects. The source which notes this adds: 'And this was in spite of the fact that rabbi had a bodyguard of *qetzutzei*/eunuchs.'[30] The term *qetzutzei,* here, like *gevaza',* or, in other sources, *qevaza,*[31] means literally a eunuch. *Gevaza'* is *qavas* in Turkish Arabic, a term which was particularly applied to a bodyguard. The function, with small changes, was preserved through much of history. For example, in Constantinople in the 19th century, high status guests were received by this sort of official. In mandatory Palestine a *qavas* still walked in front of the chief rabbis, Rabbi Ya'aqov Meir and Rabbi Ben-Zion Meir Ḥai Uziel. Even Rabbi Abraham Isaac haCohen Kook had a *qavas* walking before him and striking his stick on the ground in the early days of his office.

---

[29] See the extensive discussion of this by M. Stern, *GLAJJ* 2 *(loc. cit.).*
[30] E. g. BT Berakhot 16b.
[31] E. g. BT Shabbat 152a: 'that *govzah,*' and cf MS Vatican 108.

It is difficult to imagine that Rabbi Judah haNasi had bodyguards who were eunuchs. Both Roman law and Jewish Halakha utterly forbade castration, although the Romans did allow the import of eunuchs from the Persian empire where castration was not forbidden. The halakhic ban on castration is mentioned in many sources, some of which rule that this ban is even included in the Seven Mitzvot of the Children of Noah, the basic commandments which non-Jews were expected to observe.[32] Rabbi himself dealt with this issue, and ruled that a castrated slave must be freed.[33] Ulpian, the Roman lawyer who was active in Rabbi's day, cites a legal ruling of the Emperor Hadrian (117–138 CE) which extended the ban on castration which preceded him, and banned definitively any sort of castration, both of a free man and of a slave, whether under duress or of his free will.[34] In contrast, castration was permitted in Babylonia and common among bodyguards there. It is reasonable to suppose, therefore, that the *qetzutzei,* which the Babylonian Talmud cites as Rabbi's bodyguards, reflect the Babylonian environment. Another possibility is that Rabbi imported his eunuch bodyguards from another country such as Babylonia, where castration was permitted.

Spreading fear was not just a function of the rulers themselves; officials in the local government or the Roman administration also used a variety of tools for this purpose, as we can see from the trepidation of the common people in their dealings with them:

---

[32] E. g. Tos. Avodah Zarah viii, 6.
[33] BT Qiddushin 25a.
[34] Digesta XLVIII 8.4.2.

… After he stood and raged against the *bouleutes* [member of the *boule*/the city council] in the market, the people who heard said to him: You are the [most] foolish [man] in the world, that you stand and rage against the *bouleutes*. What if he wanted to hit you or tear your garment or put you in prison? Even more so, would you do it to him if he were a centurion who is greater than you? Or even more so if he were a *hypatikos* [governor] who is greater than both?[35]

In the New Testament book of Acts there is a description of how a Roman soldier who was stationed in Jerusalem to preserve public order dealt with Paul/Saul of Tarsus:

In reaction the legionary ordered him to be brought into the fortress [Antonia] and ordered him to be examined by scourging, in order to ascertain why they had cried out against him like that. But when they bound him with ropes Paul said to the centurion who stood beside him: Are you allowed to scourge a Roman citizen without a trial?[36]

The authority given to the Roman army to act violently was directed only against people who did not have Roman citizenship. It is interesting to note that this episode is generally used by modern scholars as evidence of the protection that Roman citizenship gave to those who had it at that time, while those without citizenship in the provinces could not enjoy this immunity.

---

[35] Sifre Deuteronomy 209 (ed. Finkelstein, p. 348).
[36] Acts 22.24–25.

4. The Authority to Judge Capital Cases

Whether the police force was granted to the patriarchs from the days of Rabbi onwards by the Roman authorities, or whether it was instituted by the patriarchs themselves, the very existence of a body which had a threatening and frightening character and was used by the patriarch to carry out his judgements, is some sort of evidence of the recognition by the Roman rulers of the legal authority of the Jewish patriarch. Thanks to this recognition, Rabbi Judah haNasi and his descendants after him increased their ability to enforce their will and their legal and halakhic system on the Jewish public. However, in spite of this, Rabbi's leadership and that of his successors after him did not fulfil all the functions which could be desired of a national leadership which was fully independent, such as, for example, the Hasmonaean leadership at the peak of its power: thus he did not have an army or independent foreign relations.

This situation meant that the Jewish leadership institutions did not always carry out the full legal processes found in the Halakha but took an aggressive approach, which included no small measure of violence, and determined fates without properly organised trials in order to move the community and the individual to take the way laid out by them through their halakhic rulings. An approach like this, of dealing out the death penalty without due legal process in front of a court, but where 'zealots attack him' – a possibility recognised by the Halakha – was also derived from what was accepted practice in the world around them at the time. Against this background it is also possible to understand the activities of the patriarchal police force, as reflected in the sources cited above about 'the members of the household' of Rabbi.

The most extensive tradition about Roman recognition of Jewish legal procedure in the time of Rabbi is to be found in the evidence of the church father Origen, who writes about the authority to judge capital cases, which was given to the patriarch *de facto*. As is well known, the Romans did not usually recognise the authority of provincials to pass the death sentence. In a letter of Origen to Julius Africanus, a Christian writer at the turn of the second and third centuries CE, Origen replies to the questions of his correspondent as to whether the story of Susannah and the Elders – one of the apocryphal books which is an addition to the biblical book of Daniel – is not in fact a forgery. One of the proofs presented by Julius Africanus that this book is a forgery is that it describes a death penalty given under foreign rule. Origen rejects this proof, saying:

And even now, under Roman rule, when the Jews pay the two dinars in tax, the ethnarch acts as the authority for the Jews, and, as it were with the connivance of the emperor, he is in no way different from a king over his people. For cases are tried surreptitiously according to the [Jewish] law, and people are even condemned to death, albeit not entirely openly, but certainly not without the knowledge of the emperor. Indeed we learned this and ascertained it when we lived in their land for many days.[37]

Origen stresses in his letter that he is relying on direct evidence obtained as a result of living in Palestine, and indeed

---

[37] Origen, *Ep. ad Africanum* 14 (*PG* 11, cols. 82–84). See also, S. Katz, *Die Strafe im talmudischen Recht* (Berlin, 1936).

we know that he was in the country during the patriarchate of Rabbi Judah ha-Nasi, and immediately afterwards.[38] He gives evidence that although the Jews were still subject to the tax of two dinars since the days of the destruction of the Temple,[39] the power of the patriarch was so great that he gave *de facto* death sentences. In spite of the doubts cast on this by many scholars, and the variety of suggestions proposed to cope with this evidence, there is no real reason to doubt its veracity. This is contemporary evidence: Rabbi's status *vis à vis* the Jews and the Romans is entirely in keeping with the silent delegation of power to judge in capital cases. This fits the evidence of judicial autonomy granted to free communities under Roman rule elsewhere.[40]

The question which remains unanswered is whether the letter is talking about the sort of case in the *dinei nefashot/* laws of capital cases, which took place before a small *sanhedrin* of twenty-three judges, as the Halakha demands. This possibility is most unlikely, for there is in fact no evidence that this sort of 'small *sanhedrin*' functioned during the

---

[38] Eusebius, *Historia Ecclesiastica* vi 19.15–19; vi 8.4; vi 23.4.

[39] This tax was imposed on the Jews in Palestine and all over the empire after the destruction of the Temple. It was especially humiliating because it was paid to the *Fiscus Iudaicus*, the Jewish treasury in Rome, in honour of Jupiter, the chief Roman god, replacing the half-shekel tax which they paid in Temple times to the Second Temple.

[40] For a different view of this matter, see, E. Habas (Rubin), *The Patriarch in the Roman-Byzantine Era: The Making of a Dynasty* (Ph.D. Thesis, Tel Aviv University, 1991, Heb.), pp. 64–71, 265–273; see discussion and a survey of scholarship on the issue in M. Jacobs, *Die Institution des jüdischen Patriarchen* (Tübingen, 1995), pp. 248–251 and bibliography *ad loc.;* for authority to punish in the free cities see, J. Colin, *Les villes libres de l'Orient gréco-romain* (Brussels, 1965), chap. 2.

period of the Mishnah and Talmud. Another possibility, much more likely, is that Origen is referring to some sort of field court-martial where the judges might have been aided by the police force which stood at the beck and call of the patriarch, in order to carry out the sentences. For in certain cases the Halakha itself allows zealots to attack someone whom they consider to be guilty, such as an *agent provocateur,* without taking due legal process.[41]

It should be noted that the Roman emperor himself was constantly surrounded by armed soldiers and barbarian guards. There was considerable importance to this for the government, for one of the methods of instilling fear in his subjects came from the actual frontal meeting between an individual and the entourage of the emperor, which could easily become violent.[42] We must suppose that the patriarchs mentioned above were influenced by the behaviour of the Roman emperor, which they imitated to some extent. In a similar way, the patriarchs imitated the various signs of honour towards the emperor which were current at the time, such as the *salutatio,* the daily audience which was held in Rome by the emperor and other central political figures for hundreds of years.[43] Daily receptions of this sort are recorded for Rabbi's successors,[44] but we may presume that this belonged to the accepted patterns of po-

---

[41] See G. Alon, 'On Philo's Halakha,' *Jews, Judaism and the Classical World* (Jerusalem, 1977), pp. 123–124.

[42] F. Millar, *The Emperor in the Roman World* (London, 1992²), pp. 61–66.

[43] *Op. cit.,* pp. 20–21, 30, 209–210.

[44] E. g. JT Shabbat xii, 13c, col. 428; JT Horayot iii, 48c, cols. 1431–1432.

lite behaviour in the house of Rabbi himself, for we find details of the behaviour of the rich and the rabbis around him, some of which seem to conform to the same pattern as the *salutatio*.

Another aspect of Rome's recognition of Jewish jurisdiction in Palestine can be seen from the fact that the Roman ruling authorities themselves were apparently sometimes involved in violent enforcement of sentences which the Jewish courts had ruled on matters of personal status. This is explicit in the Mishnah:

A divorce under compulsion is valid if ordered by a Jewish [court], but invalid if ordered by a non-Jewish [court]. If the non-Jews beat a man [who refuses to give a divorce] and say to him, 'Do what the Jews bid you,' it is valid [for the non-Jews are forcing the man according to the decision of the Jewish court, and thus simply acting as agents of the Jewish court].[45]

It is not clear when this Halakha was ruled, but a similar practice is also reflected in a Baraita which is clearly from the days of Rabbi:

Rabbi Ḥiyya taught: If non-Jews compel [a man] according to a decision [of a Jewish court], their action is valid.[46]

The involvement of the Roman authorities in the forced imposition of decisions of the Jewish courts in matters of personal status can also be seen from the following Halakha:

A *ḥalitzah* imposed on a man in a Jewish court is valid, [but] in a non-Jewish court it is invalid, [unless] the non-Jews beat him [the

---

[45] M Gittin ix, 8 according to the Kaufmann and Parma MSS.
[46] JT Gittin ix, 50d, col. 1094.

man who refuses to release his sister-in-law] and say to him: You
do what Rabbi So-and-so tells you.[47]

5. The Attempt to Cancel the Fast of Tish'a beAv

Rabbi was convinced that in view of the peace, prosperity
and autonomy given to the Jewish people in general – and
the Jewish leadership institutions in particular – under
the rule of the Severans, there was no longer any reason
to fast on the fasts that commemorated the destruction of
the Temple, even though the Temple had not been rebuilt
and the people did not have complete independence. Apart
from the political implications of this attitude, it is clear
that he saw his own time as the beginning of the Messianic
age and wished to communicate this feeling to the Jewish
people. All this appears to be reflected in his attempt to
cancel the fast of *tish'a be'av*/ the Ninth of Av, which had
been fixed as a day of fasting and mourning in memory of
the destruction of the First and Second Temples:

Rabbi Ba bar Zevda in the name of Rabbi Ḥanina: Rabbi wanted
to uproot Tish'a beAv and they would not let him. Rabbi El'azar
said to him: I was with you and you did not say this, but that Rabbi
wanted to cancel Tish'a beAv which fell on a Sabbath, and they did

---

[47] Tos. Yevamot xii, 13 (ed. Lieberman, p. 44). Lieberman has an
extensive, reasoned discussion of this source in his *Tosefta ki-Feshuta,*
where he distinguishes between *ḥalitzah* imposed by a non-Jewish court,
which is invalid, as opposed to *ḥalitzah* according to the ruling of a Jewish rabbinical court, but imposed under compulsion by non-Jews. In
the second case the *ḥalitzah* is valid.

not let him. He said since it is postponed, let us postpone it [for good]. They said to him: It shall be postponed till tomorrow.[48]

In the parallel in the Babylonian Talmud these statements are attributed to different rabbis, and the source also says that Rabbi Judah haNasi bathed in public on the fast of the Seventeenth of Tammuz, even though this is also one of the fasts linked to the stages of the destruction of the Temple, whether to the breach in the walls by Titus, or the ending of the *qorban tamid*/the continual sacrifice.[49]

Bathing is one of the bodily pleasures forbidden on a fast day, but in spite of this Rabbi bathed in public in the spring of Sepphoris on the Seventeenth of Tammuz. Rabbi certainly meant this action to serve as a personal example, and give more force to the *taqqanah* he wished to rule on cancelling this fast. Moreover, he also wanted to cancel the fast of Ninth of Av. This is a very significant reformatory process, for the Ninth of Av is a day on which there have been redoubled evils, and the fast is in memory of the destruction of both the First and the Second Temple. The Mishnah writes that it was also on this day that Beitar was taken and the fate of the Bar Kokhva revolt was sealed.[50] Rabbi's father, Rabban Shim'on b. Gamliel, said (in a Baraita) that 'Anyone who eats and drinks on the Ninth

---

[48] JT Ta'anit iv, 69c, col. 737.

[49] BT Megillah 5a–b. See the discussion of Y. Shahar, 'Rabbi 'Aqiva and the Destruction of the Temple: The Establishment of the Fast Days' (Heb.), *Zion* 68 (2003), pp. 159–165.

[50] M Ta'anit iv, 6. This does not mean that this was the historical date of the fall of Beitar.

of Av – it is as if he had eaten and drunk on *Yom Kippur*/
the Day of Atonement.[51]

The tradition about Rabbi is cited in the source under
discussion by Rabbi Abba bar Zevda in the name of Rabbi
Ḥaninah bar Ḥama, the Av Beit Din in the first generation
of the Palestinian Amoraim, who was Rabbi's pupil. The
rabbis of the third generation of Palestinian Amoraim –
Rabbi Elʿazar b. Pedat in the Jerusalem Talmud but Rabbi
Abba bar Zevda in the Babylonian Talmud (with reversal
of the names of the tradents) – are already unwilling to
accept the tradition that Rabbi Judah wanted to cancel
the fast of the Ninth of Av entirely, claiming that he was
referring to an occasion when the Ninth of Av fell on the
Sabbath, and was anyway postponed to Sunday. At any
rate, the rabbis of the generation of Rabbi were not willing
to accept this *taqqanah,* and Rabbi Judah haNasi himself
went back on this *taqqanah* when he saw he could not persuade them (see the section dealing with the opposition to
Rabbi, pp. 157–165).

It is possible that this statement expresses a double attempt by Rabbi. First of all, he wanted to cancel the fast
of the Ninth of Av entirely, and then when he did not
succeed in this because of rabbinical opposition, he tried
to cancel the fast on those occasions when it is postponed
because of the Sabbath. Rabbi used similar tactics when,
having gone back on the total cancellation of the sabbatical
year, he still chose to nibble away at these mitzvot, as we
shall see below. Here, however, the cancellation of the fast

---

[51] BT Taʿanit 30b.

in those cases when it was postponed from the Sabbath to Sunday was also not accepted by the rabbis.

There is further support for the claim that Rabbi's reason for the *taqqanah* which he wanted to rule on the cancellation of the fasts in memory of the destruction of the Temple was the clement political climate of his time. This can be found in a tradition in the Babylonian Talmud, although it is true that it is somewhat later, being attributed to Rav Pappa, one of the fifth generation of the Babylonian Amoraim, who lived in the middle of the fourth century. This tradition distinguishes between times of *shemad/* repression; times of *shalom/* peace, in the form of political independence; and 'days in which there is neither peace nor repression,' i. e. foreign rule without repression. From this we can see that the criterion for judging whether or not to fast on the fasts commemorating the destruction of the Temple is indeed the political situation.[52]

---

[52] BT Rosh haShanah 18b.

Chapter 3

Economic Reforms

1. Rabbi's Economic Status

Rabbi Judah haNasi was well-known for his great wealth. The Talmudic traditions, in the usual way of these sources, exaggerated his riches to such an extent that they put them on the level of the wealth of the Roman emperor and the king of Persia:

And the Lord said unto her [Rebecca]: 'Two nations' *(goyim)* (Genesis 25.23): Do not read 'nations' *(goyim),* but two very rich men *(ge'im),* i. e. Antoninus and Rabbi, on whose table neither radishes nor lettuce nor cucumbers ever ceased, neither in the days of sun nor in the days of rain.[1]

---

[1] BT Berakhot 57b according to the Munich MS. In comparison with the King of Persia it is said about Rabbi that even the head of his stables was richer than King Shapur, the member of the Sasanian dynasty who ruled the Persian empire, including Babylonia: 'The head of the stables of the house of Rabbi was richer than king Shapur, and when he took fodder for the animals, the noise [of the horses neighing happily] could be heard for three miles [4.5 km]' (BT Bava Metzia 85a). This comparison is not contemporary with Rabbi, for Shapur I ruled between 240–270, i. e. after the death of Rabbi around 220. Perhaps it is because of this that the source talks about 'the house of Rabbi,' i. e. Rabbi's dynasty. Unlike the possible example given in the comparison with the Roman emperor, the comparison with the Sasanian Persian king is noteworthy for its exaggeration, which can be attributed to the addition of another layer by the Babylonian Talmud, which wants to set Rabbi's riches above the riches of the king reigning in Babylonia. Indeed, the Babylonian Talmud is full of examples of exaggerations about the huge wealth of Rabbi. On Rabbi's stable master, see G. Herman, 'Ahasuerus,

The verse from Genesis quoted by the Talmudic source refers to Jacob and Esau in their mother's womb. This is significant, for Esau appears often in Midrashim as Rome or the Roman emperor. In this case, the riches of Antoninus and Rabbi are seen in the fact that they could eat vegetables on every day of the year, even out of season.[2] Rabbi was able to indulge in such luxuries because he had land in various different parts of Palestine, and when certain vegetables were out of season in Galilee, he could bring them to his table from the Jordan valley and the South. Indeed, there is an interesting source in the Jerusalem Talmud which relates that Rabbi Judah haNasi used to bring his early cucumbers to the 'authorities' *(malkhut)*.[3]

The patriarchal dynasty was well-known for its wealth even before Rabbi. His grandfather, Rabban Gamliel of Yavneh, already owned much property, and it is reasonable to suppose that some of this was inherited by Rabbi Judah haNasi. This would explain the property which he had in Judaea, even though he lived all his life in Galilee. The firm economic status of those who stood at the head of the rabbinic leadership helped them get close to the Roman authorities, and receive acknowledgement from

---

the Former Stable Master of Belshazzar, and the Wicked Alexander of Macedon: Two Parallels between the Babylonian Talmud and Persian Sources,' *AJS Review* 29 (2005), pp. 288–297.

[2] The emperor Tiberius (1st century) is noted by Pliny the Elder and Columella to have enjoyed cucumbers, one of the vegetables mentioned in the Midrash, which were grown for him artificially under glass, so he could eat them all year round. Pliny, *Natural History* xix 64; Columella xi 3.51–53. I am grateful to Susan Weingarten for these references.

[3] JT Ma'aser Sheni iv, 54d, col. 298.

their leadership. Rabbi was not only acknowledged by the authorities, but even received actual property from them. It looks as if there was a spiral effect operative in his time: not only was he acknowledged by the authorities because of his strong economic status, but this status also contributed to the fact that they strengthened him economically more and more.

In fact, most of Rabbi's wealth lay in the extensive lands in his possession, part of which he received from the Roman authorities, either on lease or as an outright gift.[4] Thus the lands of Beit She'arim belonged to Rabbi, and the lands of Mahalul (biblical Nahalal, north-east of present-day Nahalal) which adjoined them were permanently leased to him. A tradition in the Jerusalem Talmud states: 'Antoninus gave Rabbi two fertile [tracts of land] as leasehold.'[5] These lands appear to have been in the Golan, in the light of the context of this passage, which deals with the question of whether it is possible to exempt the Golan from the rules of the seventh, sabbatical year. Other traditions talk of land in his possession around Tiberias and in the area of the Bashan. Villages *(qerayot)* or waggons *(qeronot)* in the area of Lod belonging to Rabbi will be discussed below (p. 135). They point to the fact that he had land in the territory of Judaea proper. Rabbi was involved in agricultural export and trade, and his networks reached as far as Sidon in Phoenicia. One piece of evidence in the Jerusalem Talmud discusses a halakhic problem relating to

---

[4] On the habit of the emperors to hand out land see, F. Millar, *The Emperor in the Roman World* (London, 1992[2]), pp. 137–139.

[5] JT Shevi'it vi, 36d, col. 199, according to MS Vatican 133.

an episode which took place in a waggon belonging to the house of Rabbi which contained wine, and was brought by non-Jews to the vicinity of Sidon.[6] The plantations of balsam[7] which belonged to Rabbi demonstrate that he had land in the area of the Jordan Valley or the Dead Sea, as this plant could not be grown except in very hot areas. Thus it is clear that he had land in all areas of the country. The balsam plantations from which the perfume was made are mentioned in the same context as the plantations of the emperor: 'You do not make the blessing "who created spice trees" except over the balsam of the house of Rabbi and the balsam of the house of the emperor.'[8] Growing balsam was a monopoly of the emperor in the Roman period. Thus the fact that we find the plantations of this tree in the hands of Rabbi Judah haNasi and they are compared with those which belonged to the emperor is some evidence not only of Rabbi's wealth, but also of his status and the exceptional rights which he received from the Roman authorities – provided that we accept the evidence of the Babylonian Talmud as authentic. A further interesting piece of evidence on his relations with the authorities notes that 'the herd of Antoninus used to mate with the herd of Rabbi.'[9]

---

[6] JT Avodah Zarah v, 44d, col. 1408.

[7] This was a plant from which an aromatic oil was extracted by making cuts in its bark. This oil was thought of as the best possible perfume, see, H.M. Cotton & W. Eck, 'Ein Staatsmonopol und seine Folgen: Plinius, *Naturalis Historia* 12, 123 und der Preis für Balsam,' *Rheinisches Museum für Philologie* 140 (1997), pp. 153–161.

[8] BT Berakhot 43a.

[9] Genesis Rabbah 20,6 (eds. Theodor & Albeck, p. 190).

2. Rabbi and Roman Taxes

Zucker thought that Rabbi was responsible for exacting the Roman taxes from all the Jews of Palestine.[10] This suggestion is most unlikely, since not a single one of the Roman provinces had a central body or person who exacted taxes from all the inhabitants of the province, or even from the majority. Usually the taxes were imposed on cities or regions.[11] However, it is clear from the Talmudic literature that Rabbi was involved, and had an important say on questions related to paying the Roman taxes, and he was the sole judge on questions related to the division of the tax burden.

The involvement of Rabbi in matters of Roman taxation finds significant expression in the following ruling *(taqqanah)*:

Rabbi ruled that *'arnona, gulgolet* and *'anafarot* (ἀναφορά) should be like [the ruling] of Ben Nanas.[12]

This *taqqanah* mentions three Roman taxes. *'Arnona* (= *annona militaris*) was an extraordinary tax, i.e. a special extra tax which was imposed from time to time, and not a regular annual tax. It was imposed on produce according the economic needs of the Roman army units. *Mas gulgolet* or head tax / *tributum capitis,* was an annual tax imposed on everyone who had not paid land tax. *'Anafarot*

---

[10] H. Zucker, *Studien zur jüdischen Selbstverwaltung im Altertum* (Berlin, 1936), p. 159.

[11] See, B. Isaac, *The Limits of Empire* (Oxford, 1990), pp. 282–304.

[12] JT Ketubbot x, 34a, col. 1004.

appears to have been land tax/*tributum soli,* an annual tax imposed on owners of land which exempted them from *mas gulgolet.* Rabbi ruled that in the case of these taxes, the Halakha of the Tanna ben Nanas should apply. It would appear that Rabbi thought that it could be deduced from the ruling of ben Nanas in the Mishnah that paying the money agreed in the marriage contract/*ketubbah,* of a woman takes priority over other debts of her husband.[13] For example, if a man dies and the property he leaves is not sufficient to pay all his debts, the woman can demand the payment of her *ketubbah* first, and the other claimants have to divide what is left. Rabbi thus rules that paying the taxes to the authorities takes precedence over the other debts of her husband.

Following the legislation of Septimius Severus and Caracalla, Jews were enabled to become members of the leadership institutions of cities. The result of this was that in cities where the majority of the inhabitants were Jews, there were also leadership institutions manned by Jews. In everything related to the fixing of the division of the Roman tax burden, these institutions accepted the authority of Rabbi Judah haNasi. This is expressed in the following episode which is found in the Babylonian Talmud:

When Rav Yitzḥaq b. Joseph came he said: There was a case about the crown tax which the imperial house imposed on the *boule* and *strategoi* (the city leadership institutions). Rabbi said: The *boule* [should give half] and the *strategoi* should give half![14]

---

[13] M Ketubbot x, 5.
[14] BT Bava Batra 143a, according to the Munich MS. The addition in square brackets follow the printed version.

In the parallel source in the Jerusalem Talmud, we find the background to the episode described here: a disagreement between the members of the *boule* and the *strategoi* as to the division of the tax burden, which was brought to Rabbi Judah haNasi for his decision:

> When the *boule* and the *strategoi* had a payment to the authorities imposed on them, and the case was brought before Rabbi, he said: Are not the two *strategoi* included in the *boule*? So what did the authorities mean when they mentioned [both] *boule* and *strategoi*? Obviously they meant: these should give half and these should give half.[15]

As the Babylonian Talmud tells us, this is a case of the imposition of *demei kelilah*/crown tax (*aurum coronarium*[16]) on the Jewish leadership institutions of a particular city. This is a well-known Roman tax, which began as a tax imposed when an emperor succeeded to the throne, but over time developed into a tax which was also imposed on other occasions. To begin with, this tax was paid in the form of an actual gold crown which was given to the emperor, but eventually the crown was exchanged for a monetary payment like any other tax. The debate between the members of the *boule*/ the city council, and the *strategoi,* who were also members of the *boule,* was over the size of the contribution of each of these institutions. The number of members of the *boule* was far greater than the number of *strategoi,* so that the members of the *boule* wanted each

---

[15] JT Yoma i, 39a, col. 546. The translation of the word קריבו as payment to the authorities follows M. Sokoloff, *A Dictionary of Jewish Palestinian Aramaic of the Byzantine Period* (Ramat Gan, 1990), p. 505.

[16] On the crown tax see, F. Millar, *Emperor* (above, n. 4), pp. 139–144.

of the institutions to pay half the sum, without relating to the number of members of the institution. The *strategoi,* in contrast, wanted each member of the *boule* and each *strategos* to pay an equal amount. Rabbi came down on the side of the members of the *boule,* and according to the Jerusalem Talmud, explained his decision as reflecting the Roman ruling, which distinguished between the members of the *boule* and the *strategoi,* showing that the intention was not that the tax burden should be imposed equally on each member. Otherwise the Roman authorities would have simply used the term *boule,* and the *strategoi* would have been included automatically, since they were also members of the *boule.* It is possible that Rabbi ruled like this because after paying the tax it would be easier for the *strategoi* to exact the sum they had paid from the local population, because their status was greater than that of an ordinary member of the *boule.*

From this episode it is clear that the obligations of the city leadership institutions to Rome were a considerable burden on them. Thus, two generations later, at a time when there appears to have been a financial crisis, Rabbi Yoḥanan, the most important rabbi of the second generation of Amoraim in Palestine, says: 'If they propose you for the *boule,* make the Jordan your border!'[17] In other words, if someone's name comes up as a candidate for membership of the city council, he should flee and go east of the Jordan River. There is a similar midrash:

---

[17] JT Moʿed Qatan ii, 81b, col. 808.

This is the kingdom of evil [= Rome] which puts its evil eye on a man's money: So-and-so is rich, let us make him an *archon* [the highest position in the city]; so-and-so is rich, let us make him a member of the *boule* [the city council].[18]

Many scholars have discussed the *strategoi,* and there have been many suggestions as to the nature of this institution.[19] It is necessary to clarify this, not only to find out what the *strategoi* were, but also to understand the status of Rabbi Judah haNasi in relation to them, as well as his connection to Roman taxation. The term is not common in the Talmudic literature, so we shall have to examine its occurrence in city administrations in other Roman provinces. Thus we find that it is quite clear that *strategoi* is the Greek term parallel to the Latin *duoviri,* which means literally 'two men.' This term denoted the two most senior office holders in the city administration in cities which had the status of a Roman colony, parallel to the two consuls who were the most important office holders in the city of Rome in the time of the Republic.[20] It is well known that this administrative body, the duovirate, existed in various

---

[18] Genesis Rabbah 76,6 (eds. Theodor & Albeck, p. 904).

[19] See e.g., A. Büchler, *The Political and Social Leaders of the Jewish Community of Sepphoris in the Second and Third Centuries* (London, 1909), pp. 39–40; A. Gulak, '*Boule* and *strategoi:* On the Roman Tax System in the Land of Israel' (Heb.), *Tarbiz* 11 (1940), pp. 119–122; G. Alon, 'The *strategoi* in the Palestinian Cities during the Roman Epoch,' in idem, *Jews, Judaism and the Classical World* (Jerusalem, 1977), pp. 458–475; A. Oppenheimer, *Galilee in the Mishnaic Period* (Jerusalem, 1991, Heb.), pp. 71–78.

[20] For this office see, C. Gizewski, 'Duoviri, Duumviri,' *Der Neue Pauly,* vol. 3 (Stuttgart, et al., 1997), cols. 843–845.

different cities in the eastern provinces.[21] In several places in the Talmudic literature it is possible to deduce that there were indeed two *strategoi*.[22]

A third source found in the Babylonian Talmud may also refer to the same episode, thus opening the possibility that the disagreement already noted between the *boule* and the *strategoi* took place in Tiberias:

There was a case when crown tax was imposed in Tiberias. They appeared before Rabbi and said to him: The rabbis should also take part in paying this tax. He said to them: No! They said to him: So we will flee. [He said to them:] Flee! Half of them fled. They removed half [the tax]. The remaining half came before Rabbi and said to him: Let the rabbis pay together with us. He said to them: No! – So we will flee. – Flee! They all fled. Only one laundryman

---

[21] The term *strategos* is mentioned, for example, in an inscription from the city of Gerasa in Trans-Jordan, as well as in an inscription from a basilica from the time of the Severans discovered in Sebaste, the central city in the mountains of Samaria which was granted the status of a *colonia* by Septimius Severus. When Tadmor/Palmyra, the oasis in the Syrian desert, became a *colonia* it followed the custom of appointing *duoviri,* and during the years 224–262 the holders of this high office are referred to as *strategoi*. The institution of the *strategoi* is also referred to in a bill of sale written in Edessa in North Mesopotamia which was found in the excavations at Dura Europos, the city on the banks of the Euphrates, at present in Syria close to the Iraqi border. (In this city they also found the remains of a synagogue from the time of the Talmud, with wonderful painted frescoes.) *Strategoi* are also mentioned in connection with the cities of Petra and Gaza: F. Millar, 'The Roman *Coloniae* of the Near East: A Study of Cultural Relations,' *Roman Eastern Policy and Other Studies in Roman History* (eds. H. Solin & M. Kajava; Helsinki, 1990), pp. 46–48.

[22] E. g. Deuteronomy Rabbah 3,3 (ed. Lieberman, p. 84, according to the Oxford MS); JT Berakhot viii, 12c, col. 63; Genesis Rabbah 3,4 (eds. Theodor & Albeck, p. 22).

was left. They imposed [the crown tax] on the laundryman. The laundryman fled, and they cancelled the crown tax.[23]

It is clear that this source is mythical, but it may include authentic elements, which may not add up to a single episode, but might have been drawn from different traditions which relate to Rabbi's time. The following elements may be authentic:

a. The members of the leadership institutions of Tiberias come before Rabbi and ask for the rabbis to be included in tax payments. (This episode is parallel to the sources above, which describe the *strategoi* and the members of the *boule* coming before Rabbi to apportion the payment of crown tax.)

b. The existence of an indemnity from certain Roman taxes for rabbis – rabbis also ask to use their indemnity from taxation when Rabbi Judah Nesiah, Rabbi's grandson, imposes the funding of building a wall around the city on the inhabitants of Tiberias. The rabbis of Tiberias ask to realise their indemnity, claiming that the study of Torah guards them. In the words of Resh Laqish, one of the leading Amoraim of the time: 'Rabbis don't need guarding.' In the case in question, they are refused by Rabbi Judah Nesiah.[24]

c. Abandoning settlements because of the heavy tax burden is known from other provinces from the time of the imperial crisis in the third century.[25]

---

[23] BT Bava Batra 8a. For various opinions on this source see, L. I. Levine, *The Rabbinic Class of Roman Palestine in Late Antiquity* (Jerusalem/New York, 1989), pp. 147–151 and bibliography *ad loc.*

[24] BT Bava Batra 7b.

[25] See e. g. B. Isaac, *Limits* (above, n. 11), p. 302.

d. The laundryman who is left behind – the laundryman appears frequently as a representative of the simple people, who do the hard and dirty work for small rewards.[26]

e. Cancellation of the crown tax – there were occasions when a Roman emperor cancelled this tax after it was imposed. Thus, for example, Alexander Severus cancelled the crown tax which was imposed in 222 in honour of his accession to the imperial throne, although this does not necessarily relate to this episode.

If the *boule* and *strategoi* who turn to Rabbi in these sources were members of the leadership institutions of Tiberias, and if, as noted, the *strategoi* can be identified with the *duoviri,* then Tiberias must have had the status of a *colonia,* for the institution of the *duoviri* only existed in the *coloniae.* A mention of the status of Tiberias as a *colonia* is to be found in the Babylonian Talmud, included in a collection of legends about the relations between Rabbi and Antoninus. Here there is also a story which relates to making Tiberias a *colonia:*

Antonius [sic] said to Rabbi: I want my son Severus to reign after me, and Tiberias to be made a *colonia,* and if I tell them [the Senate] one of these, they will do it for me; if I tell them both things, they will not do it. [Rabbi] brought in a man riding on another man, and put a dove in the hand of the man on top, and said to the man below: Tell the man above to release the dove from his hand. [Antoninus] said, Understand from this, that he hinted to me as

---

[26] Cf BT Ketubbot 103b: There is a story about a laundryman who came every day to Rabbi, but on the day he [Rabbi] died, he did not come.

follows: You ask them for Severus my son to succeed me, and tell
Severus that he should make Tiberias a *colonia*.[27]

This source clearly has a legendary atmosphere.[28] It is only
logical to assume that it was in fact Rabbi who asked the
emperor to give Tiberias the status of a colony, and not
'Antoninus' who put this request to Rabbi. There is no
basis for the supposition presented here and attributed
to 'Antoninus,' that the Roman senators would not grant
him two requests. The parable of the released dove is reminiscent of animal stories common in antiquity and its
purport is not entirely clear (it would appear to relate to
the freedom of the *colonia*). However, this evidence does
fit in with what is known of a number of different cities in the eastern empire, to which emperors of the Severan dynasty granted the status of a *colonia* (see examples
below). Moreover, it has been suggested that it also fits
with some inscriptions on coins of Tiberias from the time
of Elagabalus – who was proclaimed emperor in 218 after
the murder of Caracalla, following a rumour spread by his
mother, Julia Soaemias, that he was the son of Caracalla.
On these coins, so Meshorer thinks, the letters COL (for
col[onia]) appear to have been added to the name of Tiberias.[29] It should be noted that such a finding alone should

---

[27] BT Avodah Zarah 10a.

[28] This is discussed by a number of scholars, together with literary
analysis: see, e. g. A. M. Gray, 'The Power Conferred by Distance from
Power: Redaction and Meaning in b. A. Z. 10a–11a,' *Creation and Composition* (ed. J. L. Rubenstein; Tübingen, 2005), pp. 23–99.

[29] Y. Meshorer, *City-Coins of Eretz-Israel and the Decapolis in the
Roman Period* (Jerusalem, 1985), p. 35, coin 86.

have been enough to demonstrate that Tiberias did indeed become a colony, and that this happened in the time of Elagabalus. This, indeed, is the claim of Meshorer, based on the Latin letters COL, which he identifies on the reverse of the coins. However, these coins clearly bear Greek letters also, and coins do not generally have inscriptions in Latin on one side and Greek on the other.[30] In a document written in 1035, found in the Genizah in Fustat, which is ancient Cairo in Egypt, we find the words *medinta Tiberia qolon[ia]*/ the city colony of Tiberias. We may assume, then, that this wording reflects a tradition that Tiberias was a colony in ancient times.[31]

A city with the status of a colony was highly important, enjoying many privileges of self-government, and its institutions were similar to those of Rome, as we have already noted for the institution of the duovirate or the *strategoi*. According to the Talmudic tradition, it was the son of 'Antoninus' who gave Tiberias the status of a colony. If we accept the identification of 'Antoninus' with Caracalla, this indeed fits in with what is known about Elagabalus, who certainly behaved as if he was the son of Caracalla. As noted, according to the letter of Rav Sherira Gaon, Rabbi was still active as patriarch in 219. In other words, if we accept this scenario, it is quite possible that Rabbi lived to

---

[30] Contra Meshorer: A. Kushnir-Stein, 'Coins of Tiberias with: Asclepius and Hygieia and the Question of the City's Colonial Status,' *Israel Numismatic Research* 4 (2009), pp. 99–101.

[31] A. Friedman, *Jewish Marriage in Palestine*, vol. II (Tel Aviv, 1981), pp. 207–212.

see the granting of colonial status to Tiberias by Elagabalus, who became emperor in 218.

Accepting the possibility that Tiberias received colonial status in the days of Rabbi can throw light on the reasons and meaning for the move of the leadership institutions from Sepphoris/Zippori to Tiberias in the first half of the third century. The leadership institutions (the patriarch and the leaders of the rabbis) continued to increase in power from the time of their low-profile rehabilitation at Ushah (and possibly Shefaram too), following the repressive legislation in the wake of the Bar Kokhva revolt, through their move to Beit She'arim and Sepphoris in the days of Rabbi Judah haNasi (see below pp. 149–152). The final station was Tiberias, which now became the most important of the cities of Galilee once it had received colonial status. The move to Tiberias took place after the death of Rabbi and the subsequent beginning of the process of separation between the patriarchate and the Beit haVa'ad.[32] In any event, by the time of Diocletian, who became emperor in 284 CE, the patriarchate was already seated in Tiberias. Thus the long process which lasted over a hundred years in Galilee came to an end. It had begun in the little town or village of Ushah and ended in Tiberias, capital of Galilee, with colonial status. From now on, the patriarch-

---

[32] The Beit haVa'ad first moved to Tiberias in the third century, and Rabbi Yoḥanan b. Nappaha was appointed head of its Beit Din (= Beit haVa'ad). Following this, the patriarchate moved too, at the latest in the time of Rabbi Judah Nesiah II, the great-great-grandson of Rabbi. See A. Oppenheimer, *Galilee in the Mishnaic Period* (Jerusalem, 1991, Heb.), p. 86.

ate and rabbinical leadership did not move from Tiberias until the abolition of the patriarchate after the death of Rabban Gamliel VI, in the middle of the first half of the fifth century.

3. Rabbi's Enactments on the Cities and the Severan Urbanisation Initiative

The Severans were very active in raising the status of towns in the eastern provinces and in North Africa to that of a city, *polis* or *colonia.* The founder of the dynasty, Septimius Severus, gave the status of *polis* to Lydda/Lod in 199/200, as a result of which it received the name Diospolis (= City of Zeus), and to Beit Guvrin, which received the name Eleutheropolis (= City of Free Men). Apparently, he had earlier promoted Sebaste, which was already a *polis,* to the status of a *colonia,* while in contrast the status of *polis* was temporarily removed from Neapolis/Shechem, which lost its status because it had supported his rival Pescennius Niger in the year 194.[33] The urbanisation policies of

---

[33] For Lydda/Lod see, G. F. Hill, *Catalogue of the Greek Coins of Palestine (Galilee, Samaria, and Judaea)* (A Catalogue of the Greek Coins in the British Museum 27; London, 1914; repr. Bologna, 1988), p. 141, nos. 1–2; M. Rosenberger, *City Coins of Palestine,* vol. II (Jerusalem, 1975), pp. 28–31; *ibid.,* vol. III (Jerusalem, 1977), p. 80; A. Kindler & A. Stein, *A Bibliography of the City Coinage of Palestine: From the 2nd Century B. C. to the 3rd Century A. D.* (BAR International Series 374; Oxford, 1987), pp. 96–99. For Beit Guvrin see, A. Spijkerman, 'The Coins of Eleutheropolis Iudaeae,' *Liber Annuus: Studium Biblicum Franciscanum* 22 (1972), pp. 369–374, pls. 1–4; Kindler & Stein, *op. cit.,* pp. 112–116. For Sebaste see Digesta L 15.1.7. (From the numis-

Severus can also be seen in other cities outside the borders of *provincia Syria-Palaestina.* Thus, for example, he gave the status of *colonia* to various cities in the new province of Mesopotamia, including Resaina (about 80 km east of Haran in North Mesopotamia), Nisibis (present-day Nusaibin in Turkey, next to the Syrian border), and Haran.[34] Caracalla (211–217) and Elagabalus (218–222) carried on this policy. Caracalla granted the status of colony to Edessa (the capital of Osrhoene in North Mesopotamia, Sanlıurfa in present-day Turkey). Colonial status was also granted to Emesa (present-day Homs in Syria, on the banks of the Orontes) and to Antioch (present-day Antakya on the Orontes, in Turkey).[35] Palmyra also became a colony, perhaps as early as the time of Septimius Severus himself.[36] In *Syria-Palaestina,* Elagabalus gave the status of a city to Emmaus (in the present-day Canada Park, next to Latrun), which was re-named Nicopolis (= City of Victory), and to Antipatris (Aphek, next to present-day Rosh haAyin).[37] As

---

matic evidence it would seem that the change took place between the years 201–211, probably in 201/202. See Hill, *op. cit.,* pp. xxxix, 80 and nos. 12–13; Kindler & Stein, *op. cit.,* pp. 222–229.) For Neapolis, see SHA, *Septimius Severus* 9,5.

[34] A. Oppenheimer, 'Politics and Administration,' *Rabbinic Texts and the History of Late Roman Palestine* (eds. M. Goodman & P. Alexander; Proceedings of the British Academy 165; Oxford, 2010), pp. 377–388.

[35] For Emesa see, Digesta L 15.1.4; cf L 15.8.6; W. Wroth, *Catalogue of the Greek Coins of Galatia, Cappadocia, and Syria* (A Catalogue of the Greek Coins in the British Museum 20; London, 1899), pp. 237–241. For Antioch see, Digesta L 15.8.5; Wroth, *Catalogue,* pp. lviii–lxiii, 151–232.

[36] Digesta L 15.1.5; D. Schlumberger, 'Les gentilices romains des Palmyréniens,' *Bulletin d'Études Orientales* 9 (1942–43), pp. 53–82.

[37] For Emmaus see, A. H. M. Jones, *The Cities of the Eastern Roman Provinces* (Oxford, 1971²), p. 279 and n. 72; E. Schürer, *The History of the*

noted, it is possible that he made Tiberias a colony. He also gave the status of colony to Petra in *provincia Arabia* (present-day Jordan), and to Sidon and Caesarea (= Acra) in Lebanon. In the days of Severus Alexander, Bostra (south of the Hauran mountains), the capital of *provincia Arabia,* also became a colony.

The acceleration of the process of urbanisation, as noted, took place in the time of the Severans, that is in the days of Rabbi. We can learn about the administrative organisation of the Roman province at this time from the *Onomasticon,* a lexicon of biblical sites composed by Eusebius (about 260–340), bishop of Caesarea in Palestine. This document is most important for the historical geography of the province in the Roman period.[38] Unlike the works of Josephus, Pliny the Elder and the documents from the

Jewish People in the Age of Jesus Christ (revised and edited by G. Vermes et al.; 3 vols., Edinburgh, 1973–87), vol. I, pp. 512–513, n. 142; Kindler & Stein, *Bibliography* (above, n. 33), pp. 177–179. For Elagabalus' grant of city status to Emmaus see, A. Stein, *Studies in Greek and Latin Coin Inscriptions on the Palestinian Coinage* (Ph.D. Thesis, Tel Aviv, 1990), pp. 153–195. For Antipatris, seven kinds of coins are known, all of them from the days of Elagabalus. See G. F. Hill, *Catalogue of the Greek Coins of Phoenicia* (A Catalogue of the Greek Coins in the British Museum 26; London, 1910), pp. xv–xvi, 11; N. van der Vliet, 'Monnaies inédites ou très rares du médaillier de Sainte Anne de Jérusalem,' *Revue biblique* 57 (1950), pp. 116–117, nos. 11–12; Meshorer, *City-Coins* (above, n. 29), p. 54, nos. 149–152; Kindler & Stein, *op. cit.,* pp. 41–42; Schürer, *op. cit.,* vol. II, pp. 167–168, see also, *Inscriptiones Graecae ad Res Romanas Pertinentes,* vol. I, no. 631, republished by L. Robert, *Les gladiateurs dans l'Orient grec* (Limoges, 1940), pp. 103–104, no. 43; see also *ibid.,* pp. 101–103, nos. 41–42.

[38] Eusebius, *Das Onomastikon der biblischen Ortsnamen* (ed. E. Klostermann; Leipzig, 1904, repr. Hildesheim, 1966). See also A. Oppenheimer, 'Urbanisation and City Territories in Roman Palestine,' idem,

Judaean Desert, Eusebius' lists do not contain any record
of a village which belongs to another village; they are all
made up of towns and cities together with the villages
which are to be found in their territories. The administrative development which led to there being a city in the
centre of every territory appears to be rooted in the period
of urbanisation in the days of the Severan dynasty. In other
words, in the days of this dynasty, the process which created the toparchies, most of which were centred round a
village, came to an end, and from now on territories are
concentrated round cities only.

Ulpian[39] mentions the legislation of Septimius Severus
and Caracalla in relation to the status of Jews in the cities,
as recorded in the *Digesta:*

> The divine Severus and Antoninus allowed those who follow the
> way of the Jewish religion to be appointed to offices, but also im-
> posed duties on them, as long as they did not contravene their
> religion.[40]

It is clear from this record that up to this point Jews were
barred from holding administrative offices, and from the
context this clearly refers to offices in the city administration. It is well known that Hadrian in his time encouraged
the organisation of the cities of Palestine along pagan lines,

---

Between Rome and Babylon: Studies in Jewish Leadership and Society
(Tübingen, 2005), pp. 30–46.

[39] Ulpian, who came from Tyre, was one of the outstanding Roman
jurists in the first quarter of the third century CE, i.e. at the same time
as Rabbi.

[40] Digesta L 2.3.3 (eds. Mommsen & Krüger, p. 896). See A. Linder,
The Jews in Roman Imperial Legislation (Detroit, MI & Jerusalem, 1987),
pp. 103–110.

keeping the Jews out of the leadership institutions of the cities.[41] In contrast, the emperors Septimius Severus and Caracalla ruled that Jews were allowed to take office, and serve, for example, as members of the *boule.* Similarly, the same Severan emperors ruled that Jews who were appointed to these offices were to undertake to pay for liturgies, in other words those official outlays which were not in conflict with their religious observances. Thus the sources discussed in the previous passage about Jewish members of the *boule* provide evidence for this opening up of access to city offices for the Jewish population in the days of Rabbi Judah haNasi.

There is a considerable degree of overlap between the urbanisation policy of the Severans in *Syria-Palaestina,* and Rabbi's policies and rulings on the cities. Thus Rabbi gave exemption from the mitzvot dependent on the produce of the Land of Israel, such as the sabbatical year and tithes, to cities whose inhabitants were mostly non-Jews:

Rabbi exempted Beit She'an [from mitzvot dependent on the Land of Israel], Rabbi exempted Caesarea, Rabbi exempted Beit Guvrin, Rabbi exempted Kefar Tzemaḥ.[42]

Rabbi stressed that there was no intent to remove these cities from the halakhic borders of the Land of Israel, and that they were still subject to the purity of the Land of Israel. This step of his was intended to give an incentive to

---

[41] See Jones, *Cities* (above, n. 37), p. 278; B. Isaac & I. Roll, 'Judaea in the Early Years of Hadrian's Reign,' *Latomus* 38 (1979), pp. 63–64 (= B. Isaac, *The Near East under Roman Rule* [Leiden/New York/Cologne, 1998], pp. 87–111).

[42] JT Demai ii, 22c, col. 121.

Jews to settle in these cities. With these *taqqanot*/corrective rulings, Rabbi joined in the urbanisation policies of the Severans. Indeed, one of the very cities mentioned – Beit Guvrin/Eleutheropolis – received the status of *polis* from Septimius Severus in Rabbi's own time.

Among the settlements listed above, which Rabbi exempted from the mitzvot dependent on the produce of the Land of Israel, only Kefar Tzemaḥ was not a city. This village was probably included in the territory of the city of Susita/Hippos, which was one of the cities of the Decapolis. Tzemaḥ would seem to have been sited near wadi a-Sameq in the Golan, and to have received its name from this valley. It is possible to deduce the reason for the exemption of Kefar Tzemaḥ from a Baraita which is found in the continuation of the discussion in the Jerusalem Talmud,[43] in its parallels, and in the halakhic inscription found in the mosaic floor of the ancient synagogue at Reḥov.[44] In these sources, the only place mentioned from the list of places which Rabbi exempted from the mitzvot dependent on the produce of the Land of Israel, is Kefar Tzemaḥ. The Baraita lists Jewish agricultural settlements on the periphery of the Jewish settlement in the area of Susita, which were obliged to take tithes and observe the

---

[43] JT Demai ii, 22d, col. 122; cf Tos. Sheviʿit iv, 10 (ed. Lieberman, p. 181).

[44] Near the tel which is generally identified with the biblical settlement of this name, about 5 km south of Beit She'an, in Khirbet Parvana in the fields of Kibbutz Ein haNatziv. See on this, Y. Sussmann, 'An Halakhic Inscription from the Bet She'an Valley' (Heb.), *Tarbiz* 43 (1974), pp. 88–158; idem, 'Baraita di-Tehumei Eretz Yisra'el' (Heb.), *Tarbiz* 45 (1976), pp. 213–257.

sabbatical year, in spite of the fact that they were sited in an area of pagan settlements. Kefar Tzemaḥ is mentioned among these Jewish settlements, but, as noted, eventually: 'Rabbi exempted Kefar Tzemaḥ' and released it from tithes and the sabbatical laws, apparently to make it easier for its Jewish inhabitants in their economic competition with their non-Jewish neighbours. It should be noted that Rabbi is mentioned explicitly in the mosaic from Reḥov, in spite of the fact that all the evidence points to this being made in the Byzantine era, in other words, much later than Rabbi's own time.[45]

In the continuation of the discussion in the Jerusalem Talmud, it says that Rabbi relied on a precedent of Rabbi Meir, the central Tanna of the Ushah generation, for the exemption which he gave to Beit She'an:

Rabbi exempted Beit She'an following Joshua b. Zeruz, the son of Rabbi Meir's father-in-law, who said: I saw Rabbi Meir take greens from the garden in the sabbatical year, and he exempted them all.[46]

It is reasonable to suppose that this precedent is simply a support for the ruling of Rabbi, and not the cause of this ruling, which, as we have said, was political and economic, stemming from his wish to encourage Jewish settlement in mixed cities.

The process of granting an exemption to Ashkelon is to be found in the Tosefta and the Jerusalem Talmud. Ashkelon was also a city where most of the inhabitants were

---

[45] Another possibility of identification for Kefar Tzemaḥ is the site of present day Tzemaḥ, on the southern shore of the Sea of Galilee.
[46] JT Demai ii, 22c, col. 121; cf BT Ḥullin 6b.

non-Jews, and it was sited on the halakhic border of the Land of Israel. The process of giving the exemption was carried out by a group of rabbis, headed by Rabbi Judah haNasi, which met in Lydda/Lod, the most important Jewish centre in Judaea proper in those days. At first they ruled that Ashkelon was not subject to the impurity of *ʾeretz ha-ʿammim*/gentile territory (abroad), and is thus included within the halakhic borders of the Land of Israel. In that case, the city would be subject to the mitzvot dependent on the produce of the Land of Israel, so that in the second stage they gave Ashkelon an exemption from tithes, and presumably also from the sabbatical laws.[47] The episode is related thus in the version in the Jerusalem Talmud:

> Rabbi Shimʿon said in the name of Ḥilfai: Rabbi and Rabbi Ishmaʿel b. Rabbi Yose and Bar haQappar came to a conclusion on the air of Ashkelon, and purified it, following Rabbi Pinḥas b. Yair, who said: We [priests] used to go down to the market of Ashkelon, and take wheat and go up to our town and bathe and eat [it] with our *terumot*/priests' share. The next day they wanted to vote on it to exempt it from tithes …[48]

In this version, Rabbi arrives in the South with a group of rabbis from the centre in Galilee. They receive assistance from the local rabbi, Pinḥas b. Yair, a *ḥasid,* who lived in Lod or Ashkelon (on him and the *ḥasidim,* see below, pp. 121–125). From him they learn that people who go to the market in Ashkelon do not become subject to the impurity of *ʾeretz ha-ʿammim,* and thus do not have to undergo the long process of purification. They only become

---

[47] Tos. Ahilot xviii, 18.
[48] JT Yevamot vii, 8a, col. 862; cf JT Sheviʿit vi, 36c, cols. 197–198.

subject to the lesser impurity of non-Jews, and can thus
be re-purified within a day. Thus priests going to Ashkelon
can be purified by immersing in the *miqveh*/ritual bath,
on the same day, and the next day can eat their *terumah*/
priests' portion, in a state of purity, and apply the purity
of the Land of Israel to Ashkelon. On this basis, Rabbi
and the rabbis who accompany him purify Ashkelon, and
rule that the city is to be considered as lying within the
borders of the halakhic Land of Israel.[49] As a result of this,
Ashkelon becomes subject to the mitzvot dependent on
the produce of the Land of Israel, and they need to make
a ruling which exempts the Jews of the city from observing
the mitzvot of priests' portions and tithes, otherwise they
will have lost all the advantage they gained.

Another Halakha from the Tosefta explains the halakhic
status of Ashkelon in the light of this:

Cities which are enclaves in the Land of Israel, like Susita and its
surroundings, and Ashkelon and its surroundings, even though they
are exempt from tithes and from the sabbatical year, are in no way
ʾ*eretz ha-ʿammim*/gentile territory.[50]

Note that Rabbi did not absolve Sepphoris, his place of
residence, or Tiberias, or Lod from the mitzvot dependent
on the produce of the Land of Israel, because their population was mostly Jewish. From all this, it would seem
that Rabbi's intention was to strengthen the Jewish settlement in those cities which he exempted from the mitzvot
dependent on the produce of the Land of Israel, giving

---

[49] On the purification of Ashkelon see, A. L. Baumgarten, 'Rabbi
Judah I and His Opponents,' *JSJ* 12 (1981), pp. 161–170.

[50] Tos. Ahilot xviii, 4.

an incentive for Jews to settle there, and helping them in their daily and seasonal economic competition with their non-Jewish neighbours in those mixed cities.

The city of Akko/Ptolemais was a port at a central cross-roads in the province of Phoenicia, which, like Ashkelon, was close to the halakhic borders of the Land of Israel, but outside them. It was not included among the cities which Rabbi ruled as being pure in status. It is possible that this was because of its extremely pagan character.[51] In an episode linked to a visit he made to Akko, he stresses its impurity:

Rabbi was in Akko. He saw one man going up from the *kippa*/cupola, northwards. He said to him: Are you not the son of So-and-so the priest? Was not your father a priest? He replied: My father looked too high and married a wife who did not behave decently towards him and profaned *(ḥillel)* that man.[52]

The man whom Rabbi meets tells him about himself, that he is a *ḥalal*/a profaned person, i.e. the child of a marriage which was forbidden to a priest, so that he does not need to observe the laws of purity like a priest.

The fair of Akko was one of the three fairs where Rabbi Yoḥanan, the head of the second generation of Palestinian Amoraim, continued the ban on Jews participating in them, in contrast to fairs in other places, because of the extreme manifestations of pagan cult which characterised them.[53]

---

[51] See on this, A. Oppenheimer, 'Das Verhältnis der Stadt Akko zum Land Israel und zu Galiläa,' idem, *Between Rome and Babylon* (Tübingen, 2005), pp. 83–92.

[52] JT Sheviʿit vi, 36c, col. 197; JT Gittin i, 43c, col. 1056.

[53] JT Avodah Zarah i, 39d, col. 1379.

The fact that Akko was not included in Rabbi's conces-
sions was probably because the pagan nature of the city was
more firmly rooted, and its Hellenistic and Roman culture
more marked than in other cities. Thus he left Akko as
impure, i.e. outside the boundaries of the halakhic Land
of Israel. Jews did live in Akko, and important rabbis, including Rabbi himself, visited the city, but the picture we
get from the statements and Halakhot shows a shunning
of the city and its pagan culture.

To sum up, without the Romans forcing or asking for it,
Rabbi joined in the urbanisation policies of the Severans,
and exempted mixed cities from the sabbatical year and
from tithes in order to strengthen their Jewish population.
The result can be seen clearly, for example, in Caesarea.
Not only did the number of Jewish inhabitants grow considerably, but an important Beit Midrash was even set up
there in the time of the Amoraim. This was also the result
of internal Jewish factors, such as the separation of the patriarchate from the Beit haVaʿad after Rabbi's death. Some
of the rulings of the rabbis of the Beit Midrash in Caesarea
are cited in the name of *'rabbanan deQisrin'*/ the rabbis of
Caesarea. There can be no doubt that this is evidence of
the importance of this Beit Midrash.[54]

The main purpose of the Reḥov inscription mentioned
above was to detail the Halakhot of the sabbatical year
and the tithes that were in force in Beit Sheʾan and its

---

[54] According to Lieberman, the tractate Neziqin of the Jerusalem
Talmud (which includes all three Bavot) was edited in the Beit Midrash
in Caesarea: S. Lieberman, *The Talmud of Qisrin* (Supplement to *Tarbiz*
II 4; Jerusalem, 1931, Heb.).

surroundings, where Tel Reḥov is sited. The Amoraic literature, indeed, does not give evidence of any growth in the Jewish population of Beit She'an after Rabbi 'exempted Beit She'an,' but archaeological finds show that there was a considerable Jewish settlement in Beit She'an and its surroundings. In other words, in Beit She'an too there was a noticeable growth in Jewish settlement as a result of Rabbi's ruling. The situation was similar in the other cities we have already mentioned which Rabbi included in his rulings.

4. The *taqqanot* of Rabbi on Mitzvot Dependent on the Produce of the Land of Israel

As we have already noted, Rabbi aimed at normalising the economic life of the Jews of Palestine. Agriculture was the main branch of the economy engaged in by the local population, including city dwellers. Thus the mitzvot dependent on the produce of the land, above all those of *shemitah* and the tithes, naturally interfered with carrying out normalisation, for the ban on working the land in the seventh year and the giving of its fruits to the poor did not allow the farmer fair economic existence in the sabbatical year. The tithes, especially the first tithe, in other words a tenth of the produce which was intended for the priests and the Levites, were taxes on top of those already imposed by the Roman authorities, and they put the Jewish farmer at a disadvantage in comparison with his pagan counterpart in Palestine. Moreover, the reasons for giving tithes to the priests and the Levites no longer existed: even in Second Temple times the tribe of Levi no longer lacked lands, whatever the situation might have been in biblical times. The reason for the tithe had been given as *ḥelef ʿavodatam/* an exchange for their service (Numbers 18.21), in other words in exchange for their office as priests and Levites in the Temple cult, but this was no longer valid after the destruction of the Second Temple.

Rabbi wanted to bring about a revolution, aiming at a complete cancellation of the ban on working the land in the sabbatical year in the Land of Israel. However, it is impossible to know whether he began by a slow erosion of the regulations of the sabbatical year, until, in his opinion, the time had come to cancel it altogether, or whether the opposite is true, and he began with an attempt to carry out a revolutionary reform of cancelling the sabbatical year completely, and when this did not work, decided to cancel a number of the laws of the sabbatical year.

Rabbi's attempt to cancel the sabbatical year met with opposition from Rabbi Pinḥas b. Yair the *ḥasid,*[55] who did, however, cooperate with him on the purification of Ashkelon, and the exemption from the sabbatical year and from tithes which he gave to the city, as decribed in the Jerusalem Talmud:

Rabbi wanted to cancel the sabbatical year. Rabbi Pinḥas b. Yair came up to him. He [Rabbi] said to him [Rabbi Pinḥas b. Yair]: What is the corn doing [in the field]? He replied: [Wild] endives are

---

[55] On Rabbi and the *ḥasidim* in general, and Rabbi Pinḥas b. Yair in particular, see below, pp. 121–125.

good. What is the corn doing? He replied: [Wild] endives are good.
So Rabbi understood that he did not agree with him.[56]

Rabbi turns to Rabbi Pinḥas b. Yair during the sabbatical
year and asks him what the corn is doing in the field, in
other words, hinting that it should be reaped. Rabbi uses
the term ʿivurayya as used in the book of Joshua 'and they
ate of the corn of the land (Joshua 5.11).' But Rabbi Pinḥas
b. Yair answers that it is possible to survive on eating wild
endives. When he finds himself unable to persuade Rabbi
Pinḥas b. Yair, Rabbi gives up his attempt to cancel the
sabbatical year. There can be no doubt that it was not accidental that it was to Rabbi Pinḥas b. Yair to whom Rabbi
turned when he wanted to cancel the sabbatical year. Rabbi
Pinḥas b. Yair, the head of the *ḥasidim,* who emphasised
the social mitzvot, would be expected to be against cancelling the sabbatical year, for the poor enjoyed its fruits.[57]
Rabbi abandoned his attempt to cancel the sabbatical year
not because Rabbi Pinḥas b. Yair was greater than him in
status or learning, but because he did not want to create
a division in the people on this important subject. A division of this sort could have, for example, caused the people
of the South to follow Rabbi Pinḥas b. Yair, who lived in
Lod or Ashkelon, so that in the light of this they would
not have agreed to trade agricultural produce with people

---

[56] JT Demai i, 22a, col. 118; cf JT Taʿanit iii, 66c, col. 719.

[57] The Talmudic Aggadah tells of the she-ass of Rabbi Pinḥas b.
Yair, which refused to eat uncertainly tithed produce *(demai)* which
was put before her, in spite of the fact that according to the Halakha
it was permissible to feed animals with such produce: JT Demai i,
21d–22a, col. 117.

from Galilee because they suspected them of not keeping the laws of the sabbatical year properly.

Apart from Rabbi's attempt to cancel the sabbatical year entirely, which he did not manage to carry out, he made numerous rulings which eroded the sabbatical year and also most certainly led – because of his lenient attitude – to a further rise in the numbers of those who did not observe it carefully. We have already noted the exemption from the sabbatical year and tithes which he gave to the mixed cities, and he added many other rulings which we will detail below.

In Rabbi's attitude to the mitzvot of the sabbatical year there is, on the one hand, revolutionary reform, compared with what was acceptable in the Yavneh period after the destruction of the Temple, but on the other hand we can also see the continuation of a process which began in the Ushah period during the economic crisis in the period after the Bar Kokhva revolt. The mitzvah of the sabbatical year was the only significant mitzvah among the mitzvot depending on the produce of the Land of Israel whose existence was always independent of Jerusalem and the Temple. Unlike the priests' portions and the tithes, for example, which were given to the priests and Levites and were the compensation for their service in the Temple, the laws of the sabbatical year are only linked to the poor who benefit from its fruits, who can be found everywhere. Thus the rabbis of Yavneh were very stringent about the observance of these laws.[58]

---

[58] On the development of the laws of the sabbatical year see, S. Safrai, 'The Mitzvah of the Sabbatical Year after the Destruction of the Second Temple' (Heb.), *Tarbiz* 35 (1966), pp. 26–46; 36 (1967), pp. 304–328

The change in this direction and the transition from stringency to leniency in the observance of the sabbatical Halakhot had begun in the Ushah period, and the incentive was without doubt the economic crisis precipitated by the Bar Kokhva revolt.[59] Even the Romans apparently cancelled the exemptions from Roman taxes in this year.[60]

Meanwhile, by the time of Rabbi Judah haNasi, things had returned to normal. The Romans no longer intended to punish the Jews; the large number of soldiers encamped in the country after the repression of the Bar Kokhva revolt returned to their stations; and we can presume that the exemption from taxes given to Jews during the sabbatical year was reinstated. Rabbi was faced with two ways in which to relate to the sabbatical year: the first was to return to the line taken during the Yavneh period, which was stringent about the laws of the sabbatical year and set them as the only significant mitzvah of those dependent on the produce of the Land of Israel whose observance was not linked to the Temple; the second was to be lenient about the laws of the sabbatical year in order to promote the economy. Naturally he chose the second option, which fitted his general policies.

One of Rabbi's *heterim*/exemptions, related to the sabbatical year was on vegetables from the year after, the eighth year, which was also the first year of the next seven year cycle. It is quite clear that vegetables sold in the mar-

---

(= idem, *In Times of Temple and Mishnah: Studies in Jewish History* [Jerusalem, 1994, Heb.], pp. 421–466).

[59] M Sanhedrin iii, 3.
[60] BT Sanhedrin 26a.

ket immediately following Rosh haShanah/the New Year of the next year would have been sown in contravention of the regulations in the seventh year and should have been forbidden:

> When may a man buy vegetables after the close of the seventh year? When enough time has passed for the same crop to ripen again. When the early ripening crop ripens, the later ripening crop is permitted. Rabbi permitted buying vegetables immediately after the close of the seventh year.[61]

In this case too, there had been a *taqqanah,* presumably from the Ushah period, which relaxed the regulations to a certain degree. In other words, it had been permitted to buy any sort of vegetable in the eighth year after the first fruits of this vegetable which had been sown in the eighth year came on to the market. From now on, it was also permitted to buy this particular vegetable in an area where it ripened later, i. e. in the hill country, even if there was a suspicion that it had been sown in the seventh year. However, Rabbi allowed the purchase of vegetables without any restrictions right from the beginning of the eighth year. In permitting this, he was clearly recognising and accepting the knowledge that some people had sown them in the seventh year in contravention of what was said in the commandment, so that they would have a harvest of vegetables to sell immediately at the beginning of the eighth year.[62]

---

[61] M Shevi'it vi, 4.

[62] In the Talmudic literature the rabbis tried to find various reasons for Rabbi's exemption, from an halakhic standpoint and with an aggadic approach: see a possible analysis in the paper by Safrai cited in n. 58.

A further exemption by Rabbi, which was intended to ease the regulations of the sabbatical year, allowed drying and pickling vegetables in the seventh year.[63] In other words, until this exemption, an owner was only permitted to pick fruits for his immediate food needs. From the time of Rabbi's exemption onwards, the owner was also allowed to pick produce for drying and pickling, in order to preserve the fruits for a longer time. Rabbi made these *taqqanot* in stages: first he allowed people to eat vegetables which had been imported from abroad to the Land of Israel, as well as vegetables which grew near the halakhic borders of the country. After this, Rabbi allowed the purchase of vegetables immediately after the end of the sabbatical year. Similarly, Rabbi first allowed the import of figs and grapes from abroad in order to dry and preserve them in the halakhic border areas, and only afterwards allowed this in the Land of Israel itself.[64]

Thus even without the attempt of Rabbi Judah haNasi to cancel the sabbatical year entirely, it would appear that his *taqqanot* brought about a basic change in the laws of the seventh year, and certainly undermined its status among the people. The seventh year is a *mitzvah de'oraita'*/a regulation from the Torah, but Rabbi ruled through his exegesis that the sabbatical year was now only obligatory as a *mitzvah derabbanan*/a rabbinical regulation. By this ruling Rabbi achieved two goals. First of all, it gave him legitimisation to nibble away at the laws of the sabbatical

---

[63] Tos. Shevi'it iv, 16 (ed. Lieberman, p. 183).

[64] See Safrai, 'Mitzvah" (see n. 58).

year and even to try to cancel them altogether, for even
he was not allowed to root out a mitzvah from the Torah,
but he could make a reform within the Halakhot which
had been ruled by the rabbis. Secondly, the fact of the ruling certainly brought other rabbis to be lenient over other
matters forbidden by this regulation and led many of the
people to neglect to observe it:

As it says in a Baraita, "And this is the manner of the release of *shem-
itah/shemitah shamot* (Deuteronomy 15.2)." Rabbi says: The reduplication of *'shemitah'* refers to *shemitah* and the *yovel/* the fiftieth year,
[when all land returned to its original owners]. When the *yovel* is
observed, *shemitah* is observed, [according to the Torah]. [From the
moment when] the *yovel* ceased, *shemitah* is only observed according
to their words [i. e., as a rabbinical regulation].[65]

The reduplication of *shemitah shamot* in the verse refers, in
Rabbi's opinion, to the interdependence of *shemitah* and
yovel, when the mitzvot of the sabbatical year were also observed. Since the jubilee was cancelled and not observed
even in Second Temple times, in Rabbi's opinion the obligation to the sabbatical year from the Torah was also cancelled, and it only continues as a rabbinical regulation.[66]

---

[65] JT Shevi'it x, 39c, col. 214. Cf BT Gittin 30a–b.

[66] A similar concept is found in the Talmudic literature in respect of
ma'asrot/ tithes: 'From then on they took on themselves [i. e. the rab-
bis] the tithes.' JT Maasrot ii, 49c, col. 268 and parallels. These statements mean that the obligation of tithes is only a rabbinical regulation.
This conception is not only related to the days after the destruction of
the Temple, but it goes back to the days of Ezra. Similarly, in relation
to the *terumah* tithe, to which they usually related more strictly than
to *ma'asrot,* both in Halakha and in actual practice, we find the concept: *terumah* nowadays is a rabbinical regulation (BT Yevamot 81a).
This concept in relation to *terumot* and *ma'asrot* is not handed down
in Rabbi's name, but it is reasonable to suppose that it was produced

There is also a very interesting episode where a teacher is brought to court before Rabbi Judah haNasi because of a suspicion that he did not observe the laws of the sabbatical year:

A teacher was suspected of [trade in] the fruits of *shemitah*. They brought him before Rabbi. [Rabbi] said to them: And what should this wretched man do? He did what he did in order to make a living.[67]

Rabbi Judah haNasi acts with extreme forgiveness to the poor teacher, and excuses him from everything. Rabbi is known from the sources as a forceful patriarch who has no hesitation in handing out punishments even to important and rich people, but in the respect of not observing the sabbatical year properly he changes his habits in judgement, for in his opinion it would have been preferable to cancel it altogether.

It thus becomes clear that Rabbi's many regulations tending to leniency over *shemitah,* his ruling that *shemitah* in his time was a rabbinical regulation and not from the Torah, his ruling of 'not guilty' in the case of people brought before him on a charge of non-observance of *shemitah,* as well as his attempts to cancel *shemitah* completely – all these challenged the status of *shemitah* in his generation, as well as in the period of the imperial crisis after his time.[68]

---

by his school/Beit Midrash, although it is possible that it crystallised only later in the time of the Palestinian Amoraim. In one of the parallel sources, this approach is attributed to Rabbi El'azar b. Pedat, from the third generation of the Palestinian Amoraim, who lived at the turn of the third and fourth centuries (JT Shevi'it vi, 36b, col. 196).

[67] JT Ta'anit iii, 66b–c, col. 719.

[68] It should be noted that in the time of the Amoraim there was a

5. *Siqariqon*

Rabbi Judah haNasi also brought about a reformation and normalisation of the subject of land ownership, when he made a new ruling about the renewal of Jewish ownership of lands which had been confiscated by the Romans. This ruling was important because it ensured maximum Jewish ownership of land in the Land of Israel, and at the same time improved political and economic relations with the Roman authorities.

The Romans used to confiscate land as a punishment measure in extreme cases. This punishment was not specific to the Jews of Palestine, for the authorities acted in the same way in Rome itself towards someone who, for example, consistently refused to pay taxes. When the death penalty was imposed on a Roman citizen it automatically included the confiscation of his property by the authorities, and they did not return it to his heirs if it had been confiscated in this way. The confiscation of land as a means of punishment was used against rebels in Palestine, just like rebels at Rome. For many years the scholarly consensus was that after the First Jewish Revolt the Romans took over all the territories of the Land of Israel. However, both the Graeco-Roman sources and the Talmudic literature give evidence that Jews still owned some land in *provincia*

---

kind of reaction which brought about a new strengthening of the status of *shemitah,* similar to the new stringency in the *shemitah* regulations which took place after the destruction of the Second Temple in the Yavneh period, although not to the same extent.

Iudaea even after the failure of the revolt and the punishments which followed.[69]

This is not to say that the Romans did not confiscate any territory at all. They confiscated the lands of those who took part in the revolt, and sometimes the territory of whole villages which joined the rebellion. After some time had passed, the Romans would often put up the confiscated lands for sale, and here the legal question arose of whether it was permissible for a Jew to buy land which had belonged to another Jew from the Romans. This legal question is called *siqariqon* in the Talmudic literature.[70] Sometimes the use of this Greek term in the Talmud relates to the legal question, and sometimes to the Roman who has taken over the land. The exact linguistic origin of the term is debatable, and has not been clarified. When the leadership institutions of the rabbis came to rule Halakha on this question, they were faced with a dilemma: on the one hand, there was a clear tendency to enable the purchase of land, and thus strengthen the Jewish holdings of territory in the Land of Israel; on the other hand, there was a tendency not to allow purchase of lands, for in the eyes of the rabbis the Romans did not have the authority to confiscate territory in the Land of Israel, so that from the point of view of the Halakha, the land remained the

---

[69] See B. Isaac, 'Judaea after AD 70,' idem, *The Near East under Roman Rule: Selected Papers* (Leiden, 1998), pp. 112–119; Postscript, pp. 120–121.

[70] See S. Safrai, *'Siqariqon'* (Heb.), *Zion* 17 (1952), pp. 56–64 (= idem, *In Times of Temple and Mishnah* [Jerusalem, 1994, Heb.], pp. 259–267), and bibliography *ad loc.*

possession of its original owner. Moreover, if a Jew were to buy the land, and its original owner were then to come to the rabbinical leadership to ask for legal aid in getting back the land which had been his, from the buyer, they would be obliged to give him such aid.

Up to the time of Rabbi, there had been a number of stages in the rulings of the rabbis about *siqariqon*.[71] At first they tended towards forbidding purchase, unless the buyer bought the land both from the Romans and from the original owner. Following this, they gradually made things easier for the buyer. Finally, Rabbi's *taqqanah* made these rulings almost meaningless:

> Rabbi set up a court and they decided by vote that after the [land] had been in the possession of the *siqariqon* for twelve months, whoever first bought it secured the title, but he [must] give a quarter to the owners.[72]

This ruling meant that buying confiscated land was freed from restrictions, for after a year from the time that the land was confiscated, there was no longer any obligation for the buyer to find the original owners, for they no longer had the first right to buy the land, so that it was possible to buy it freely from the Romans. The only element which still restricted the buyer to some extent was that if the original owner happened to turn up, he would have the right to get a quarter of the land, or its monetary equivalent, from the buyer as compensation.

---

[71] See especially, M Gittin v, 6; Tos. Gittin iii, 10 (ed. Lieberman, pp. 257–258); JT Gittin v, 47b, cols. 1076–1077.

[72] M Gittin v, 6 (tr. Danby, adapted) and cf Tosefta *ad loc.*

Rabbi lived and worked in a time when the economy was in a good state. What could have led him to rule a *taqqanah* which was the opposite of that ruled by the rabbis of Yavneh? First of all, he was not a reformer who wanted to turn everything upside down all at once, but he followed the same path which had already been taken, which gradually nibbled away at the *taqqanah* ruled at Yavneh: there had been an emergency ruling after the Bar Kokhva revolt which allowed the free purchase of confiscated lands in the area of Judaea, followed by a *taqqanah* ruled by the centre at Ushah, which was similar to Rabbi's ruling, but required the buyer to look for the original owner first, and to compensate him. Secondly, Rabbi aspired to reach maximum normalisation of the economy, and a market which was as free as possible. Thirdly, there was, of course, the tendency to encourage Jewish settlement of the Land of Israel, in other words to act so that there should be as much land as possible in Jewish ownership. Fourthly, as noted, the massive confiscation of lands was a thing of the past, which had last taken place at the time of the repressive legislation following the Bar Kokhva revolt, in other words, decades before Rabbi's time. Most of the original owners must have long since died or left the country, and it was not always possible to find their heirs, so that buying the land which had once been taken from them by the Roman authorities was no longer likely to cause them real damage. However, above all, what was most influential in this matter was the improved relationship with the Roman authorities, which led Rabbi to legitimise their confiscation of land. The moment they had been given this legitimation, there was no longer any reason to forbid anyone to buy land which they had confiscated from them. There can be no doubt that Rabbi aspired to complete independence, but he recognised the legitimacy of Roman authority, which he was close to and which was recognised by him, and obviously in this light he was no longer able to stick to a *taqqanah* which underlined the lack of legitimacy of the Roman authorities by its very nature.

6. Whitewashing Interest and Stolen Money

A further Talmudic *taqqanah* which aimed at normalisation of economic and social life rules: 'The thief, and [a man] who lends out his money at interest who repent and return what they have stolen – anyone who receives from them is not approved by the rabbis.'[73] The following tradition attributes this *taqqanah* (in a slightly different version) to Rabbi Judah haNasi:

Rabbi Yoḥanan said: In the days of Rabbi they repeated this mishnah: There is a Tannaitic tradition, which relates a case of one man who wanted to repent. His wife said to him: Fool, if you repent, even your belt will not belong to you! So he stopped and did not repent. At the same time they said: Thieves and people who lend for interest, if they give [it] back, you should not take it from them, and anyone who does take from them, the rabbis do not approve of him.[74]

This tradition is found in the Babylonian Talmud, and it is possible to raise doubts over the attribution to Rabbi.

---

[73] Tos. Shevi'it viii, 11 (ed. Lieberman, p. 202).

[74] BT Bava Qama 94b. This *taqqanah* does not add 'they repented,' but this can be presumed from the context and from the *taqqanah* itself.

However, it is attributed to Rabbi Yoḥanan who was Rabbi's pupil and is generally considered reliable on the subject of historical traditions. From this source, it appears that the economic development in the time of Rabbi developed to the stage when loans with interest became necessary, and he was therefore interested to allow this *de facto*. This is similiar to Hillel the Elder, who made the ruling of the *prosbul*, which cancelled *shemitah*/the release of loans in the seventh, sabbatical year *de facto*. Rabbi could not, of course, uproot a law from the Torah, but he looked for a way to get round the ban. Thus he ruled that if someone who lends out for interest repents and wants to return the interest he has taken, one should not take it back from him, and if someone does decide to take it back, 'the rabbis do not approve of him.'

It is clear that loans with interest were indeed common in those days, as we learn from a statement of Rabbi Yoḥanan himself:

They asked in front of Rabbi Yoḥanan: Should judges rule on interest? He said to them: If they do not, there will be nothing left for the great ones of the Land of Israel.[75]

In other words, when Rabbi Yoḥanan is asked whether it is part of the function of a court to extract the interest from people who took a loan, he replies that if they do not do so, the whole economic fabric of society will be damaged, for the rich would get no profit at all. Rabbi used to 'honour' the rich for his own reasons, as we shall see below (pp. 112–116).

---

[75] JT Bava Metzia v, 10a, col. 1226. Cf JT Bava Batra iii, 14a, col. 1244.

It is more difficult to see why the same *taqqanah* was applied to thieves as to those who lent out at interest and changed their mind, except for rather far-fetched suppositions, which naturally add a question mark to the authenticity of the whole *taqqanah,* for what was wrong with someone who took back something stolen from himself by a thief who repented? Alon puts forward the proposition that this is not a case of simple thieves, but people 'who took for themselves other people's possessions without a proper right to them, but not actual theft.'[76] Thus, for example, we find similar statements from Shemuel, the head of the Yeshivah at Nehardeʿa in the first generation of the Babylonian Amoraim (who may have studied in Palestine with Rabbi himself), on the subject of those who wished to be strict about the laws of possession: 'Shemuel said: If it is like this, then there will be nothing left for the great ones of the Land of Israel.'[77] It is possible that Alon is right, but it is also possible that the text is referring to real thieves, when we must make the problematic suggestion that when Rabbi and Rabbi Yoḥanan after him ruled this *taqqanah,* they wanted to help thieves return to good behaviour, and at the same time preserve the stability of the extant economic and social strata of society.

---

[76] This is the version in Alon's book in Hebrew: G. Alon, *Toledot ha-Yehudim be-ʾEretz Yisraʾel bi-Tequfat ha-Mishnah ve-haTalmud,* vol. II (Tel Aviv, 1956), p. 156. Compare this with the way the translator reads this in the English version of Alon's book: G. Alon, *The Jews in Their Land in the Talmudic Age* (Jerusalem, 1984), p. 734.

[77] JT Bava Batra iii, 14a, col. 1244.

Chapter 4

Rabbi Judah haNasi's Social Stances

1. Rapprochement with the City Elites

Rabbi Judah haNasi's social stances were very much the result of his closeness to the Romans, his great riches and his centralised leadership. Rabbi was interested in rapprochement with the Jewish city elites in order to subordinate them to his authority. He was successful in this aim – we have already noted the episode of the members of the *boule* and the city *strategoi* who asked him to distribute the tax burden among them (above, pp. 76–82) – but his approach and its practical implications aroused the criticism of the rabbis.

An example of an episode which aroused this sort of criticism can be found in the following source, where Rabbi Judah haNasi is presented as someone for whom personal riches were a criterion for determining where a man should sit at public events:

Ben Bunias [who was well-known for his extensive wealth] came before Rabbi. He said to them: Make way for the wealthy man. Another man came, [and] he said to them: Make way for this even wealthier man. Rabbi Ishmaʿel b. Rabbi Yose said to him: Rabbi, this man's [ben Bunias'] father has a thousand ships at sea and a thousand villages on land. He said to him: When you go to his father, tell him: Don't send him to me in such clothes! Rabbi honours rich men, Rabbi ʿAqiva honours rich men.[1]

---

[1] BT Eruvin 85b–86a.

In the period under discussion much importance was attached to the place where people sat in the leadership institution, for example, next to the patriarch, and so on. Someone who sat in the first row was not the same as someone who sat in the third row, someone who had a seat was not the same as someone who had standing room only, and so on. Rabbi Judah haNasi gave a certain degree of honour to the son of Bunias (or to Bunias himself according to the Munich MS) who owned much property, and also used to send him presents, but gave preference to another rich man who arrived later. He is criticised for this by one of the important rabbis, his colleague Rabbi Ishmaᶜel b. Rabbi Yose Ḥalafta, who tells him it would be better to prefer the son of Bunias, who was a really rich property-owner. Here Rabbi answers him that he fixed the place of ben Bunias not just on the basis of his riches, and his father's property, but also because of his unsuitable clothes. Following this the source adds a statement, without noting the name of its author but certainly with a hint of irony or criticism, that Rabbi honours the rich and Rabbi ᶜAqiva did too.

This is strange, since we might have expected that the source would mention another rabbi opposed to Rabbi's ideas, but in fact it mentions Rabbi ᶜAqiva, to whom it attributes the same social stance as that of Rabbi. This does not fit what we know of Rabbi ᶜAqiva, who made no distinction between rich and poor.[2] The solution, according to Safrai, is to accept a variant text which reads: Rabbi honours the rich, Rabbi Yaᶜaqov honours the *ḥasidim* / the

---

[2] See for example M Bava Qama viii, 6.

pietists.[3] It is thus reasonable to suppose that the intent here is to show that in contrast to Rabbi, who honours the rich, one of his teachers, Rabbi Ya'aqov b. Qursi,[4] honoured the *ḥasidim,* who were mostly involved in social activities with the poor.

Rabbi's closeness to the rich and the criticism which this aroused in rabbinic circles is clearly expressed in the evidence on Ben El'ashah, the husband Rabbi chose for his daughter, who was not from rabbinic circles but from the circles of the rich, and was not very intelligent:

Ben El'ashah was the son-in-law of Rabbi, and very rich ... as is written [in a Baraita]: Ben El'ashah did not spend his money without a reason, but to copy the hairstyle of the high priest, as it is written: *But they shall crop their heads* (Ezekiel 44.20). It is written [in a Baraita]: In a sort of *lulyanit/* spiral.[5]

Ben El'ashah's appearance in the 'hairstyle of the high priest,' the construction of which cost a great deal of money, was excessive in the eyes of the rabbis. The hairstyle itself was apparently constructed of rows of hair where the hair of the first row was inclined in the direction of the roots of the hair of the second row and so on, in a way which produced a spiral. The description is reminiscent of the permission granted by the rabbis to the house of Rabbi

---

[3] *Teshuvot haGe'onim,* copied from an Italian MS (ed. and comm. Y. Musafia; Lyck, 1864), para 2,6, p. 1. 'Ya'aqov' became ''Aqiva' in the standard version, while *ḥasidim* became '*ashirim/* the rich, two pairs of words where the letters are similar. See S. Safrai, 'Teaching of Pietists in Mishnaic Literature,' *JJS* 16 (1965), p. 33, n. 52.

[4] It is possible that his name alludes to his origins from Qursi on the east bank of the Sea of Galilee.

[5] BT Nedarim 51a.

to wear a *qome* hairstyle, such as was worn by Romans of aristocratic families, so that the prestigious Roman appearance would make it easier for them in their relations with the authorities:

They allowed the house of Rabbi three things: They could look in a mirror; they could wear a *qome* hairstyle; and they could teach their children Greek, for they needed [all these] for the authorities.[6]

Bar Qappara, one of Rabbi Judah haNasi's contemporaries, who had an ambivalent relationship with Rabbi himself, mocked Ben El'ashah because of his ignorance:

Rabbi used to honour Ben El'ashah. Bar Qappara said to him [Ben El'ashah]: All the people ask questions of Rabbi, but you, you don't ask him anything. He replied: What should I ask? He said to him: Ask:[7] [What] is seen from the heaven? [What] yearns in the depths of her house, makes all the winged creatures fear, the youth see and hide, old men get up and leave, the one who flees say 'ho ho,' and the trapped to be trapped in his iniquity?

Rabbi turned round and saw him mocking him. Rabbi said [to Bar Qappara]: I do not recognise you as an Elder [= ordained rabbi], and he [Bar Qappara] understood that he would not be appointed in his days.[8]

---

[6] JT Shabbat vi, 7d, col. 395. We cannot know the sort of hairstyle this was, for the Greek word *qome* (κόμη) simply means 'hair.' See also G. Veltri, 'Magic, Sex and Politics: The Media Power of Theatre Amusements in the Mirror of Rabbinic Literature,' *"The Words of a Wise Man's Mouth are Gracious" (Qoh 10,12): Festschrift for Günter Stemberger on the Occasion of His 65th Birthday* (ed. M. Perani; Berlin & New York, 2005), pp. 253–255.

[7] Ask: שאל. It is possible that this is a play on words from a proverbial saying about the fox, שאול.

[8] JT Mo'ed Qatan iii, 81c, col. 810.

Bar Qappara wants to show up Ben El'ashah, Rabbi Judah haNasi's son-in-law. At first he mocks him because he does not ask Rabbi questions about studying, as was accepted practice, and thus marks him out as someone who does not know how to ask. After this he primes him with a question which is a riddling trap.[9] At the end of all this Rabbi understands that Bar Qappara has made a laughing-stock of Ben El'ashah, and because of this he punishes Bar Qappara, telling him that he will not be able to be ordained all the time that he, Rabbi, is alive. At the beginning of the episode it is stressed, clearly in a tone of criticism, that Rabbi honoured Ben El'ashah, his rich and ignorant son-in-law. This is similar to the criticism voiced above by the rabbis against Rabbi: 'Rabbi honours rich people.'

It is reasonable to presume that Rabbi respected the rich not only because he was rich himself, but also for political reasons. Rabbi naturally aimed at increasing the power of the Jewish self-governing institutions which he headed. As already noted, the rich members of the city councils were close to the Romans, and by the time of Rabbi Judah ha-Nasi they recognised the leadership of the rabbis and its head. The relations of Rabbi with the Romans and the honours he gave to the rich played a major part in bringing the city elite, i.e. the Jewish office holders on the city councils, to submit themselves to his leadership.

---

[9] Many scholars have debated the meaning of this riddle. In the opinion of Tur-Sinai, for example, it is about folly: q.v. N. H. Tur-Sinai, *The Language and the Book,* vol. III (Jerusalem, 1955, Heb.), pp. 209–312.

2. The Change in Rabbi's Attitude to the ʿammei haʾaretz

On the one hand Rabbi Judah haNasi continued to reflect the attitude to the ʿam haʾaretz which had been current up to his time,[10] as in the example here:

It says in a Baraita: Rabbi said: An ʿam haʾaretz is forbidden to eat meat, as it is written: *This is the Torah of the animal and the bird* (Leviticus 11.46). Everyone who is engaged in Torah is allowed to eat the meat of animals and birds, and anyone who is not engaged in Torah is forbidden to eat the meat of animals or birds.[11]

In other words, eating meat – which was considered a luxury in Palestine – was only allowed for those engaged in studying Torah, and was forbidden for the ʿam haʾaretz. Similarly, the following statement was also attributed to Rabbi:

No trouble comes to the world except through the ʿammei haʾaretz.[12]

In contrast, Rabbi Judah haNasi clearly changed his attitude to the ʿammei haʾaretz, as is clear from the following aggadic episode:

Rabbi opened his stores [of grain to the public] in a year of drought. He said: Let those who know *miqraʾ* come in, and those who know *mishnah,* those who know *gemaraʾ,* those who know *halakhah,* those who know *aggadah,* but the ʿammei haʾaretz should not come in. Rabbi Yonatan b. Amram insisted on coming in. He said to him: Rabbi, feed me! He said to him: My son, did you study Scripture?

---

[10] See, A. Oppenheimer, *The ʿAm ha-Aretz: A Study in the Social History of the Jewish People in the Hellenistic-Roman Period* (Leiden, 1977), pp. 170–195.

[11] BT Pesaḥim 49b.

[12] BT Bava Batra 8a.

He said: No. He said: Did you study Mishnah? He said: No. If so, how can I feed you? He said: Feed me like a dog or a raven. He gave him food from his store. After [Rabbi Yonatan b. Amram] left, Rabbi sat down and was sorry. He said: How could I have given my food to an *ʿam haʾaretz*? Rabbi Shimʿon b. Rabbi said to him: Was that not Rabbi Yonatan b. Amram, your pupil, who never wanted to profit from the study of Torah? They checked, and it was he [Rabbi Yonatan b. Amram]. Rabbi said: Let everyone come in.[13]

This episode, even if it does have some aggadic elements, reflects the change which took place in Rabbi Judah haNasi's attitudes to the *ʿammei haʾaretz*. At the beginning he was only prepared to give food in a drought year to those who had studied Scripture and Mishnah. The expressions *miqraʾ, mishnah* and *gemaraʾ* clearly do not mean the works we know by these names today, for Gemara (Talmud) did not yet exist in the days of Rabbi Judah haNasi. They must therefore be there to signify the different ways of studying: *miqraʾ* as reading, *mishnah* as repetition and *gemaraʾ / talmud* as study in depth. When his pupil Yonatan b. Amram comes to him incognito, he tells him he has not read or repeated any texts, and asks for Rabbi to feed him like a dog or a raven, who are entitled to receive food even if they do not learn. At this point Rabbi changes his ways: in the first stage he gives grain from his store to Yonatan b. Amram, but immediately regrets it. In the second stage, after his son Shimʿon shows him that it is possible that this was a rabbi who was not prepared to take advantage of the honour of the Torah in order to achieve economic advantage, Rabbi calls to all the needy, without differen-

---

[13] BT *loc. cit.*

tiating between education or status, to come in and eat from his stores.

It is reasonable to presume that Rabbi Judah haNasi's decision to open up his grain stores to the ʿammei haʾaretz was not only due to his pupil who came incognito because he did not want to gain advantage from honouring the Torah, but also reflects other factors. Above all, it relates to Rabbi's own social policy, where we have seen a rapprochement between him and the city elite, where he does not investigate how much knowledge of Torah the rich and honourable had. The episode of his son-in-law Ben Elʿashah might even show that the rich as a whole group were known at the time for their ignorance of Torah. Even Rabbi Judah haNasi could not do two things at once: on the one hand, make friends with rich people ignorant of Torah, and even make them part of his family, and on the other to continue to decry the ʿammei haʾaretz as the rabbis had in preceding generations. Moreover, it should be noted once again that the main reason for the rejection of the ʿammei haʾaretz by the rabbis of Ushah was their fear that as a result of the circumstances of the time the study of Torah would not return to the central place it had held after the destruction of the Temple. The scornful and rejecting attitude to the ʿammei haʾaretz then was intended to serve as a stick to push them towards the study of Torah. By the time of Rabbi, the institution of Torah study now stood on firm foundations because of the clement political and economic climate, and there was no longer any fear that it would not take the place it deserved within Judaism. Thus there was room for change in the attitudes towards the ʿammei haʾaretz who still remained, and it was possible to stop deriding them and rejecting them from the normative community. This change is reflected in the aggadic episode under discussion, where Rabbi changes his practice and opens his stores in a drought year even to those who had not studied Torah.

There is also evidence of a change in Rabbi's attitude to the *ʿammei haʾaretz* in the following statement:

> Rabbi was of the opinion that it is preferable for a *ḥaver* [in a fellowship which is extraordinarily strict about purity and tithes] to commit a minor transgression so that an *ʿam haʾaretz* should not commit a major transgression. But Rabban Shimʿon b. Gamliel was of the opinion that it is preferable for a *ḥaver* to allow an *ʾam haʾaretz* to commit a major transgression so that he should not even commit a minor transgression.[14]

It is true that the source here is referring to tithes, and halakhically it is related to the concept of an *ʿam haʾaretz letaharah ulemaʿasrot* at the time when the Temple still stood, but the difference in attitude between Rabban Shimʿon b. Gamliel of the generation of Ushah, and his son, Rabbi Judah haNasi, is some evidence of the change which occurred in the attitude to the *ʿammei haʾaretz le-Torah* in their times.

The change in the attitude to *ʿammei haʾaretz leTorah* was possible because they did not belong to any sort of religion, sect or party: they were a social stratum, and thus could return to the mainstream when the time was right. Generally speaking, it seems clear that Rabbi Judah haNasi was as interested in social normalisation as he was in economic normalisation.

---

[14] BT Eruvin 32b.

3. Rabbi and the *ḥasidim*

Rabbi Judah haNasi was a legally constituted leader, a member of the leadership dynasty recognised by all Jews, including the members of the city councils. Similarly, he was also recognised by the Roman authorities with whom he had come to a rapprochement. However, he was also uncompromising and concentrated on Halakha. It is thus little wonder that he should be estranged from the *ḥasidim* and their popular leader, Rabbi Pinḥas b. Yair, who not only laid his stress on Aggadah, but also concentrated his efforts on promoting the well-being of the lowest and weakest strata of Jewish society.

The *ḥasidim* were a group who were active on the fringes of the Pharisees and the world of the rabbis. It is possible to identify a Hasidic stream as early as the time of the Second Temple, from the first century BCE. This stream continued to develop during the period of the Tannaim, but gradually disappeared at the beginning of the period of the Amoraim. The *ḥasidim* were known in three primary arenas: they laid considerable stress on doing good deeds in the social arena; they set prayer as their leading value; and they relied on miracles in order to fulfil their social aims.

The antithesis between Rabbi Judah haNasi, the domineering authority figure and owner of extensive properties, and Rabbi Pinḥas b. Yair, the popular leader, can be seen in the evidence about the clashes between them, as we shall see below. However, the gap between them was not totally unbridgeable, and sometimes Rabbi Judah haNasi and Rabbi Pinḥas b. Yair actually cooperated, as we have already seen, for example, over the purification of Ashkelon, and its inclusion within the halakhic borders of the Land of Israel, while at the same time gradually releasing the Jews of the city from the mitzvot dependent on the produce of the Land.

Rabbi Pinḥas b. Yair sets out a sort of scale of values of *ḥasidim* and *ḥasidut* in the following statement:

And Rabbi Pinḥas b. Yair used to say as follows: Speed leads to cleanness, cleanness leads to purity, purity leads to holiness, holiness leads to humility, humility leads to fear of sin, fear of sin leads to *ḥasidut*, *ḥasidut* leads to the holy spirit, the holy spirit leads to the revival of the dead, the revival of the dead leads to Elijah, may he be remembered for good.[15]

In the version in the Babylonian Talmud, as opposed to the Jerusalem Talmud, there is no eschatological ending, and the statement ends with the value of *ḥasidut,* ruling 'and *ḥasidut* is greater than all of them.' The holy spirit and the revival of the dead are missing from this version. In this case we should see the Babylonian Talmud text as the original and earlier version of the tradition, which describes a scale of values which begins with speed in carrying out mitzvot and sets *ḥasidut* at its peak. In the Palestinian version, the tradition was broadened and eschatological elements were added.[16] In any event, in the Jerusalem Talmud, *ḥasidut,* in Rabbi Pinḥas b. Yair's opinion, also stands at the top of the scale of human behaviour.

---

[15] JT Sheqalim iii, 47c, col. 613, and cf the Baraita added to the end of M Sotah ix, 15; BT Avodah Zarah 20b.

[16] See S. Safrai, 'The Pious *(Ḥassidim)* and the Men of Deeds' (Heb.), *Zion* 50 (1985), pp. 147–149 (= idem, *In Times of Temple and Mishnah* [Jerusalem, 1994, Heb.], pp. 532–534).

Rabbi Judah haNasi and Rabbi Pinḥas b. Yair sometimes clashed with one another. For example:

Rabbi Pinḥas b. Yair used to go to redeem captives. … Rabbi heard, and went out to meet him. He said to him: Do you want to eat with me? He replied: Yes. Rabbi's face glowed [with pleasure]. [Then] he said to him: … But now I refuse, because I am engaged in a mitzvah. When I get back I will come in to you. When he came he happened to come in at the same entrance where the white mules were to be found. He [Rabbi Pinḥas b. Yair] said: The Angel of Death is in the house of this man [Rabbi] and I am going to eat with him?! Rabbi heard and went out to him, and said to him: I will sell them. He said to him: *Thou shalt not put a stumbling block before the blind* (Leviticus 19.14). [Rabbi said:] I will let them go. [Rabbi Pinḥas b. Yair said:] They will cause much damage. I will hobble them. That is causing pain to animals. I will kill them. That goes against [the command]: Do not waste (cf Deuteronomy 20.19). He pleaded with him, and a mountain grew up between them. Rabbi wept and said: If in our lives [we did not manage to get close to one another], how much less so after death![17]

Rabbi Judah haNasi invites Rabbi Pinḥas b. Yair, a southerner from Lod or perhaps Ashkelon, to eat at his table, when the latter was passing through Beit Sheʿarim or Sepphoris on his way to redeem captives, one of the good deeds that the *ḥasidim* used to engage in. This implies that the patriarch approved of the *ḥasid*, but also, and perhaps most importantly, it assumes acceptance of the leadership of the patriarch by the *ḥasid* when he agrees to be present at his table. The episode of the white mules in the Babylonian Talmud is not at all clear, for it is difficult to understand what damage they could cause which was so great that they should be compared to the Angel of Death. The episode is

---

[17] BT Ḥullin 7a–b.

much easier to understand in the parallel in the Jerusalem Talmud, where Rabbi Pinhas b. Yair defies Rabbi and says:

All these [asses] eat at the expense of the people of Israel. You may not see me being so friendly to you again.[18]

From the Jerusalem Talmud it becomes clear that Rabbi Pinhas b. Yair is antagonistic to Rabbi Judah haNasi because of his public demonstrations of authority. He therefore refuses to eat with him, so that he does not have to recognise his office publicly and symbolically in this way. The episode in the Jerusalem Talmud deals at one and the same time with the clash between Rabbi and Rabbi Pinhas b. Yair against the background of the attempt by Rabbi to cancel the sabbatical year, and the antagonism of Rabbi Pinhas b. Yair to Rabbi because of his domineering behaviour. Thus the Jerusalem Talmud appears to be uniting two separate traditions on the conflict between Rabbi Judah haNasi and Rabbi Pinhas b. Yair. In contrast, the episode in the Babylonian Talmud deals with him against a single backdrop, although it is difficult to understand this without the parallel in the Jerusalem Talmud.

It may not be accidental that Rabbi Ḥanina b. Dosa, the head of the *hasidim* in the days of Rabban Yoḥanan b. Zakkai, lived in Galilee when the leadership institution was at Yavneh, while Rabbi Pinhas b. Yair lived in the south at a time when the leadership institution headed by Rabbi Judah haNasi was active in Galilee. There were also several other Galilean *hasidim* apart from Rabbi Ḥanina b. Dosa in the Yavneh period: the *hasid* priest from Ramat Benei

---

[18] JT Demai i, 22a, col. 118.

Anat in Galilee, as well as an anonymous *ḥasid* from Kefar Imi[19] mentioned in the Jerusalem Talmud.[20] In contrast, after the central leadership moved to Galilee following the Bar Kokhva revolt, we find the important *ḥasidim* active in Lod in Judaea, like Rabbi Pinḥas b. Yair, and in the generation after Rabbi we find Rabbi Joshua b. Levi there too. Thus if indeed there is any historical explanation for the geographical situation of the *ḥasidim,* it may well be connected to their physical distance from the centre of leadership and settlement. In the Yavneh period, when the leadership institutions were in Judaea, the *ḥasidim* lived and were active in Galilee, while in contrast, when the centre of leadership and settlement moved to Galilee, we find the most important *ḥasidim* in Judaea. We see here the frictions within the world of the rabbis: between the legally recognised and rational leadership of patriarchal domination and the charismatic popular leadership of the wonder-working *ḥasidim.* The tensions and differences are also evident from the fact that the leaders of the *ḥasidim* distance themselves geographically from the areas of activity of the leadership institutions.

The clashes between Rabbi and Rabbi Pinḥas b. Yair marked the height of the tensions and the polarisation within the world of the rabbis: Rabbi Judah was the pa-

---

[19] This was a *ḥasid* who was said to have brought down rain after he prayed. Kefar Immi has been identified with Kefar Iamma near Yavneʾel, called by this name presumably because of its propinquity to the Sea of Galilee (see e.g. Y. Tsafrir, et al., *Tabula Imperii Romani* [Jerusalem, 1994], s.v. Kefar Iamma, p. 163).

[20] JT Taʿanit i, 64b, col. 708.

triarch, while Rabbi Pinḥas b. Yair was the leader of the *ḥasidim;* Rabbi Judah was the legal leader, a member of the patriarchal dynasty, who was also recognised by the Roman authorities, while Rabbi Pinḥas b. Yair was a popular charismatic leader; Rabbi Judah haNasi was the representative of Halakha, the redactor of the Mishnah, while Rabbi Pinḥas b. Yair was a man of Aggadah and deeds within the social sphere, although he was also concerned about Halakha, and especially about the concrete mitzvot with social aspects to them, such as the sabbatical year; Rabbi Judah haNasi was an inhabitant of Galilee who carried out his office with a high hand in Bet She'arim, and later in Sepphoris/Zippori, while Rabbi Pinḥas b. Yair distanced himself from the domination of the centre in Galilee and lived, as noted, in Lod or perhaps even in Ashkelon in the south; Rabbi Judah haNasi was purely a realist, Rabbi Pinḥas b. Yair was a wonder-worker who brought about miracles. In addition, Rabbi Judah haNasi strongly supported economic normalisation, while Rabbi Pinḥas b. Yair was a conservative who stood for observing the commandments in the strictest way, especially if they were intended to care for the weakest strata immediately without let or hindrance.

4. The *qahala' qadisha' di-b'Yerushalayim* and Rabbi

The *qahala' qadisha' di-b'Yerushalayim*/ the holy community in Jerusalem, was the name of a *ḥavurah*/fellowship, of the pupils of Rabbi Meir which was active in the time of Rabbi Judah haNasi. The members of this *ḥavurah* settled in Jerusalem and took on themselves a way of life which was similar in many ways to that of the *ḥavurot* of the Pharisee elite in the time of the Second Temple, who had come together in order to observe the taking of tithes and the purity regulations more strictly. This *ḥavurah* was an exceptional social phenomenon, and its leaders were closely linked to Rabbi Judah haNasi. Like all the important rabbis of this period, they also took part in creating Halakha and editing the Mishnah.

There is evidence in the works of the Church Fathers that the repressive legislation following the Bar Kokhva revolt included a ban on Jewish settlement in Jerusalem. In the light of this, there are scholars who claim that the name of the *ḥavurah* should be *qahala' qadisha'* mi-*Yerushalayim*/the holy community *from* Jerusalem, and that it refers to a *ḥavurah* of refugees from Jerusalem who settled in Galilee. According to another view, this was a *ḥavurah* which was originally active during the Yavneh period and settled in Jerusalem, but those rabbis who are noted in the sources as being from the time of Rabbi Judah haNasi belonged to a later period in the history of the *ḥavurah* when it no longer existed in Jerusalem. However, these theories have no basis in the sources. It is reasonable to suppose that in the fifty or so years which had passed between the days of the repressive legislation following the Bar Kokhva revolt and the days of Rabbi Judah haNasi, the legislation was cancelled in all or some respects. It is very possible that in the days of the Severans, a time of improved relations with the Jews of Palestine in general and with their leader

Rabbi Judah haNasi in particular, the Roman authorities did not apply the ban on Jews settling in Jerusalem very strictly, so that what we have here is a *havurah* which really was active in Jerusalem, just as it says.

The following source demonstrates the principles of the *qahala' qadisha' di-b'Yerushalayim* and the way of life of its members:

Enjoy life with a woman you love (Ecclesiastes 9.9). Rabbi said: This relates to the holy community: Get yourself a craft together with Torah. What does this mean? *Enjoy life etc.* And why does he call them a holy community? Because they included Rabbi Yose b. Meshullam and Rabbi Shim'on b. Mansia who used to divide the day into three: a third for Torah, a third for prayer, and a third for work. But there are those who say: They used to labour over Torah in the winter, and over their work in the summer.[21]

In the first part of the source we find Rabbi Judah haNasi's exegesis of the name of the holy community. In this exegesis it is stressed that a man must not rely only on learning Torah, which is compared to the beloved woman in the verse from Ecclesiastes, but he must also learn a craft, i.e. work, which is parallel to the word 'life' in the verse in question. In other words, if a man wants to be able to learn a great deal of Torah, he must learn a craft so that he will have an income which will enable him to learn. In the second part of the source, there is a search for a balance between studying Torah, stressing prayer as the *hasidim* did, and engaging in work for an income. Unlike the rest of the rabbis, who made their motto learning Torah only, the rabbis who belonged to this *havurah* laid equal stress

---

[21] Ecclesiastes Rabbah ix, 9.

on prayer and work, as well as Torah. We can assume that
the *havurah* also stressed purity as well, for the very term
qedushah in the Talmudic literature is often a synonym for
Pharisaic norms and for purity. Rabbi Yose b. Meshullam,
one of the heads of the *havurah* of the *qahala' qadisha'
di-b'Yerushalayim,* was very strict over the Halakha when
dealing with the laws of purity of the *haver* in a *havurah*
at the time of the Second Temple. It is even possible that
the members of the *qahala' qadisha'* were strict over eating
hullin/unsanctified food, in a state of purity, like the *havurot* from the time of the Temple. The Halakha requires,
for example, priests to eat tithes in a state of purity, but it
does not oblige them to eat unsanctified food in purity, so
that this an extremist demand.

The stress on prayer and work, and the strictness about
purity are flagged in the name of Rabbi Meir, one of the
most important rabbis of the Ushah generation, if not the
most important of all. Like Rabbi Judah haNasi after him,
Rabbi Meir was one of the few rabbis who received the
title 'holy.' He was among those who repeated the Halakhot and customs of the *havurot* from the Pharisaic elite at
the end of the time of the Second Temple, and was considered as exceptionally rigorous about the Halakhot of
the *havurot,* in comparison with his colleagues. We must
remember that rabbis who were active after the destruction of the Temple still continued to deal with Halakhot
related to Temple times, such as the Halakhot of the Temple itself, or the Halakhot of the Pharisaic *havurot.* Thus it
is clear that in the time of Rabbi Judah haNasi there were
still some pupils of Rabbi Meir who continued to carry

out his teachings in reality, and organised themselves into a *ḥavurah* which chose to live in Jerusalem.

Among the pupils of Rabbi Meir who became heads of the *qahalaʾ qadishaʾ* the sources mention Rabbi Shimʿon b. Mansiah and Rabbi Yose b. Meshullam. It is also possible that Rabbi Shemuel of Phrygia (in present-day Turkey), a pupil of Rabbi Meir, whose tombstone inscription has been found in Jerusalem and dates to around this period, was also one of the heads of the *qahalaʾ qadishaʾ* in Jerusalem.[22]

It is interesting to note that, in spite of the fact that the *ḥavurah* was active in Jerusalem and had links with Rabbi, none of the sources mention that Rabbi Judah haNasi himself had any tendency to settle in Jerusalem. Similarly, there is no hint that he brought up the subject of increasing the Jewish population of Jerusalem with the Roman authorities, or tried to get permission to rebuild the Temple. Rabbi Judah haNasi continued to administer the leadership centre in Galilee, like the rabbis of Ushah before him, and the rabbis who were responsible for the transfer of the leadership institutions to Tiberias after him. He followed in the footsteps of Rabban Yoḥanan b. Zakkai and Rabban Gamliel of Yavneh in filling the vacuum which had been created with the destruction of the Temple, mostly through stressing the importance of studying Torah. As we have noted, he saw the political situation of his time

---

[22] See S. Safrai, 'The Holy Assembly of Jerusalem' (Heb.), *Zion* 22 (1957), p. 192 (= idem, *In Times of Temple and Mishnah* [Jerusalem, 1994, Heb.], p. 180; idem, 'The Holy Congregation in Jerusalem,' *Scripta Hierosolymitana* 23 [1972], p. 77).

as so favourable to the Jews that he wanted to cancel the fast of the Ninth of Av, but even if building the Temple was included in his hopes of salvation, he did not return to Jerusalem and did not try to rebuild it there.

Chapter 5

Rabbi Judah haNasi as a National and Religious Leader

1. Fixing the Calendar

The Jewish calendar regulates the pulse of the life of the Jewish people: the cycle of the festivals and fasts, and some of the mitzvot dependent on the produce of the Land of Israel. This calendar is common to the Land of Israel and the Diaspora, and thus acts as a unifying factor for all Jewish communities.[1]

Fixing the calendar was one of the most important sources of authority for the leadership institutions in Palestine, including hegemony over the Diaspora. In the Yavneh period, tensions arose between Rabban Gamliel of Yavneh and the Beit haVaʿad on the question of who should fix the calendar. The patriarch saw this as his own prerogative, while the rabbis saw the patriarch as *primus inter pares*. By the days of Rabbi Judah haNasi, no-one questioned his right to fix the calendar, and because of this, he himself slighted this authority to some extent through his *taqqanot*.

Unlike earlier patriarchs, Rabbi Judah haNasi was somewhat ambivalent over the question of fixing the calendar. On the one hand, he was an assertive patriarch, for whom

---

[1] On the Jewish calendar see, S. Stern, *Calendar and Community: A History of the Jewish Calendar, Second Century BCE – Tenth Century CE* (Oxford, 2001).

it was reasonable to keep the fixing of the calendar in his own hands. On the other hand, he had enough authority, and did not need to strengthen it by keeping the sanctification of the month and the intercalation of the year in his hands only. It is against this background that we should understand his far-reaching *taqqanah* which 'allowed [the evidence of] a murderer, and allowed [the evidence of] a witness who heard from another witness' in order to sanctify the new month.[2] This far-reaching permission, to accept even the statement of a murderer and hearsay evidence as allowable evidence of seeing the crescent moon, and to sanctify the month on the basis of this evidence, almost takes all meaning from the evidence about the new month, for in every other matter the rabbis banned the evidence even of someone who had committed small sins, such as dice players (i.e. gamblers), and certainly did not allow murderers. This is also the case with a witness who had heard from another witness, i.e. hearsay evidence, which was certainly not admissible on a subject which was all based on autopsy. In the same context, we hear that 'Rabbi cancelled the bonfires.' A line of bonfires used to be lit on fixed hill-tops in order to announce the sanctification of the month, but these were already cancelled in the days of the Second Temple because of the Samaritans. The Samaritans 'spoiled' this custom, in other words, they used to light bonfires on the night following the twenty-ninth day, in order to mislead the Jews into thinking that they had sanctified the month that day. Thus the Beit haVa'ad

---

[2] JT Rosh haShanah ii, 58a, col. 669.

used to send messengers instead of lighting beacons.[3] The question here, then, is how Rabbi Judah haNasi could cancel the bonfires, when these had been cancelled already more than a hundred years before his patriarchate. It would appear that the bonfires which Rabbi cancelled and which are referred to here were local internal bonfires only, such as from the hills of Safed to Tiberias. It also says in the same place in the Jerusalem Talmud that Rabbi 'allowed them to go out in the evening, presuming that the sanctification would take place.' In other words, after the crescent moon had been seen, it was already permitted for the messengers to go out to announce the sanctification of the month, before those entitled to had proclaimed the month as sanctified. These far-reaching *taqqanot* are demonstrations that Rabbi had no need of fixing the calendar to fortify his authority, and that in effect they relied on the calculation of the month which was already known from the days of his grandfather Rabban Gamliel, more than they relied on the witnesses of the moon. However, Rabbi Judah haNasi did not cancel the sanctification of the month by witnesses, and indeed continued to use his authority to fix the calendar as a political tool in various different situations.

In this context it is very interesting indeed to see how Rabbi Judah haNasi relates to the question of where the calendar is to be fixed. The Tannaitic Halakha rules: 'You should not intercalate the year except in Judaea, but if it

---

[3] M Rosh haShanah ii, 2.

is intercalated in Galilee, then it is intercalated.[4] In the days of Rabbi, the territory of Judah, which had almost become a desert following the Bar Kokhva revolt, underwent a real restoration. The status of Lod is particularly noteworthy, for the city went back to being a centre of Torah study, as it had been when the leadership institutions were still at Yavneh. Modern scholars even think that the leadership institutions moved to Lod before the Bar Kokhva revolt.[5] Rabbi himself returned some of her former status to Lod when he decided that the act of fixing the calendar should take place in this city. Thus we find a Baraita on the intercalation of the year by two of the rabbis of his generation:

> The rabbis taught in a Baraita: It happened that Rabbi Simai and Rabbi Zadoq went to intercalate the year at Lod, and passed the Sabbath at Ono [in the area of present-day Qiryat Ono].[6]

The status of Lod gradually improved in the days of Rabbi Judah haNasi, until it became a threat to the status of the centre in Galilee. Rabbi thus clearly understood that he stood to lose if Lod became more important. He changed his mind, therefore, about giving permission to intercalate the year in Judah, and returned this privilege to Galilee. The sanctification of the month was less important, however, and Rabbi left this in Judah at the request of Rabbi Shimʿon (who is the same Rabbi Simai who intercalated

---

[4] Tos. Sanhedrin ii, 13 according to codex Vienna and *editio princeps*.

[5] See this trend already in G. Alon, *The Jews in Their Land in the Talmudic Age* (Jerusalem, 1984), pp. 462–465.

[6] BT Ḥullin 56b.

the year in Lod together with Rabbi Zadoq), but they took this privilege away from Lod and fixed it in the adjacent village of Ein Tav. This has been identified with the settlement called ENETABA which appears on the Madaba map.[7] Thus we find:

Rabbi said to Rabbi Ḥiyya: Go to Ein Tav and sanctify the month, and send me the sign: Long live David, king of Israel![8]

Among Rabbi's *taqqanot* on the sabbatical year, or those of other rabbis following in his footsteps, we find some conclusions related to the calendar about years which it was not possible to intercalate. Before his *taqqanot* which nibbled away at the institution of the sabbatical year, they did not intercalate the sabbatical year for economic reasons, so as not to lengthen the year in which it was forbidden to work the land by yet another month. Similarly, they did not intercalate the year after the sabbatical year, in other words the eighth year, so as not to postpone the permission to eat new produce, for this new produce, as we have

---

[7] The Madaba map is a mosaic map from the sixth century CE. It is the only original map of Palestine from antiquity, and appears to have been drawn following the *Onomasticon* of Eusebius. The map is still *in situ* on the floor of a Greek Orthodox church in the Jordanian town of Madaba, 30 km south of Amman. See, M. Piccirillo & E. Alliata (eds.), *The Madaba Map Centenary 1897–1997: Travelling through the Byzantine Ummayad Period* (Jerusalem, 1999); M. Piccirillo, 'The Madaba Mosaic Map,' idem, *The Mosaics of Jordan* (Amman, 1993), pp. 81–95.

[8] BT Rosh haShanah 25a, on this see, S. Safrai, 'The Places Where They Sanctified the Months and Intercalated the Year in the Land of Israel after the Destruction of the Temple' (Heb.), *Tarbiz* 35 (1965), pp. 27–38 (= idem, *In Times of Temple and Mishnah* [Jerusalem, 1994, Heb.], pp. 247–258).

noted, was only allowed after Nisan 16th, when they had waved the *'omer* sheaf in the Temple.[9]

You do not intercalate the year in the sabbatical year or the year after the sabbatical year … Rabbi Zeira in the name of Rabbi Abbahu [said]: What you say here [that you do not intercalate in the sabbatical year or the year after], this was when Rabbi did not allow the import of vegetables from abroad to the Land of Israel, but when Rabbi allowed them to import vegetables from abroad, they allowed [the intercalation] in the sabbatical year and the year after.[10]

In other words, Rabbi's *taqqanah* ruled that in the sabbatical year it was permissible to import vegetables from abroad to Palestine, so that there would be enough to eat in the country during the sabbatical year and the year after. On the basis of this *taqqanah,* they intercalated the year in the sabbatical year and the year after, whenever necessary, as in all the other years of *shemitah.*

2. *Semikhah/*Ordination

Rabbi's power can be seen in particular in the fact that he alone held the exclusive authority to give *semikhah/*ordination. In his time *semikhah* (or *minui* as it is termed in the Jerusalem Talmud) included bestowing the title 'rabbi,' and giving those who held this office certain powers in judging laws of property and fines, and teaching the laws on what was forbidden and permitted. All the members of the Beit haVaʿad (or Sanhedrin as it is termed in the

---

[9] Leviticus 23.9–14.
[10] JT Peah v, 18d, col. 98 and parallels.

Babylonian Talmud), were rabbis with *semikhah*. It is clear that the man or institution who had the authority to give *semikhah* held great power, and it was against this background that tensions appeared between the patriarchs, who wanted to keep the authority to give it in their hands only, and the rest of the Beit haVaʿad, who wanted to share it with the patriarch.

There are many sources which inform us that Rabbi granted ordination exclusively, and that he also used this right for political ends, especially in order to increase the centrality of his authority. One of the best known sources is the request of Rabbi Ḥiyya to grant ordination to one of his pupils, who was also his relative:

When Rabbah bar Ḥana went down to Babylonia, Rabbi Ḥiyya said to Rabbi: The son of my brother is going down to Babylonia. *Yoreh*/may he rule [on the laws of forbidding and permitting]? He may rule. *Yadin*/may he judge? He may judge. *Yatir*/may he exempt first-born animals? He may exempt [them]. When Rav went down to Babylonia, Rabbi Ḥiyya said to Rabbi: The son of my sister is going down to Babylonia. May he rule? He may rule. May he judge? He may judge. May he exempt first-born animals? He may not exempt [them].[11]

Rabbi Ḥiyya was an important rabbi. He would presumably have fulfilled the function of the head of the Beit haVaʿad alongside Rabbi Judah haNasi had such a position existed then. The source also tells us about three fields to which *semikhah* relates: *yoreh, yadin* and *yatir bekhorot*. *Yoreh*/he may rule, implies that the ordained rabbi may rule on Halakhot on what is forbidden and what is al-

---

[11] BT Sanhedrin 5a.

lowed. *Yadin*/he may judge, implies that the ordained rabbi is allowed to sit as a member of a Beit Din and also to judge in cases which are not actually a matter of laws of property but where there is likely to be a fine imposed. *Yatir bekhorot*/he may exempt the first-born, grants him the authority to allow the priest who received the first-born of a clean animal to slaughter or sell it. When the Temple was still standing, the first-born of a clean animal was given to the priest as an offering, and the meat from it was eaten by him in Jerusalem. After the destruction of the Temple, the first-born was given to the priest, and used to join his flock until the animal produced a defect which would have made it forbidden to sacrifice. The ordained rabbi had the authority to release the animal for use by the priest after he had ruled that it did indeed have the right sort of defect, and that the priest had not deliberately made it defective. Rabbah bar Ḥana received this final authority, whereas Rav, in spite of the fact that he was more learned in Torah than his cousin, did not receive it.

The wording of Rabbi's will in the Jerusalem Talmud (see below, pp. 215–219) gives us further information about Rabbi's exclusive authority to grant ordination and some of the ways he carried this out. According to this, Rabbi set up a standard for the number of rabbis to be ordained. They were subject at first to a trial period, and only after they had proved themselves were they given a permanent ordination. If they did not succeed in their trial period, they would lose their ordination. The standard was two rabbis a year, and the trial period was for a year. In his will Rabbi instructed that the trial period should be cancelled and that they should immediately ordain all those who were suitable:

Rabbi used to appoint two people to be ordained;[12] if they were suitable, they would stay; if not, they went.[13]

Anyone who objected to Rabbi Judah's methods of control was in danger of not receiving ordination, even if they were suitable candidates. One of the outstanding cases, which we have already mentioned previously, was that of Judah and Hezekiah, the sons of Rabbi Ḥiyya, who expressed their antagonism to Rabbi's demonstrations of power by comparing the patriarchate to the exilarchate, saying that the messiah would not come until these two dynasties came to an end.[14] The Midrash gives evidence here:

Rabbi Zeira said: How many *ḥasidim* and people learned in Torah were suitable for ordination, like Judah son of Rabbi Hezekiah, about whom it is said, 'and also the last ones' (Ecclesiastes 1.11). But in the Time to Come, the Holy One blessed be He will appoint a *ḥavurah*/fellowship of his own righteous men for himself, and they will sit with him in a great Yeshivah.[15]

It is reasonable to assume that the Midrash is not speaking here of one rabbi, i.e. Judah b. Rabbi Hezekiah, but of two, Judah and Hezekiah, for it speaks of them here in the plural, presumably referring to the two sons of Rabbi Ḥiyya. The quotation here, therefore, appears to relate to these two sons of Rabbi Ḥiyya, who like others in Rabbi's time, were not granted *semikhah,* in spite of the fact that

---

[12] Two per year: cf Lamentations Rabbah vii, 7.

[13] JT Taʿanit iv, 68a, col. 728.

[14] See below, p. 158–159.

[15] Ecclesiastes Rabbah i, 11.

they deserved it, and in the opinion of the exegete they would only receive the place due to them in the World to Come. They do indeed appear often in the sources with just their names – Judah and Hezekiah – without the title 'rabbi.' It is interesting that the Midrash also emphasises that Rabbi withheld ordination from the *ḥasidim,* which reminds us of the tensions between him and Rabbi Pinḥas b. Yair discussed in the previous chapter.

Another rabbi whom Rabbi Judah haNasi did not ordain all his life because he criticised him was Bar Qappara. As already noted, Bar Qappara used his literary abilities to satirise Rabbi on the subjects of his riches, his power and his close relations with the city elite. When Bar Qappara attacked Ben El'ashah, Rabbi's rich and ignorant son-in-law, Rabbi reacted: 'I do not recognise you [as an] Elder.'[16] From this Bar Qappara understood that he would not receive *semikhah* all the time Rabbi was alive.

An even more striking example of this sort of behaviour on the part of Rabbi, is the way he refrained from granting ordination to Rabbi Ḥanina bar Ḥama, who became Av Beit Din, a sort of head of the Beit haVa'ad, after Rabbi's death. This was the result of Rabbi's instructions to his son in his will, where he told him not to behave as he, Rabbi, had done in matters of ordination, and to grant ordination first and foremost to Rabbi Ḥanina bar Ḥama: 'And appoint Rabbi Ḥanina bar Ḥama first.'[17]

---

[16] JT Moʿed Qatan iii, 81c, col. 810.
[17] JT Taʿanit iv, 68a, col. 728.

The Jerusalem Talmud asks a series of questions about this:

And why did he [Rabbi Judah haNasi] not ordain him [Ḥanina bar Ḥama]? Rabbi Drosa said: Because the people of Zippori/Sepphoris were angry with him in Zippori. And because of this anger should one do this [i. e. refrain from ordaining him]? Rabbi Elʿazar b. Rabbi Yose said: It was because he contradicted [Rabbi's] words in public. Rabbi used to sit and repeat: And their refugees remembered me and were on the mountains like the doves of the valleys, all *homiot*/yearning (cf Ezekiel 7.16).[18] He said to him: *homot*/moaning. He said to him: From where [do you get] this reading? He said to him: From Rav Hamnuna of Babylonia. He said to him: When you go down there tell him to ordain you as a rabbi. Thus he [Ḥanina bar Ḥama] knew that he would not be ordained in his [Rabbi's] lifetime.[19]

The source tells us that Rabbi Ḥanina bar Ḥama dared to correct Rabbi's quotation in public (to the version in the masoretic text, i. e. in our text of the Hebrew Bible), and because of this Rabbi did not grant him ordination. According to another version, which is rejected because it is not sufficient reason for withholding ordination, Rabbi did this because Rabbi Ḥanina bar Ḥama brought on himself the anger of his fellow inhabitants of Zippori, because he had rebuked them. In the parallel version of Rabbi's will in the Babylonian Talmud, Rabbi instructs his son not just to give *semikhah* to Rabbi Ḥanina bar Ḥama, but also to appoint him as head of the Beit haVaʿad. This may also be his

---

[18] Ezekiel 7.16: 'And those fugitives that escape shall be on the mountains like the doves of the valleys, all of them moaning.'

[19] JT *loc cit*.

intention in the Jerusalem Talmud version, which we will look at in detail below in our discussion of Rabbi's will.

According to an aggadic source in the Babylonian Talmud, Rabbi Judah haNasi also granted ordination to those who were clearly not suitable for it, and certainly not at the time he gave it to them. A striking example of this is the case where he gave ordination to the son of his colleague, Rabbi El'azar b. Rabbi Shim'on, after the latter had died.[20] Even though in the end the sad boy learned Torah and made himself suitable for the ordination which he got because Rabbi was sorry for him, it is clear that when Rabbi gave him *semikhah* because of his family's merit, he was far from being an example of a rabbi who deserved it.[21]

Teaching in the open air suited the climate in Palestine, and was also accepted in the Graeco-Roman world, not to mention the world of the New Testament. However, according to the opinion brought by Rabbi, the words of the Torah include information which is not suitable for everyone, so that he forbids teachers who are preparing their pupils for ordination to continue to teach them, as had been common up till then, 'under a tree,' 'under a fig tree,' 'under an olive tree' or in the street. From the moment when Rabbi Judah haNasi ruled that teaching should take place only in the Beit Midrash, and not outside, not only was he in sole control of the actual giving of *semikhah*, but

---

[20] BT Bava Metzia 85a.

[21] A similar story to the one described here is told in the same passage of the Babylonian Talmud about the grandson of Rabbi Tarfon, to whom Rabbi promised that if he repented of his way of life, he would give him his daughter to marry.

he could also vet the suitability of the candidates coming to prepare themselves for ordination:[22] when the studies took place in a specific closed site like the Beit Midrash, it was possible to prevent the entry of someone who was found to be unsuitable.

A further convention which Rabbi changed as part of this trend to increase the centralisation of his leadership was the restriction of freedom on teaching on the subject of forbidden and permitted:

Rabbi was in Akko. He saw them [the people of Akko] eating white bread [i. e. without bran]. He said to them: How do you soak them [the grains of wheat, so that afterwards it will be easier to separate the kernels from the bran]? They said to him: A [rabbinical] student came here and instructed us about water of eggs, which is not permitted, so we boil eggs and soak [the grains of wheat] in the water [in which the eggs were boiled]. They were sure [that the student meant] the water in which eggs were boiled, and did not say 'the water [= white] of eggs.' Rabbi Ya'aqov bar Idi said: From that moment they ruled that a student [who has not yet been ordained] should not teach and instruct [on what is forbidden or permitted]. Rabbi Ḥiyya [said] in the name of Rabbi Huna: When a student teaches [about what is forbidden or permitted], his decision is not binding.[23]

Thus there was a misunderstanding between the student and the people of Akko as to the liquid in which the student ruled that it was permitted to soak the grains of wheat without fear that they might become liable to impurity. According to the Halakha, foods do not become unclean when they come into contact with a source of impurity as

---

[22] JT Ta'anit iv, 68a, col. 728.
[23] JT Shevi'it vi, 36c, col. 197. Cf BT Sanhedrin 5b.

long as they do not come into contact with water or one of the other six liquids which are liable to impurity. When the student who had not yet received *semikhah* taught in Akko that water from eggs does not make food liable to impurity, he meant the liquid white of eggs, which is not included in the liquids which make food liable to impurity. But the student did not explain himself properly, and the people of Akko thought he meant the water in which eggs were cooked, and of course the Halakha does not distinguish between this and any other water.

This episode gave Rabbi an excuse to rule a *taqqanah* which cancelled the status of a 'student who was eligible to teach' even though he was not ordained,[24] a sort of junior rabbi who sometimes took the place of the senior qualified one. Rabbi's ruling fixed that in every situation 'a student should not give a ruling.' In the parallel in the Babylonian Talmud, the wording of his *taqqanah* was: 'A student should not give rulings unless he has been given permission by his teacher.'[25] It is reasonable to prefer the version of the Jerusalem Talmud here, both because it is the talmud of the Land of Israel, and because this unmistakable *taqqanah* is more suited to the ways of Rabbi Judah haNasi.

Rabbi also used to suspend rabbis with *semikhah* who had aroused his anger temporarily, usually for a period of a month. Even his close colleague, Rabbi Ḥiyya, was punished in this way, as we saw above.[26] Rabbi Ḥiyya told him: 'Rav Huna [the exilarch] is outside,' after Rabbi had

---

[24] Cf Horayot i, 1.

[25] BT Sanhedrin 5b.

[26] Chapter 1, pp. 41–42.

said that the only person he was prepared to give up his seat to was the exilarch, if he arrived from Babylonia, for his relationship to the royal House of David was preferable to Rabbi's. When Rabbi Ḥiyya told him that the exilarch had indeed come, but in a coffin, in order to be buried in the Land of Israel, Rabbi sent Rabbi Ḥiyya to see who was looking for him outside, and when he saw that no-one was looking for him, he realised that he should not appear before the patriarch for thirty days.

On another occasion, Rabbi Ḥiyya received the same punishment, when he broke Rabbi's *taqqanah* mentioned above: 'that they should not teach students in the street,' and Rabbi Ḥiyya demonstratively taught his two nephews Rav and Rabba bar Bar Ḥanah in the street.[27]

3. Rabbi's Activities in Beit Sheʿarim and Zippori

Rabbi moved the leadership institutions from Ushah (or Shefaram) to the town of Beit Sheʿarim, and afterwards to the city of Zippori / Sepphoris (Diocaesarea).[28] These two moves demonstrate the special status and power of Rabbi Judah haNasi among both Romans and Jews. The lands which were apparently granted or leased to him by the Roman authorities (see above, Chapter 3.1) included lands at Beit Sheʿarim, which it is reasonable to suppose were already royal property at the time of the Second Temple.

---

[27] BT Moʿed Qatan 16a–b.
[28] Genesis Rabbah 97,13 (eds. Theodor & Albeck, pp. 1220–1221). Cf BT Rosh haShanah 31a–b.

To begin with, these lands were owned by the Hasmonaean kings, then they fell to Herod and his family, and were finally taken over by the Roman emperor.[29] After the Roman authorities gave them to Rabbi, he moved his residence to Beit Shecarim and transferred the leadership of the rabbis there, too. The transfer of the leadership institutions to Beit Shecarim – whose lands were royal property – is evidence of the deepening Roman recognition of Rabbi.

Rabbi appears in the Talmudic literature as ruling on halakhic questions related to Beit Shecarim:

The rabbis taught: *'Justice, justice shalt thou pursue'* (Deuteronomy 16.20). [This means:] Go after the rabbis to their Yeshivah … after Rabbi to Beit Shecarim.[30]

With the move to Zippori/Sepphoris, the institutions of the self-governing Jewish leadership in Galilee moved for the first time to a city with the status of a *polis*. The conditions for this were ripe from the time that the members of the city leadership institutions and the rest of the city elite in Sepphoris and other cities were prepared to submit themselves to Rabbi's leadership. Before his time, the Jewish city elites were not usually prepared to accept the authority of the rabbinical leadership institutions, because of their identification with the Roman authorities and

---

[29] Josephus, *Vita* 119 and see, B. Mazar, *Beth Shecarim,* vol. I (Jerusalem, 1973), pp. 15–16; B. Isaac & I. Roll, *Roman Roads in Judaea,* vol. I: *The Legio-Scythopolis Road* (BAR International Series 141; Oxford, 1982), pp. 104–106.

[30] BT Sanhedrin 32b. The Babylonian Talmud here uses the Babylonian term Yeshivah to denote the Batei Midrash of the rabbis of Palestine in the settlements where they lived.

with Hellenistic and Roman culture in general. There can be no doubt that the decisive reasons for the change were the increasing recognition by the Roman authorities of the leadership institutions headed by Rabbi in general, and the strong links of the authorities with Rabbi in particular. This is expressed, for example, in the request the city leadership institutions addressed to Rabbi, which we dealt with already in Chapter 3, that he should divide up the responsibility for payment of Roman taxes amongst them.

A Babylonian Talmudic tradition proposes a different reason for the move from Beit She'arim to Sepphoris – Rabbi's illness:

Rabbi was in Beit She'arim, but because he fell ill, they brought him to Sepphoris, which is high up with good air.[31]

It is true that there are traditions of the various illnesses suffered by Rabbi before he died. However, Rabbi and the leadership institutions were in Sepphoris for quite a long time, and there are undoubtedly a number of other places in Galilee where the climate is much better than either Beit She'arim or Sepphoris. The sources tell us that Rabbi lived in Sepphoris for seventeen years. Even if this number is there as a midrashic parallel to the seventeen years which Jacob spent in Egypt, it is still evidence of a long stay.[32]

The importance of the move from Beit She'arim to Sepphoris is that it points to a further stage in the establishment of the leadership institutions in Galilee, which

---

[31] BT Ketubbot 103b–104a.
[32] E. g. Genesis Rabbah 95, Vatican MS (eds. Theodor & Albeck, p. 1234).

reflects Rabbi's hegemony over the Jewish city elite who held the city leadership. The transfer of the leadership institutions to Sepphoris, and their functioning there also strengthened Jewish settlement in the city. Among other things, this brought about an influx of rabbis to the city, and led to the setting-up of a large number of Batei Midrash and synagogues in Sepphoris, especially in Rabbi's time.

The evidence in the Talmudic literature of the presence of Rabbi in Beit She'arim and Sepphoris/Zippori have led scholars to look for sites and buildings connected to him and his life in these two settlements. Recently it has been suggested that Rabbi's house can actually be identified in Beit She'arim. There is a building there which, according to the evidence of the pottery and coins found in it, was built in the second half of the second century, i.e. during the time of Rabbi's patriarchate. The size of the house is evidence that its owner must have been wealthy, and it includes among other things an *exedra* and large stables – which fit the Talmudic story about Rabbi's white mules, already mentioned above.[33] However, it should be noted that at that time every rich man, not just the patriarch, could have had large stables. Moreover, the Talmudic source does not say that the *exedra* was actually in the house of the patriarch, but only that Rabbi allowed carrying on the Sabbath in an *exedra* in Beit She'arim.

---

[33] Yigal & Yotam Tepper, *Beth She'arim: The Village and Nearby Burials* (Yagur, 2004, Heb.), pp. 105–106, 118–119.

A further building which might be connected historically with Rabbi is the impressive basilica uncovered south of Beit Sheʿarim. This is a large building 40 m long by 15 m wide, built of large well-worked stones with a smooth flat border on their external face. The building, like all basilicas, is divided into three spaces by two rows of pillars. There is a large courtyard in front of it, through which there is an entrance to the basilica through a narrow narthex. On the basis of the ceramic and numismatic finds, the building has been dated to the period between the middle of the second and the beginning of the third centuries, that is, more or less the time of Rabbi's patriarchate in Beit Sheʿarim, and it remained in use for nearly two hundred years. It is possible to see this building as the place where the leadership institutions sat when they were in Beit Sheʿarim for part of the time of Rabbi's patriarchate. However, as long as there is no definitive find to confirm this supposition, such as an inscription, it still remains possible that this was another sort of public building, such as a synagogue or a market, and not necessarily the place where the patriarch and Beit haVaʿad had their seats. The same is true of the similar large building which has been uncovered in Tiberias, where the dating fits the period when the leadership institutions sat in Tiberias: here too there is no proof that this was indeed the place where they sat. We shall discuss the necropolis in Beit Sheʿarim below (pp. 228–231), together with the question of whether it is possible to identify Rabbi's tomb there.

There is another theory which identifies the house where Rabbi lived in Zippori/Sepphoris after he moved there from Beit She῾arim with a building which has been excavated in the former city.[34] This is a large house sited south of the theatre, and according to the archaeological evidence it was built in the third century CE. In the wing which was used for everyday living there is a toilet with an inscription in Greek 'Hygieia' – Ὑγ(ί)ει(α) – i.e. health, on the white mosaic floor. This is reminiscent of the opinion of Rabbi Yose in a Baraita on the question 'Who is rich?' to which the answer given is 'Anyone who has a toilet near to his table.'[35] The large dining-room of this building at Zippori/Sepphoris has a figured mosaic floor which includes scenes from the life of Dionysos – the god of wine and emotion in Greek mythology – including a wine-drinking contest between Dionysos and Heracles. This mosaic is particularly well-known today because it includes a depiction of the head of a beautiful woman, wearing a laurel wreath and with earrings in her ears, in the centre of the northern part of the mosaic frame.[36] The fact that there is a pagan mosaic in the building need not rule out the possibility that this was Rabbi's house, for it is possible that in his eyes the mosaic was simply decorative, a natural expression of his closeness to Roman culture. Moreover, not long after-

---

[34] Z. Weiss, 'Between Paganism and Judaism: Toward an Identification of the "Dionysiac Building": Residents at Roman Sepphoris' (Heb.), *Cathedra* 99 (2001), pp. 7–26.

[35] BT Shabbat 25b.

[36] C. Meyers, 'The Dionysos Mosaic,' *Sepphoris in Galilee: Crosscurrents of Culture* (eds. R.M. Nagy, et al.; Winona Lake, IN, 1996), pp. 111–115; R. Talgam & Z. Weiss, *The Mosaics of the House of Dionysos at Sepphoris* (Jerusalem, 2004). The female bust is popularly known as the 'Mona Lisa of the Galilee.'

wards a synagogue was built in Ḥammat Tiberias, with an image of the sun-god Helios in the centre of its mosaic floor. Helios is depicted riding his chariot, surrounded by a zodiac, which includes a nude figure. The main donor to the building of the synagogue, mentioned in two of the inscriptions found in the building, was one Severus, who is called 'Severus the freedman of the honoured patriarchs.'[37] In Sepphoris itself a synagogue mosaic has also been found with a zodiac surrounding the chariot of Helios at its centre, although this dates to the beginning of the fifth century. If this was the situation in synagogues, there is no reason why there should not be a pagan mosaic decorating the house of Rabbi. Once again there has been no definitive find up to now which would confirm the suggestion that Rabbi did live in this house in Sepphoris.

However, these archaeological finds from Rabbi's times from Beit She'arim and Sepphoris do have something to tell us about life in this period. They clearly indicate the improved economic state of these settlements; the way of life of the rich strata of society; and the new openness of Jewish culture to what had been seen in the past as *'avodah zarah*/idol worship. All this came in the wake of the feelings of stability and power that the Jews of Palestine experienced under the leadership of Rabbi.

---

[37] See E. Habas (Rubin), 'Θρεπτοί in the Inscriptions of Palestine' (Heb.), *The Path of Peace: Studies in Honor of Israel Friedman Ben-Shalom* (eds. D. Gera & M. Ben-Zeev; Jerusalem, 2005, Heb.), pp. 487–498; C. Hezser, *Jewish Slavery in Antiquity* (Oxford, 2005), pp. 103–104.

4. The Circuits of Rabbi

Like his father and grandfather before him, Rabbi made
many journeys around Palestine and the Diaspora. These
journeys took the form of formal circuits, and were among
the most important ways by which the leadership institutions in the period of the Mishnah and the Talmud demonstrated their control over the settlements of Palestine. This
custom appears to have been adopted by the patriarchal
dynasty following the Roman emperors and governors, and
it would have increased the Jewish leaders' awareness of
popular trends and feelings, as well as allowing them closer
supervision of the Jewish settlements. During the course of
these circuits they were able to make local appointments,
answer questions of Halakha, judge various sorts of cases;
and in general act to strengthen the links between the inhabitants of the periphery and the centre.[38]

There is one source from Rabbi's time which details how
the patriarch made a local appointment during a circuit:

Our Rabbi passed near Simonia. The people of Simonia came out
and said to him: Rabbi, give us a man who can teach us Scripture
and Mishnah [or: teach us reading and repetition] and rule on our
law cases. He gave them Levi b. Sisi ...[39]

When Rabbi passed near Simonia, (Shimron, near present-day Nahalal) during his circuit, the people of the place

---

[38] A. J. Marshall, 'Governors on the Move,' *Phoenix* 20 (1966),
pp. 231–246; A. Oppenheimer, 'Rabban Gamaliel of Yavneh and His
Circuits of Eretz Israel,' *Between Rome and Babylon* (Tübingen, 2005),
pp. 145–155.

[39] Genesis Rabbah 81,2 (eds. Theodor & Albeck, pp. 969–972).

asked him to appoint them a teacher and judge. On the one hand, we can posit that this episode serves as a blueprint for other potential cases, and deduce from it that Rabbi and other patriarchs must have behaved like the Roman authorities, who used to appoint judges during their circuits. On the other hand, there are two possible reservations which should be made from this interpretation of the source. First of all, Simonia was quite near to Beit Shecarim where Rabbi lived, so that the question arises of how far this incident is applicable to Rabbi's activities in the wider context of Palestine in general. Secondly, there is a parallel source which says that the people of Simonia came to the place where Rabbi Judah haNasi was in order to place their request before him,[40] so that this was not something which happened during one of Rabbi's circuits in the country in general. At any rate, the source does underline the way in which Rabbi behaved in all the appointments he made, concentrating power in the centre, i.e. in himself.

In the traditions about the circuits which Rabbi made in the country two cities are mentioned by name: Akko and Lod.[41] The port city of Akko/Ptolemais had the status of a Roman *colonia,* and lay on an important crossroads at the border between the provinces of *Phoenicia* and *Syria-Palaestina.* Lod/Lydda also lay on a central crossroads. The city received the status of a *polis* in Rabbi's time, and the most important Beit Midrash of the time in the South

---

[40] JT Yevamot xii, 13a, col. 889.
[41] On Akko see above, pp. 94–95.

was sited there. Thus Rabbi Judah haNasi clearly continued in the tradition of his grandfather, Rabban Gamliel
of Yavneh, who aimed his circuits at the most important
towns of Judaea and Galilee.

In the Talmudic literature there are no further mentions
of places where Rabbi went during his circuits, but there
are some further details of the circuits themselves: Rabbi
is noted as 'walking along the road' with Rabbi Ḥiyya,[42]
and again with Rabbi Yose b. Rabbi Judah.[43] He is also
recorded going to a certain place with his pupils,[44] and ar-
riving at the residence of Rabbi Eliezer b. Rabbi Shimʿon.[45]
Rabbi appears to have travelled around much more than
his father, Rabban Shimʿon b. Gamliel, for there is no evidence that the latter left Galilee during his patriarchate.
We should note, however, that we have much less information about Rabban Shimʿon b. Gamliel than about his
father, Rabbi's grandfather, Rabban Gamliel of Yavneh. It
may be that the great power of Rabbi as a leader allowed
him to cut down on his journeys of supervision in the cities, towns and villages of Palestine and generally to rely on
sending his colleagues and pupils for these matters. In this
context we should point out the phrase which was coined
in Rabbi's time and also used in the days of his successors: 'so-and-so went out to the settlement.' For example,
Yoḥanan Ḥaquqah, a contemporary of Rabbi's, 'went out

---

[42] BT Hagigah 5b.
[43] Genesis Rabbah 76,8 (eds. Theodor & Albeck, p. 906).
[44] BT Shabbat 125b etc.
[45] BT Bava Metzia 85a.

to the villages;[46] 'the sons of Rabbi Ḥiyya went out to the villages;[47] and so on. In general, these sources report that the local people to whom Rabbi's representatives were sent asked them questions in Halakha and Aggadah. On Rabbi Ḥiyya we are told that he '*hirbitz*/ taught Torah in Israel' and that 'he went to the Diaspora (= Babylonia) in order to teach.'[48] A further source gives evidence that Rabbi Ḥiyya went out to various settlements in order to set up schools and supervise the education there.[49] In this context, we should mention here the rabbis who were sent out by Rabbi Judah haNasi in order to sanctify the New Moon or intercalate the year. We have already noted (above, pp. 132–134) that Rabbi's great power allowed him to delegate authority in everything related to the calendar, and he did not feel the need to fix the calendar in person, as his grandfather Rabban Gamliel of Yavneh had demanded.

As for the journeys of the Palestinian leaders to the Diaspora, there is evidence that Rabban Gamliel of Yavneh and the leaders of the rabbis of his time visited Rome during their travels, at least twice.[50] On their journeys to the Diaspora they ruled on what was forbidden and permitted, taught Torah, met people from Jewish communities, redeemed captives and also met with representatives of the Roman authorities. However, there is no tradition of a journey to Rome by Rabbi. It is possible that he did go

---

[46] BT Pesaḥim 3b.
[47] BT Berakhot 18b; BT Beitzah 9b.
[48] JT Kilayim ix, 32b, col. 175; JT Ketubbot xii, 35a, col. 1010.
[49] BT Bava Metzia 85b; cf BT Ketubbot 103b.
[50] See C. Hezser, *Jewish Travel in Antiquity* (Tübingen, 2011).

there but this was not mentioned in the sources, or that he never went there at all. At any rate, his good relationships with the Roman authorities presumably allowed him to run his patriarchate without any need for this expedient.

5. Expressions of Opposition to Rabbi

Everyone who stood at the head of the Beit haVaᶜad and all the patriarchs, both before and after Rabbi Judah haNasi, had to cope with an opposition. Rabbi was the strongest and most revered of them all, but precisely because of his power there are many not inconsiderable signs of opposition which arose against him, some of which have already been mentioned in previous chapters.

As we have noted, Rabbi was one of the most revered Jewish leaders in history. Tradition places him together with the great deliverers of the Jewish people, such as Daniel and his companions, Shimᶜon haZadiq, Mattathias the Hasmonaean and his sons, Mordechai and Esther.[51] Indeed it is said of him that 'from the days of Moses up to Rabbi we have not found Torah and greatness in one place.'[52] But the unification of Torah and greatness which was personified in the figure of Rabbi Judah haNasi was also an obstacle for him. The world of the rabbis – of Torah and mitzvot, of popular leadership and the kingdom of heaven – did not follow the same course as the earthly leadership of

---

[51] BT Megillah 11a.
[52] BT Gittin 59a; BT Sanhedrin 36a.

Rabbi, which was a sort of monarchy based on his claim to be related to the royal House of David, on his recognition by the Roman authorities, and on the relationship he built up with the city elite, where riches and domination were part of its conspicuous external expressions. The world of the rabbis was also by its nature conservative, and they were not prepared to participate in all the reforms which Rabbi made in the Halakha. Those who were prepared to accept his Mishnah as binding and unchanging related critically to his innovative rulings. These, then, were the two reasons for the opposition to Rabbi: his domination and his reforming rulings.

Those who were opposed to the domineering methods of Rabbi Judah haNasi came both from the circles of those who were near to him and from those who were far from him. The sons of Rabbi Ḥiyya, the rabbi who was closest to him, compared the domineering way in which Rabbi carried out his patriarchal functions to that of the exilarch, when they said:

The Son of David will not come until two houses in Israel have come to an end, and these are the exilarch in Babylonia, and the patriarch in the Land of Israel.[53]

It is true that there were also learned rabbis among the exilarchs, but most of their function was in the field of secular administration, and in essence they were like absolute east-

---

[53] BT Sanhedrin 38a (see above, Chapter 1, pp. 42–44 and see there the note on the paper of M. Lavi. See too, G. Herman, 'Table Etiquette and Persian Culture in the Babylonian Talmud' (Heb.), *Zion* 77 (2012), pp. 149–188.

ern potentates surrounded by their court, with conspicuous signs of riches and splendour. The words above, which the sons of Rabbi Ḥiyya directed against Rabbi Judah ha-Nasi, begin their criticism by comparing Rabbi, who stood at the head of the learned rabbis, with the exilarch, who represented dominion only. They continue to sting because they are written as a 'prophecy,' that the Messiah, son of David, will not come until the dynasties of Rabbi and the *Resh Galuta'*, who both claim relationship with the House of David, have ended.

This sort of comparison between the leadership of Rabbi Judah haNasi and that of the exilarch is also to be found in the episode which we have already discussed in Chapter 1, where Rabbi says he is not willing to give up his position for anyone unless the exilarch comes to Palestine, because the exilarch has a better genealogical relationship to the House of David through the paternal line. As noted (see above, p. 42), on one occasion Rabbi Ḥiyya mocked him and told him that the exilarch had arrived, when in fact the exilarch had arrived in his coffin to be buried in the Land of Israel.

The regal manners of Rabbi Judah haNasi angered the *ḥasidim* considerably. I have already described in Chapter 4 how Rabbi Pinḥas b. Yair, the head of the *ḥasidim,* was not prepared to come to a meal to which he was invited in the house of the patriarch, even though he had previously agreed to come, because he saw Rabbi's white mules in the courtyard. The huge gap between Rabbi Pinḥas b. Yair and Rabbi was caused first and foremost by the contrast between what was seen as the 'regal' behaviour of the legal leader, and the popular figure of the charismatic head of the *ḥasidim*.

We have already met with criticism of the relationships Rabbi built up with the city elites and the circles of the rich – another aspect of his behaviour as leader – in the episode where Bar Qappara mocked Ben Elʿashah, Rabbi's rich and ignorant son-in-law. The rabbis also expressed their disdain for the status Rabbi gave to the wealthy when they said, apparently ironically: 'Rabbi honours the rich.' Criticism of the links between wealth and power are clearly very old.[54]

Rabbi Pinḥas b. Yair and Bar Qappara were southerners. In earlier times too there had been tensions between the inhabitants of Judaea and the inhabitants of Galilee against the background of the geographical distance between them (which was quite considerable in antiquity), as well as their differences in *minhagim*/customs, the different accents, etc. It is possible that the antagonism of these two to Rabbi's demonstrations of his power are also connected to this fact. Rabbi, for his part, also contributed to ambivalent relations: first of all when he returned the fixing of the calendar to Judaea, and fixed it at Lod/Lydda, the site of the most important Beit Midrash in the south of Palestine; and afterwards, when this Beit Midrash grew too strong for Rabbi's taste, when he went back on this decision and removed the privilege from them.[55] It is clear, however, that Rabbi acknowledged the strength of the teaching centre in

---

[54] On all this see Chapter 4.
[55] See above, pp. 134–136.

the South, and the strength of Rabbi Pinḥas b. Yair. Thus when rabbi came to 'purify' Ashkelon by including the city within the halakhically bounded territory of the Land of Israel and thus exempting it from tithes and sabbatical regulations, he betook himself to Lod/Lydda, in order to consult the head of the opposition to himself, Rabbi Pinḥas b. Yair the *ḥasid.*[56]

Rabbi's reforming rulings were the second reason for the opposition to him. Throughout this book I have noted two cases when Rabbi went back on his rulings in the wake of the criticism which the rabbis voiced about him. In one case, Rabbi wanted to cancel the sabbatical year altogether, and brought down on himself the opposition of Rabbi Pinḥas b. Yair, who protected the poor because of his *ḥasidut.* The poor, indeed, would have been the first to lose had the sabbatical year been cancelled, since in this year produce is made free for all. Rabbi wanted to avoid making a *taqqanah* which would not be acceptable to all the people, and might even split Judaea from Galilee, and thus went back on his intention. In the second case, Rabbi Judah haNasi wanted to cancel the fasts of the Seventeenth of Tammuz and the Ninth of Av as mourning for the destruction of the Second Temple, but here too he went back on this intention after other rabbis did not co-operate with him. Since the source does not specify the names of his opponents, it is reasonable to suppose that the opposition was widespread.

---

[56] See at length in Chapter 3.

Some rabbis also criticised other *taqqanot* of Rabbi's which were less drastic reforms than those he withdrew. In these cases, Rabbi stood by his opinion and confirmed the validity of his *taqqanot,* as in the example below, where he wanted to exempt the mixed cities from tithes and from the sabbatical year:

Rabbi exempted Beit She'an, Rabbi exempted Caesarea, Rabbi exempted Beit Guvrin/Eleutheropolis, Rabbi exempted Kefar Tzemaḥ. Rabbi allowed them to take vegetables after the end of the sabbatical year and they all slandered him. He said: Come and judge, it is written: *And he broke in pieces the brazen serpent* (II Kings 18.4). For there was no-one more righteous than Moses, until Hezekiah surpassed him, for the Holy One blessed be He left him this ornament to be ornamented with, and in our case too the Holy One blessed be He left us this ornament to ornament ourselves with.[57]

In other words, Rabbi rejects the slanderers with the claim that it is sometimes necessary for later people to right an earlier wrong. In the parallel in the Babylonian Talmud the message is similar.[58]

While in the Jerusalem Talmud the identity of the opposition is unknown, hidden behind the anonymous statement 'they were all slandering him,' in the parallel in the Babylonian Talmud the source of the opposition is in the family of the patriarch himself: 'His brothers and the house of his father joined together against him.' Here too, Rabbi strongly opposes the conservative attitude of his relatives, who claim that it is not proper to change a Halakha which was observed by Rabbi's forefathers. He responds that, on

---

[57] JT Demai ii, 22c, col. 121.
[58] BT Ḥullin 6b–7a.

the contrary, his fathers left him a space to operate, where he can boast about his reforming *taqqanot.*

There were some rabbis who, even in Rabbi's presence, avoided accepting any of his dispensations which seemed to them too far-reaching, such as the example below. This is a case relating to the dispensation which Rabbi gave to the inhabitants of rural areas of the halakhic Land of Israel to eat vegetables grown abroad in the sabbatical year:

Ulla bar Ishmaʿel in the name of Rabbi Ḥanina: Rabbi and Rabbi Yose bar Judah went down to Akko and were received by Rabbi Mana. He said to [Rabbi Mana]: Make us a potful of vegetables. He made him meat. In the morning he said to him: Make us a potful of vegetables. He prepared them a cock. ... And why did he do this? Because he was a pupil of Rabbi Judah, and Rabbi Judah said: Vegetables are forbidden [in the sabbatical year] near the borders of the halakhic Land of Israel ...[59]

Rabbi Mana was a contemporary of Rabbi and the pupil of Rabbi Judah bar Ilaʿi, one of the chief spokesmen of the Ushah generation. In the episode noted here, on two occasions Rabbi Mana did not accede to Rabbi's request to give him vegetables when the latter came to him in his home in Akko, which at that time was sited on the border of the halakhic Land of Israel and thus considered a border city. Rabbi Mana did this because he continued to hold to the view of Rabbi Judah bar Ilaʿi, of the previous generation, that in the borders of the halakhic Land of Israel it was forbidden to eat vegetables in the sabbatical year. Thus Rabbi Mana did not accept Rabbi's *taqqanah* which allowed this.

---

[59] JT Sheviʿit vi, 37a, col. 200.

The *taqqanot* of Rabbi Judah haNasi, which were aimed at making the preparation of pupils for ordination more centralised, and restricting the freedom to teach only to those rabbis who had received ordination from himself, also roused antagonism in rabbinic circles, as has already been noted in this chapter. When Rabbi made a *taqqanah* which cancelled the possibility of learning outdoors, Rabbi Ḥiyya demonstratively transgressed it, even though he was Rabbi's friend and closest colleague. Thus Rabbi Ḥiyya taught his relatives Rav and Rabba bar Bar Ḥanah in the street, in full sight of everybody. As already noted, these pupils did eventually receive ordination from Rabbi, and Rav later went down to Babylonia, where he became the head of the academy in Sura, one of the two large Babylonian Yeshivot, and gave an impetus to the study of Torah in this Diaspora community. Here this is not a case of someone who refused to accept a *taqqanah* which Rabbi ruled to make life easier, like Rabbi Mana in Akko, but someone who transgressed a *taqqanah* which included a ban, and as noted above, Rabbi punished Rabbi Ḥiyya for this by making him suspend himself for thirty days.

Rabbi used a double standard in his treatment of his opponents. If signs of opposition appeared among the rabbis who were close to him, he punished them: he suspended those with *semikhah* temporarily from the sessions of the Beit haVaʿad, and he punished those who had not yet been ordained by withholding ordination from them. In contrast, if signs of opposition came from people far away, he handled them with velvet gloves, as in the case of Rabbi

Pinḥas b. Yair: here Rabbi even made great efforts to make peace with him.

In general, Rabbi's ability and strength as a leader stood him in good stead in his responses to the circles of opposition. With his acute political sensitivities, he knew when to punish his opponents, when to overlook their protests or when to change his wishes in their favour. In this way he succeeded in navigating his course without becoming involved in struggles or crises which might have endangered his leadership.

Chapter 6

Rabbi Judah haNasi's Relations
with the Babylonian Diaspora

1. The Rise in the Status of the Babylonian Diaspora

After the Bar Kokhva revolt, the status of the Jewish Diaspora in Babylonia gradually began to rise. This was now the largest diaspora community outside the borders of the Roman Empire, and the political, economic and social situation of the Jews who lived there was extremely good. Thus it is not surprising that Babylonia became a magnet for the refugees who fled from Palestine following the failure of the Bar Kokhva revolt and the repressive legislation which followed.

If we examine the relations between Rabbi Judah haNasi and Rabbi Ḥiyya, who originated in Babylonia according to the Talmudic literature, it is evident that Rabbi Ḥiyya was seen as a leader of the rabbis of his generation, and that he was active alongside Rabbi. As already noted, Rabbi ran his patriarchate with a high hand, without other office holders to help him, in other words, without another head for the Beit haVaʿad.[1] It is also possible to identify a certain disdain for the rabbis of Babylonia on the part of Rabbi. As noted in the previous chapter, Rabbi Ḥanina bar Ḥama did not receive *semikhah* from Rabbi Judah haNasi

---

[1] JT Taʿanit iv, 68a, col. 728.

because he corrected a mistake of his in public, based on what he had learned from Rabbi Hamnuna in Babylonia. It is clear from this source that Rabbi refused to acknowledge that Rabbi Hamnuna was able to give *semikhah*. We should note here that in his will, which we shall discuss in Chapter 8, Rabbi decided to correct his slight of Rabbi Ḥanina bar Ḥama, and perhaps even instructed his son to make him Av Beit Din.

Following Rabbi's final redaction of the Mishnah, this was quickly brought to Babylonia, where its arrival marked an important stage in the development of the Jewish community there, which eventually took over the place of Palestine as the most important Jewish centre. The first signs of this development can be identified after the Bar Kokhva revolt, but it was the foundation of the Babylonian Yeshivot after Rav arrived in Babylonia, and the discussions which took place in them on the basis of the Palestinian Mishnah, which laid the foundations of the independent Babylonian creation in the shape of the Babylonian Talmud. It is this Talmud which was finally accepted as the source for ruling Halakha by Jews everywhere, right up to the present day. The Babylonian Talmud fixed the pattern of life not only for the Jews of Babylonia, and not only for its own time, but more than any other work it formed the image of the Jewish people for generations – in their patterns of thought, way of life, relations with the world around them, laws and regulations.

2. Rabbi Judah and His Relations
with the *Resh Galuta*ʾ / the Exilarch

The first *Resh Galuta*ʾ known to us by name is Huna, who held this office in the time of Rabbi Judah haNasi, although there are hints that the first signs of the exilarchate can be identified in Babylonia at least a generation earlier. From these hints it is very reasonable to assume that the exilarchate was created in Babylonia with the arrival of the Jewish refugees from Palestine following the Bar Kokhva revolt. In the time of Huna, the exilarch began to claim a relationship with the royal House of David, in parallel to the relationship to the House of David claimed by the patriarchate in Palestine in the days of Rabbi. As already noted (above, p. 42), the relationship of the exilarch to the House of David through the paternal line was considered preferable to that of Rabbi Judah haNasi through the maternal line, so that Rabbi declared that although he did not intend to give up his seat to anyone, he would be prepared to give it up to the exilarch if he were to come from Babylonia to Palestine. It is clear that Rabbi did not dream that the exilarch would do so, and when Rabbi Ḥiyya from Babylonia told him that the exilarch had come, we are told that 'Rabbi's face fell,' since he thought that he would have to carry out his expressed intent. After Rabbi Ḥiyya calmed him and told him that 'it is his coffin which came' so that he could be buried in the Land of Israel, Rabbi Ḥiyya was forced to suspend himself temporarily from the Beit haVaʿad.

The jurisdiction of Rabbi Judah haNasi and the exilarch was similar: both of them held the secular political leadership and behaved as if they had the authority of a king. However they differed from each other in that Rabbi also held the religious and spiritual leadership of the Jews in Palestine.

3. Rabbi's Attitudes to the Purity of Lineage of Babylonian Jewry

The Jews of Babylonia saw themselves not only as preserving the legacy of Jewish tradition, but also as the faithful guardians of the purest Jewish lineage. This guardianship was carried out by extreme strictness in arranging marriages, with the exclusion of all those who were disqualified in any way for whatever reason. The Jews of Babylonia took care that their community should not be 'contaminated' by converts whose conversion was not according to Halakha, by priests who were born to women who were disqualified from marrying priests, by non-Jewish slaves who had not been legally freed, by bastards and so on.

According to the tradition in the Babylonian Talmud, when Rabbi was on his death-bed, he accused the inhabitants of different settlements in Babylonia of failing to care for purity of lineage and committing grave sins over this:

When Rabbi's soul was about to depart, he said: There is a [place called] Humaniya in Babylonia: it is all Ammonites. There is a [place called] Masgariya in Babylonia: it is all *mamzerim*/bastards. There is a [place called] Birqa [MSS: Birta] in Babylonia: there are two brothers [there] who exchange wives with each other. There is a [place called] Birta de-Satya in Babylonia: today they have turned aside from the Almighty: a fishpond overflowed on the Sabbath, and they went and caught [fish] there on the Sabbath. After this Rabbi Ahi b. Rabbi Yoshiah excommunicated them and they converted [to a different religion].[2]

From all that has been said on the meticulousness of Babylonian Jewry over purity of lineage, the words attributed to Rabbi Judah haNasi on his deathbed appear very strange, accusing settlements in Babylonia of failing to care for this. However, although there were settlements within genealogical Babylonia that prided themselves on the extreme purity of their lineage, there were also settlements which did not act with such care. But why should the purity of settlements in Babylonia worry Rabbi Judah haNasi, the Patriarch of the Jews of the Land of Israel, when the Jews of Babylonia themselves cast doubt on the purity of lineage of the Jews of the Land of Israel?

The beginning of Rabbi's words hint that we should not relate to them on their face value, for the accusation that the Ammonites are mixed in the settlement of Humaniya appears to be simply a play on words. Indeed it is reminiscent of Rabbi's statement in the continuation of this source:

A person from Guvai is like a Gibeonite, Durdonita is a village of *netinim*.[3]

----

[2] BT Qiddushin 72a (tr. Soncino, adapted).
[3] BT Qiddushin 70b.

In other words, the inhabitants of the Babylonian village of Guvai are like Gibeonites, while Babylonian Durdonita is a village of *netinim*/descendents of the Gibeonites, people who are disqualified from joining the community, in other words unable to marry Jewish women.

It would seem, therefore, that we must see this statement of Rabbi in the context of the tensions between Babylonia and Palestine over which community would take the lead. These tensions began after the Bar Kokhva revolt against Rome, when many refugees fled from the Land of Israel to Babylonia, the only significant Jewish diaspora community outside the Roman Empire. Among those leaving for Babylonia were rabbis like Rabbi Ḥananiah, son of Rabbi Joshua's brother, who tried to fix the calendar in Babylonia, thus threatening the hegemony of the Land of Israel. The fact that the Jews of Babylonia prided themselves on their purity of lineage over the Jews of Palestine was also a threat to this hegemony. It is therefore easier to understand why sneering words were attributed to Rabbi when he mentioned Jewish settlements in Babylonia, which not only failed to take care over this, but also included people who transgressed Halakhot about marriages or the profanation of the Sabbath. There is a further source which mentions criticism by Rabbi of the Jews in one of the settlements of Babylonia, also near his death, in a sort of will where he leaves instructions for his sons. Here he describes the inhabitants of Shekhanziv in Babylonia as forming a kind of 'parliament of fools':

Our Holy Rabbi commanded four things to his sons: Do not live in Shekhanziv, because they are fools and will draw you into their foolishness ...[4]

It should be noted that this censure attributed to Rabbi is found only in the Babylonian Talmud. It is reasonable to conclude that these statements were not made by Rabbi, but result from the ideas of the Babylonian rabbis discussing among themselves what was said about them in Palestine. At any rate, the statements do give evidence of a certain amount of tension between Palestine and Babylonia. However, it should be noted that there are also Babylonian Amoraim who themselves accuse settlements like these of a lack of proper care in matters of purity of lineage, or other improper modes of behaviour.

In the final event, the hegemony of the Land of Israel over Babylonia, at least in everything connected with the study of Torah, continued after the final redaction of the Mishnah and after the death of Rabbi.

4. The Jews of Mesene Turn to Rabbi

The Babylonian Talmud speaks disparagingly of the areas which were outside 'Talmudic Babylonia,' because they did not preserve the purity of lineage with the required strictness:

---

[4] BT Pesaḥim 112b. On the settlements in Babylonia mentioned in the sources attributed to Rabbi, see, A. Oppenheimer, in collaboration with B. Isaac & M. Lecker, *Babylonia Judaica in the Talmudic Period* (Beihefte zum Tübinger Atlas des Vorderen Orients B/47; Wiesbaden, 1983), s.v., and in the index.

Rav Pappa the Elder said in the name of Rav: 'Babylonia [from the point of view of purity of lineage] is healthy, Meshan [Mesene] is dead [because everyone there is disqualified], Media is sick [because most Jews there are kosher and the minority are disqualified], Elam is fatally ill [because most Jews there are disqualified and the minority kosher]. And what is the difference between 'sick' and 'fatally ill'? Most sick people live, but most fatally ill people die.[5]

We may presume that these statements also reflect the general tension between Jewish Babylonia and the Jews of the neighbouring regions, in present-day southern Iraq (Mesene) and Iran (Elam and Media). It is thus not surprising that the Jews of these regions turned to the centre in Palestine with their questions on halakhic matters, circumventing the Babylonian centre which was nearer to them, as in the following episode, described in tractate Pesaḥim of the Jerusalem Talmud, where the Jews of Mesene turned to Rabbi Judah haNasi:

For thus said Rabbi Ba: 'The people of Mesha/Mesene took it upon themselves not to sail on the Great Sea.' They came and asked Rabbi, saying to him: 'Our fathers used not to sail on the Great Sea, what should we do?' He said to them: 'Since your fathers kept this ban, do not change the custom of your fathers' …[6]

The people of Mesene turn to Rabbi to ask him to absolve them from their fathers' vow not to sail on the sea, presumably for the purpose of trade. There is no clear explanation of why the Jews of Mesene restricted themselves from

---

[5] BT Qiddushin 71b, according to the MSS from Munich and Vatican MS III. The printed version has 'Meshon.' These would appear to be different versions due to different pronunciations.

[6] JT Pesaḥim iv, 30d, col. 517 (and see *Ahavat Zion veYerushalayim*, *ad loc.* [pp. 60–62]).

sailing on the sea, and why Rabbi supported the continuation of these restrictions, apart from his statement that the Jews of Mesene should continue to follow their fathers' customs. We may propose different solutions for Rabbi's stance: fear of exposure to pagan influences while engaging in international trade, fear of leaving the Jewish centre in Mesene and sailing to distant lands, or the fear of sailing on the sea on the Sabbath.[7]

The importance of Mesene derived from its position in an area which controlled the routes which linked Mesopotamia and the Persian Gulf. As a result of this, Mesene controlled the trade with India, the Far East and the southern Arabian peninsula. In the Syriac work *The Hymn of the Soul,* from around the time of Rabbi, Mesene is described as 'a Garden of Eden for traders, sited on the sea shore.'[8] In the first and second centuries CE, Mesene was also an important centre of trade with Rome. The timing of the approach of the Jews of Mesene to Rabbi fits the period of the transfer of control over the trade from India to the west from the people of Tadmor/Palmyra in Syria to the inhabitants of Mesene. A series of inscriptions discovered in Palmyra give evidence of the involvement of the people of the region in this trade route. They cease for the first time in 161 CE, in parallel with the war of the emperor Lucius

---

[7] See, A. Oppenheimer, 'Links between Mesene and 'Eretz Yisra'el' (Heb.), *Zion* 47 (1982), pp. 335–341 (German translation, idem, 'Beziehungen zwischen Messene und Palästina,' *Between Rome and Babylon* [Tübingen, 2005], pp. 409–416).

[8] A. A. Bevan, *The Hymn of the Soul Contained in the Syriac Acts of St. Thomas* (Texts and Studies V, No. 3; Cambridge, 1897).

Verus on the Parthians, and later they cease altogether in the year 193 CE, with the conquest of North Mesopotamia by Septimius Severus.[9] Against this background the timing of the approach of the Jews of Mesene to Rabbi gains more significance, for he was at this time at the height of his leadership.[10]

Thus the Jews of Mesene made a direct approach to Rabbi, in spite of the fact that there were already beginnings of Yeshivot in Babylonia adjacent to Mesene at this time. This underlines the tensions we have already noted between the Jews of Mesene and those of Babylonia on the background of the purity of lineage, and is a further demonstration of the status and authority of Rabbi in the eyes of this diaspora community. The links of Mesene with the Land of Israel are also clear from a wall inscription which was discovered at Beit She'arim, the place where Rabbi was buried:

Μισηνη Σαρα η Μαξιμ[α] (Sarah of Mesene, [also] called Maxima).

This would appear to tell us that some at least of the dead of Mesene were brought for burial in the Land of Israel.[11] The network of connections between Mesene and Palestine

---

[9] See, M. Rostovtzeff, 'Les inscriptions caravanières de Palmyre,' *Mélanges Gustave Glotz,* vol. II (Paris, 1932), pp. 792–811.

[10] On the involvement of the Jews of Mesene in sea trade we must link the presence of Jews at Mashmahig, the present-day port of Samahig on the island of Muharraq, north-east of Bahrein (cf BT Rosh haShanah 23a; BT Yoma 77a).

[11] M. Schwabe & B. Lifshitz, *Beth She'arim,* vol. II (Jerusalem, 1974), no. 101, p. 38; A. Oppenheimer, 'Links between Mesene and 'Eretz Yisra'el' (see above, n. 7), p. 341.

also carried on after Rabbi's time. In a negotiation over the Halakhot of the Sabbath it is recorded that Babylonian Jewry ruled according to the Babylonian Amoraim, while the Jews of Mesene followed the Amoraim of the Land of Israel.[12]

Mesene was not the only place adjacent to Babylonia which had links with Palestine and Rabbi at the time. There is further evidence about a question which was addressed to Rabbi by the Jews of Nineveh:

The people of Nineveh sent to Rabbi: People like us, who even in *tequfat tammuz* / the summer need rain, what should we do?[13]

The Jews of Nineveh claim that they need to ask for rain in their prayers even in the summer months, while it is usual to ask for rain in the prayers only in the winter, and they ask in which of the blessings of the Shemoneh Esrei / Eighteen [Blessings] they should insert their petition. This is problematic, for there are no summer rains in Nineveh. A number of scholars have proposed that the text is referring to Naweh in the Bashan, and note that Rabbi held land in the Bashan. This suggestion, however, does not stand up, for there is no rain in the summer in the Bashan either, while it is clear that Rabbi is relating to Babylonia and its environs, as is clearly seen from these sources.[14]

---

[12] BT Shabbat 37b.

[13] BT Ta'anit 14b. Biblical and Talmudic Nineveh is sited on the eastern bank of the Tigris, opposite present-day Mossul in North Iraq. Cf JT Berakhot v, 9b, col. 45.

[14] D. Levine, *Communal Fasts and Rabbinic Sermons: Theory and Practice in the Talmudic Period* (Tel Aviv, 2001, Heb.), p. 127.

Two pieces of evidence in the Babylonian Talmud mention Avimi, from the second generation of Babylonian Amoraim, who lived in the first half of the fourth century in the area of Be Ḥozai (Khuzastan in present-day Iran) adjacent to Mesene, and who brought Tannaitic traditions to the Yeshivot of Babylonia which were unknown to them, and presumably originated in Palestine.[15]

5. Rabbi Exchanges Gifts with Artaban, the Persian Ruler

In the Jerusalem Talmud there is a legendary tale from which it would appear that Rabbi Judah haNasi had good contacts not only with the Roman emperor Antoninus, but also with King Artaban V (or IV), the last king of the Parthian dynasty who ruled between 213–224.

Artaban sent our Holy Rabbi a single pearl of untold value. He said to him [Artaban to Rabbi]: Send me something which is of equal value. He sent him a single Mezuzah. He said to him [Artaban to Rabbi]: What! I sent you something which is of untold value, and you send me something which is worth a single *follis* [coin]. He said to him: Your possessions and my possessions cannot equal [the Mezuzah]. And not only this, but you sent me something which I have to guard, and I sent you something that will guard you while you sleep, as it says: *Wherever you turn, it will guide you* [Proverbs 6.22, which ends: When you lie in bed it will guard you].[16]

Chronologically the Artaban mentioned in this source fits the time of Rabbi Judah haNasi. Exchange of gifts be-

---

[15] BT Ḥullin 68b; BT Niddah 5b.
[16] JT Peah i, 15d, col. 82.

tween rulers and leaders was common at that time, and is also mentioned in the sources on the relations between Antoninus and Rabbi. The fact that this exchange is found in the Jerusalem Talmud gives it a chance of being true, even though it is clear that the episode as presented here has legendary aspects.

However, the authenticity of this episode is even more problematic, both because of the tensions which existed between the patriarch in Palestine and the exilarch in Babylonia, and because of the hostility between the Roman Empire and the Parthian Empire, which included Babylonia. But there was mutual appreciation between Rabbi and the Jewish leadership in Babylonia as well as tensions, while as for Rome, this was not an incident which could be interpreted as a conspiracy between Rabbi and Artaban, but a routine exchange of gifts.[17]

Artaban also had a good relationship with Rav, the head of the Yeshivah at Sura. It is possible to deduce this from the following saying, in BT Avodah Zarah, which even compares these relations to those between Rabbi and Antoninus:

Antoninus served Rabbi, Adrakhan [Artaban] served Rav, for when Antoninus died, Rabbi said: The bundle has fallen apart. When Adrakhan died, Rav said: The bundle has fallen apart.[18]

---

[17] See too the suggestion by J. Neusner, 'The Jews East of the Euphrates and the Roman Empire, 1st–3rd Centuries AD,' *ANRW* II 9.1 (Berlin & New York, 1976), pp. 59–64.

[18] BT Avodah Zarah 10b. In the Spanish MS edited by S. Abramson (see above, p. 50, n. 10), it has 'Artaban.' See on this, S. Raiskin, 'The Bundle Has Fallen Apart (נתפרדה החבילה): Which Bundle?' (Heb. with English summary), *Sidra* 23 (2008), pp. 133–135.

6. Artichokes for Rabbi from Nawsah

When dealing with the economic status of Rabbi Judah haNasi a tradition is mentioned that various vegetables were to be found on his table both in summer and winter, which were sometimes brought from places distant from Palestine (see above, p. 70). From the following source it is clear that among other things, Rabbi received vegetables as a gift brought from Nawsah:[19]

When Rav Dimi came [from Palestine to Babylonia] he said: Bonias sent Rabbi a measure of *kinras* [artichokes] from Nawsah, and Rabbi estimated that [it was equivalent to] two hundred and seventeen eggs [a common unit of volume].[20]

Bunias[21] was a man known for his wealth who had various different connections with Rabbi Judah haNasi. Above we noted an episode where ben Bunias came to Rabbi and received a seat more suited to someone of a lower economic rank, for he was wearing unsuitable clothes (see above, p. 113). From this evidence from Rav Dimi, one of the *naḥotei,* the Amoraim whose function was to bring the Torah of the Land of Israel to Babylonia, who lived

---

[19] A settlement on an island in the Euphrates river north-west of Talmudic Ihi Deqira, present-day Hit, in North Iraq. This settlement is known from classical sources and is sited about 100 km north-west of Pumbedita, next to present-day al-Fallūǧa.

[20] BT Eruvin 83a. *Kinras* (var. *kundas*) comes from *cynara,* an artichoke (s. v. קינרס in Krauss' *Griechische und lateinische Lehnwörter im Talmud, Midrasch und Targum,* vol. II [Berlin, 1899], p. 534; and s. v. קונרסא in Sokoloff's *A Dictionary of Jewish Babylonian Aramaic of the Talmudic and Geonic Periods* [Ramat Gan, 2002], p. 1000).

[21] Munich MS: 'ben Bunias.'

at the turn of the third and fourth centuries, it appears
that Bunias sent artichokes from Nawsah to Rabbi Judah
haNasi.[22]

---

[22] On artichokes at that time, as a very expensive luxury, the long-dis-
tance trade in them and what Pliny and the Talmudic literature say
about them, see, S. Weingarten, 'Wild Foods in the Talmud: The Influence of Religious Restrictions on Consumption,' *Wild Food: Proceedings
of the Oxford Symposium on Food and Cookery 2004* (ed. R. Hosking;
Totnes, 2006), pp. 326–327.

Chapter 7

Rabbi Judah haNasi's Literary Creation: The Mishnah

1. The Nature of the Mishnah

Rabbi's great legacy for posterity was the final redaction of the Mishnah, the book second in importance to the Torah in Judaism. It is impossible to know whether it was thought of as his most impressive work in the time of Rabbi himself, but it certainly was so from the point of view of the impact it had on all of Jewish history from his days up to ours, for about eighteen hundred years. The Mishnah formed the basis for the two Talmuds, the Jerusalem (Palestinian) and Babylonian, and the Halakhot included in it form the basis for all of Jewish law to this day. Thus it is the Mishnah which shaped and still shapes the patterns of Jewish life.

There are those who think that the redaction of the Mishnah was influenced to some extent by the processes of organising the framework of Roman law, which took place in the time of Rabbi. They cite the activities of important Roman legal authorities, such as Ulpian of Tyre, who was active in the first quarter of the third century, and began the work of collating and editing the laws of Rome.[1] However,

---

[1] Domitius Ulpianus was a government official, and one of the outstanding Roman jurists. He rose to fame in the time of the emperor Severus Alexander.

the systemisation of Roman law began many years before
Ulpian and Rabbi Judah haNasi, and the published collections of Roman laws appeared after Rabbi's time. Moreover,
these were collections of the edicts of the Roman emperors,
so that they can scarcely be considered as influencing the
very different Mishnah. It is true that the clement political
climate in Rabbi's time, his good relations with the Roman
authorities, and their recognition of Rabbi's authority to
judge court cases all contributed to the redaction of the
Mishnah. However, essentially the redaction of the Mishnah was the end of an independent internal process of editing the Halakha. This had already begun in the Yavneh
period and reached its peak in the Ushah period after the
Bar Kokhva revolt: its crowning glory was the final redaction by Rabbi.

There are those who think that the very name 'Mishnah' indicates that this work should take second place
to the Torah, but it is more reasonable to assume that
the name simply signifies one of the ways of studying. In
other words, the name Mishnah comes from the root שנה /
shanah, which means 'to repeat.' The names of the different works in the Talmudic literature all signify methods
of study: Tosefta from הוספה, *hosafah*/addition; Midrash
from דרש, *darash*/seeking and examining; Talmud from
לימוד, *limud*/study, and so too the Aramaic name for the
Talmud, Gemara, from the Aramaic גמר/*gamar,* which
also means to study.

In the Mishnah itself there is no mention that this work
was finally redacted by Rabbi. However, it is possible to
reach this conclusion from the fact that the rabbis of Rab-

bi's generation are not mentioned in the Mishnah, but appear mostly in the Tosefta and the Baraitot. Rabbi himself is only mentioned in the Mishnah a few dozen times, while the Amoraim of the generations after him only appear in the Amoraic literature. There are also a number of comments in the Talmud on different parts of the Mishnah, such as *Rabbi satam* – in other words, it was Rabbi who cited this Halakha as an anonymous statement *(setam)* without stating the name of the author. The Talmud also writes on occasion: *shanah Rabbi/*Rabbi repeated in a mishnah, and a further explicit statement which is quite common: *matnitin man taqin – Rabbi,* i.e. it was Rabbi who ruled this mishnah which we have here.

In the project that became the Mishnah, the Halakhot of the oral law were collated and edited according to a certain order of subjects. Roman law distinguishes between the *jus scriptum/* the written law, and *jus non scriptum/* the unwritten law. On the face of it, this looks similar to the distinction in Judaism between the written Torah and the oral Torah, but this is not the case. The Romans' unwritten law meant the laws of Nature, which were based in the order of the natural world, and not fixed by a lawgiver, whereas the Jewish oral law includes Halakhot which were ruled by lawgivers, i. e. the rabbis.

The meaning of the term *Torah she-be͑ al peh/* oral law, is apparently *torah* which it is forbidden to write down. Indeed, there are sources which include evidence of a ban on writing down the oral law, e. g.:

Things *she-be'al peh*/which are oral – you are not allowed to say them in writing.[2]

Similarly, in the name of Rabbi Yoḥanan:

Those who write down Halakhot are like those who burn the To-rah.[3]

And even when it comes to writing down Aggadah/moral narrative, the Jerusalem Talmud says:

Rabbi Joshua b. Levi said: This Aggadah – anyone who writes it down has no portion [in the World to Come].[4]

In spite of all this, there is evidence that rabbis in all generations did write things down – even Halakha. Megillat Ta'anit/the Scroll of Fasting, includes the dates of the victories of the Hasmoneans and the Pharisees which are defined as festivals so that it is forbidden to fast on them. It was written down already in the time of the Second Temple. Similarly, the rabbis used to write private notes, notebooks and scrolls for themselves. According to tradition, when Rabban Shim'on b. Gamliel punished Rabbi Natan and Rabbi Meir by excluding them from the Beit haVa'ad because of their attempt to remove him from his patriarchate, they noted down their questions and sent them to the Beit haVa'ad. Whatever the Beit haVa'ad knew how to answer, they answered, whatever they did not know, they wrote down answers and sent them to them.[5]

---

[2] BT Gittin 60b.
[3] BT Temurah 14b, according to the Munich MS and other versions.
[4] JT Shabbat xvi, 15c, col. 437.
[5] BT Horayot 13b.

The ban on writing should be understood in the terms of the ancient world, in other words, the ban was placed on writing which was liable to give authority to what was written. This is how Rabbi Yannai, from the first generation of the Palestinian Amoraim, saw the giving of the oral law:

[Moses] wrote thirteen [copies] of the Torah, twelve for the twelve tribes, and laid one in the Ark, so if someone tried to forge something, they would be able to find the copy in the Ark.[6]

In other words, Moses wrote a *Sefer Torah/*a Scroll of the Law, for each of the twelve tribes, and in addition put a *Sefer Torah* in the Ark of the Covenant, so that its version would be binding. It was in this context that disputes arose between the Pharisees and Sadducees: the Pharisees saw the renewed Halakhot as oral law, so that the dynamics of the process of creating Halakha was preserved and it was possible to change them, whereas the Sadducees used to write down their Halakhot, so that they gave them authority and fixed them. An echo of this is preserved in the following tradition:

El'azar b. Poerah [a Sadducee] said to King Yannai: If you hear my advice, crush them [the Pharisees]. And what will be with the Torah? Look, this is bound/כרוכה and laid down [in the Spanish printed version: written/כתובה and laid down] in full view. Let all who want to learn come and learn.[7]

In other words, one of the leaders of the Sadducees suggests to Yannai, the Hasmonaean king, that he should destroy the Pharisees. As for the question of what will happen to

---

[6] Deuteronomy Rabbah ix, 9.
[7] BT Qiddushin 66a.

the Torah, he replies that there is no need for the rabbis of the Pharisees, because the Torah is available to everyone.

In Megillat Taʿanit there are six dates of festivals which the *scholion* commentary (which is a kind of *gemaraʾ* to this mishnah) explains were founded as 'victories' of the Pharisees over the Sadducees, or over the Boethusians, a sect close to the Sadducees. One of the victories of the Pharisees fell

on the fourth of Tammuz [when the] *Sefer Gezerata/* the book of the Halakhot of the Sadducees, was burnt.[8]

The *scholion* in the Parma manuscript explains this date as follows:

Because it is written and laid down that the Sadducees had a book of *gezerot*, … the day it was destroyed they made into a festival.

The Oxford manuscript of Megillat Taʿanit has a different version:

The Boethusians used to write Halakhot in a book, and a man would ask and look it up for himself in the book. The rabbis said to them: Is it not written …: *According to the Torah which they shall teach you,* etc (Deuteronomy 17,11). [This] teaches that you do not write [things down] in a book.[9]

By describing their Torah as the 'oral law,' the Pharisees at one and the same time connected it to the written law, and stressed how it differed from it: there was continuity of tradition on the one hand, and the ability to develop on the other. From this we can understand the nature of the work

---

[8] Ed. Noam, p. 45.
[9] *Op. cit.,* p. 206.

of Rabbi Judah haNasi in finally redacting the Mishnah, as we have already stressed in the Introduction. This work was a huge step forward in that it created a book which became the basis for Jewish culture, together with the Torah. However, it was also a huge step backwards, for this act of finalising the Mishnah put a brake on the dynamics of the oral law to a considerable extent, and a dividing-line was created between the Tannaim, the rabbis of the Mishnah, and the Amoraim, the rabbis of the Talmud. A Tanna was allowed to disagree with the statements of another Tanna, even if he preceded him by several generations, whereas an Amora, even if he belonged to the generation immediately after Rabbi, was forbidden to disagree with the words of a Tanna, even if he preceded him only by a single generation.

2. The Six Orders of the Mishnah

The Mishnah is divided into six orders, each one of which is divided into tractates. The term *masekhet*/ tractate, denotes systems of debates, and is taken from the name of the system of warp threads stretched over the weft on a weaving loom (see Judges 16.13). Each one of these tractates is divided into chapters, and each one of the Halakhot in each chapter is again called a *mishnah* or *mishnayah*. The six orders are arranged thus according to Rabbi Shimʿon b. Laqish:

What does it say in the verse: *And he shall be the faith of thy times, a store of salvation, wisdom and knowledge* (Isaiah 33.6)? Faith – this is the order Zeraʿim/Seeds; thy times – this is the order Moʿed/

Appointed Times; a store – this is the order Nashim/Women; salvation – this is the order Neziqin/Damages; wisdom – this is the order Qodashim/Holy Things; and knowledge – this is the order Teharot/Purities.[10]

The first order, *Zeraʿim,* deals mostly with the mitzvot dependent on the produce of the earth, agricultural mitzvot obligatory only within the borders of the Land of Israel. The name of the order comes from the fact that it deals with anything connected to seeds in fields and orchards. It includes tractates dealing with the various religious taxes imposed on agricultural produce, such as *terumot* and *maʿasrot*/tithes; *maʿaser sheni*/second tithe; *demai*/produce where there is a doubt as to whether *terumot* and *maʿasrot* have been taken, and *ḥallah*/which is taken from the dough and given to the priests.

The first tractate in this order, however, is Berakhot/blessings, which is different from all the rest of the tractates in this order, as it deals with the regulations about prayers, especially the Shema prayer and its accompanying blessings and the Shemoneh Esrei/the Eighteen blessings; and with blessings, especially those connected to a meal.

Tractate Peah/the corner [of a field], which follows it, deals with the five gifts the Torah says must be given to the poor: *leqet*/sheaves left in the field after the reapers for the poor to gather; *shikhehah*/a heave-offering forgotten in the field at the time of the harvest; *peʾah*/[grain growing at] the corners of the field; *peret*/grapes left at the time of the harvest which have fallen off the bunch; *ʿolelot*/grapes

---

[10] BT Shabbat 31a.

fallen off the vine-branches at the end of the harvest season; and *maʿaser sheni* / the second tithe, which was a tenth of the produce, and must be taken every third and sixth year of the seven (sabbatical) year cycle. This tractate also deals with charity in general.

Tractate Kilayim deals with the bans on wearing clothing of mixed fibres (wool and linen, called *shaʿatnez*) and breeding animals of mixed parentage or working with two different breeds of animal together (e. g. ploughing with an ox and an ass together) as well as the ban on growing different kinds of plants together. Tractate Sheviʿit deals with the ban on working the land every seventh (sabbatical) year, as well as the release of debts in the seventh year, and the ban on demanding them from the lenders. Tractate Orlah deals with fruits from trees in their first three years, which are forbidden to be eaten or otherwise used, and have to be burned. Tractate Bikkurim deals with taking the first fruits of the *Shivʿat haMinim* / the Seven Species, to the Temple.

The second order, *Moʿed,* includes tractates dealing with the laws of the Sabbath and festivals, i. e. Shabbat; Pesaḥim / Passover; Rosh haShanah / the New Year; Yoma / the Day of Atonement; Sukkot / Tabernacles; Megillah – the reading of *megillat Esther* / the biblical book of Esther, on Purim. For example, tractate Beitzah deals with the laws of festivals in general, while tractate Moʿed Qatan deals with the laws of *Hol haMoʿed* / the intermediate festival days. The order Moʿed is the only order which is named in the singular: *Moʿed,* and not *Moʿadim,* and this is because it also includes tractate Sheqalim which deals with the half-shekel which was given every year to the Temple, and tractate Taʿanit which deals with fasts because of droughts and other natural disasters, the fasts following the destruction of the Temple, which although they are not festivals, also have fixed dates.

The third order, *Nashim,* as its name suggests, is so called because it deals with subjects relating to women. It includes Halakhot touching on marriage and divorce (tractates Qiddushin and Gittin), marriage contracts (Ketubbot), i. e. the mutual obligations of man and wife as detailed in this document, laws of *yibbum* and *ḥalitzah* (Yevamot)*,* i. e. marriage to or release of a sister-in-law in the event of her husband's dying childless, and the laws about *Sotah/*a married woman who stayed alone with another man even though her husband forbade it. In the order Nashim there are also two tractates which do not necessarily deal with women, Nedarim and Nazir. They are included in this order because the chapter in the Torah (Numbers 30) which deals with *nedarim/*oaths, deals mainly with the oaths of a woman which are cancelled by her husband, as well as the oaths of a daughter which are cancelled by her father. It is because oaths are included in this order that tractate Nazir is in Nashim too, for an oath is needed to become a *nazir/*someone who swears to forgo drinking wine, cutting his hair, or taking on impurity from contact with the dead.

The fourth order, *Neziqin,* is called after the first tractate in this order, which is divided into three *bavot/*gates: Bava Qama/the first gate, Bava Metzia/the middle gate and Bava Batra/the last gate. Two further tractates included in this order, Sanhedrin and Makkot, were originally a single

tractate, and they appear as such in some manuscripts of
the Mishnah. Neziqin deals with laws related to money,
criminal law and other matters which come before a law-
court. These subjects include monetary and bodily damage, theft and burglary; finding and taking ownership; interest and cheating; regulations about guardians of deposits
and their oaths; the conditions of employment for hired
workers; partnerships and heirs; capital punishment and
the organisation of law courts. Also included in this order
is tractate Avodah Zarah, which deals with relations with
non-Jews and the laws relating to pagan worship, and tractate Horayot, which deals with wrong instructions given
unintentionally by a court or High Priest. Tractate Eduyyot
is made up differently from the rest of the tractates in this
order, for it does not deal with a specific subject, but includes Halakhot on different sorts of subjects which have
been put together because of external similarities, i.e.
because one particular rabbi mentioned them, or gave
evidence about them. It is possible that this tractate was
organised before they organised the rest of the tractates in
this order, so that it includes Halakhot which should have
been placed in other tractates. Another exceptional tractate which has been included in Neziqin is tractate Avot/
[Sayings of the] Fathers, the only tractate in the Mishnah
whose contents are not halakhic. This includes the order of
the reception and tradition of the Torah from generation
to generation, statements about morality and proper con-
duct, wisdom literature, and above all, praise of the study
of the Torah and the observance of its mitzvot. From this
point of view, tractate Avot has similarities with the bibli-

cal book of Proverbs, the apocryphal book of Ecclesiasticus
(the Wisdom of Ben Sira), or Avot deRabbi Natan in the
Talmudic literature, which is a kind of *tosefta*/ addition, to
the tractate Avot.

The subjects of the fifth order, *Qodashim,* are mainly
matters of sacrifices and burnt offerings, both animal and
vegetable; the laws of Kashrut; the laws of firstborn men
and animals; an oath which someone makes to dedicate
something to the maintenance of the Temple treasury,
either its own value or the equivalent; the laws of substi-
tuting an unsanctified animal for one which has already
been dedicated for a sacrifice; and the laws about the use
of Temple property. Tractate Karetot in this order discusses
the sacrifices which people are obliged to bring because
of sins they have committed, which are divided into different categories. It also deals with people who are found
guilty of sins which are punished by *karet*/ punishment
from heaven, which means that the life of the sinner is
cut short and s/he will die before her or his time. Tractate
Tamid deals with the description of the morning sacrifice
in the Temple, up to the end of the offering of the *tamid*/
the continual sacrifice, in the morning. Tractate Middot
deals with the measurements of the Second Temple and
the Temple Mount. These are different in some details
from the description of the Temple found in Josephus.[11]
Tractate Ḥullin deals mainly with the Halakhot about
eating non-sanctified meat, i. e. Halakhot of Kashrut, but
in addition it deals with the parts due to the priest from a

---

[11] Especially *Bellum Judaicum* v, 238–247.

slaughtered animal – the leg, the cheeks and the stomach – as well as Halakhot on the first shearing of sheep and the law about sending a mother bird free if you take her young. Tractate Menaḥot includes some of the Halakhot about *te-fillin*/phylacteries, and *tzitzit*/ritual fringes.

The sixth order, *Teharot*, as its name suggests, deals with matters of purity and impurity. The fact that a whole order containing twelve tractates is devoted to these Halakhot shows us the great importance that was given to this subject in Judaism, as in other cultures of the time. It includes Halakhot on preserving purity related to the human body, clothes, utensils and food: the laws of impurity related to a dead body, which is the *'avi 'avot ha-tum'ah*/the source or direct cause of impurity; the impurity of the eight reptiles mentioned in the Torah; the carcass of an unclean animal; the impurity of a *zav* or *zavah*/a man or woman with discharges from their genitals; *niddah*/a woman impure because of menstruation, and *yoledet*/a woman after childbirth; as well as the impurity of *tzara'at*/a skin condition which was also identified on house walls. All these impurities are at the level of *'av ha-tum'ah*/the father or source of impurity, and someone who became impure from them became *velad ha-tum'ah*/a secondary cause of defilement, or *rishon le-tum'ah*/in the first degree of impurity. Impurity is conveyed by contact, by carrying – even if you do not touch the source of impurity – and, in the case of a corpse, simply by being in something like a tent or building where the corpse is present. The tractates in this order also discuss utensils which contract impurity; the impurity of food and drink; and the impurity of the hands and ritual hand-washing, for the hands are the only organs which are liable to contract impurity even when the body does not, when they touch the *velad ha-tum'ah* and thus contract second-degree impurity. Hands are considered to be *be-ḥezqat teme'ot/* presumed impure, because they are active, and this can be corrected by ritual hand-washing: this is the reason for ritual hand-washing with a blessing before a meal. Tractate Parah deals with the Halakhot of the *Parah 'Adumah/* the Red Cow: the Kashrut of the cow, the way it is slaughtered and burned; the sanctification of the *mei ḥat'at/* the water on which the ashes of the red cow were sprinkled after it was burnt; and the sprinkling of this water on someone who had become impure after contact with the dead. Tractate Tevul Yom deals with the laws relating to someone who had become impure who immersed him/herself during the daytime and is waiting until sunset to become pure. During the time between the immersion and night s/he would be in the category of *tevul yom.* Tractate Makhshirin deals with the factors which predispose food to become subject to impurity, for food cannot be subject to impurity unless it has come in contact with one of the seven fluids which predispose to impurity: dew, water, wine, oil, blood, milk and honey. Tractate Miqva'ot deals with the laws of ritual baths and immersion.

There are sixty-three tractates in the Mishnah (not all have been mentioned here) although the Midrash numbers them at sixty.[12] The difference is because the three Bavot in Neziqin, were originally a single tractate, and as noted,

---

[12] Songs Rabbah vi, 14.

tractate Sanhedrin included tractate Makkot. Within each order, the tractates are arranged in descending order, according to the numbers of chapters in each of them, but in Neziqin this was clearly arranged before the Bavot and Sanhedrin were divided up. Zeraʿim is exceptional in this respect, presumably because of the wish to place the unique tractate Berakhot at the beginning.

3. The Halakhot of the Mishnah and the Laws of the Torah

About half the Mishnah deals with laws which had already become outdated by the time of Rabbi in the one hundred and fifty years which had passed between the destruction of the Temple and the final redaction of the Mishnah. For example, the order Qodashim deals mostly with sacrifices related to the Temple alone; Teharot deals mostly with laws of purity and impurity related to the Temple; many Halakhot in Moʿed deal with the celebration of the festivals in the Temple, such as for example, tractate Pesaḥim, which deals mostly with the laws of the Passover offering; Yoma, which deals mostly with the service of the High Priest in the Temple on the Day of Atonement; and tractate Sheqalim which deals mostly with weighing the half-shekel tax for the Temple. In the order Zeraʿim too, there are tractates which are relevant only to the time when the Temple still stood, such as Maʿaser Sheni which deals with eating the second tithe in Jerusalem, or Bikkurim which deals with bringing the first-fruits to the Temple. The reason for including these Halakhot, tractates and orders in the Mishnah was because they were sanctified in Jewish tradition from the days of the Second Temple, and there was also the hope that the Temple would be speedily rebuilt.

In general, there is a clear link between the tractates of the Mishnah and the laws of the Torah. However, it is true that in the majority of cases the amount of detail in the Mishnah far outweighs what we find in the laws of the Torah. The Mishnah itself relates to this:

The [rules about] release from vows hover in the air and have nothing to support them. The Halakhot of the Sabbath, festival offerings and *meᶜilot*/ sacrilege, are like mountains hanging on a hair, for the [teaching] of Scripture is brief and the Halakhot are many.[13]

In other words, release from vows through a rabbi has no firm foundation in the Torah which can be relied on. The same is true of the Halakhot of the Sabbath, the Halakhot dealing with the festival offerings on the three pilgrim festivals in the Temple, and the Halakhot regulating who is allowed to benefit from *heqdesh*/ dedicated holy things. These are merely random examples, and the same is true for many areas the Mishnah deals with. We can give an example of this from the Halakhot of the Sabbath. The ban on working on the Sabbath is included in the Ten Commandments:

Thou shalt not do any work, thou, nor thy son nor thy daughter, thy manservant, nor thy maidservant, nor thy cattle, nor thy stranger that is within thy gates. (Exodus 20.10; Deuteronomy 5.14)

---

[13] M Hagigah i, 8 (tr. Danby, adapted), and see below.

However, there are no details given here of the kind of work forbidden on the Sabbath. In the Torah there are a few incidental mentions of forbidden categories of work: ploughing and harvesting (Exodus 34.21); kindling fire (Exodus 25.3); gathering sticks, where it is explained that the punishment is stoning (Numbers 15.32); as well as gathering manna on the Sabbath, which certainly cannot be regarded as a mitzvah for all time (Exodus 16.22–26, 29–30). In the rest of the Hebrew Bible several other activities are mentioned as forbidden on the Sabbath. In contrast to this, tractate Shabbat, which opens the order Mo'ed, lists 'forty minus one *'avot melakhah*/ sources of work activities,' i. e. the main work activities which are forbidden on the Sabbath,[14] and their *toladot*/ work activities derived from them. Each of these is described in detail and explained very plainly. Among the rest, tractate Shabbat details things forbidden as *shevut,* something which is not included in *'avot melakhah* and their *toladot,* but is a work activity forbidden so that the Sabbath rest from work should be total. The Tannaim defined this as an *'issur de-rabbanan*/ a prohibition made by the rabbis, which was not *mi-de'oraita'* / from the Torah. Together with these different sorts of forbidden activities, the Mishnah also goes into details about activities which were not categorised as *melakhah* or *shevut,* and are therefore not forbidden on the Sabbath, even though there are resemblances between them and activities which were forbidden.

---

[14] M Shabbat vii, 2.

The Tannaim and Amoraim wanted to point to links with the Torah, even in the number of forty minus one, which is found in other contexts, such as the number of lashes given to a sentenced criminal.[15] The same can be said of the actual definition of every single work activity forbidden on the Sabbath, where they linked their list somewhat artificially to the work activities which were needed during the building of the Tabernacle. Tractate Eruvin, which follows tractate Shabbat, also deals with the laws of the Sabbath, and some scholars think that both these tractates were originally thought of as a single entity. Eruvin contains a discussion of all the matters relating to the Sabbath boundary, that is *taqqanot* which create a mixture of boundaries and authorities in order to lighten the restrictions on movement and carrying on the Sabbath: *ʿeruvei teḥumim*/ delineated boundaries, *ʿeruvei ḥatzerot*/ courtyard boundaries, and *shituf mevoʾot*/ joined entrance-passages. It is no wonder, then, that the Mishnah cited above compares the laws of the Sabbath to 'mountains hanging on a שערה/ hair,' since they have no firm foundation in the Torah. However, the beginning of the Mishnah, as we saw, spoke of 'the [rules about] release from vows hover[ing] in the air.' Thus it is possible that what the Mishnah actually wrote was that the Sabbath laws were like 'mountains hanging on a סערה/whirlwind,' since it is common to confuse the letters *samekh* and *sin* in the Talmudic literature.

---

[15] M Makkot iii, 10, which is an exposition of Deuteronomy 25.2–3: 'How many lashes do they give him? Forty minus one, as it says: *By number forty (loc. cit.)* [that is to say], a number near forty' (tr. Danby).

There are a number of fields of Halakha which did not have separate tractates devoted to them in the Mishnah, and some which do not appear there at all. The most obvious omission from the order Moʿed is a tractate devoted to the festival of Hanukkah. There is also no special tractate devoted to the festival of Purim, only a tractate dealing with the laws of reading the *megillah*. There is also no tractate devoted to the festival of Shavuot/Pentecost, although the regulations about this festival are included in the tractates which deal with festival regulations in general. Similarly, the Mishnah did not include tractates devoted to the Halakhot of Tefillin, Tzitzit, and Mezuzah, and these important mitzvot are scarcely mentioned in the Mishnah. This lack is particularly noteable in view of the central place given to these very mitzvot in the time of the Tannaim, the rabbis of the Mishnah. Thus Rabbi did not organise the subjects of the tractates of the Mishnah so that they would give total coverage to all significant areas of Halakha. We simply do not know the exact yardsticks he used to choose the subjects for inclusion in the Mishnah: on the one hand, he devoted tractates to relatively marginal subjects, while on the other hand he did not devote tractates to relatively important subjects.

4. The Process of Editing the Mishnah

Editing the Mishnah was not the work of Rabbi alone, but it was he who brought this work to its conclusion. The beginning of the work of editing the Mishnah had begun in the Yavneh period, when the rabbis felt the need to unify the people, and to create unity and uniformity following the trauma of the destruction of the Temple.

Rabbi sat and said: It is forbidden to cover up cold foods. Rabbi Ishmaʿel b. Rabbi Yose said in his presence: My father permitted covering up cold foods. [Rabbi] said: This Elder has already ruled on this.[16]

The halakhic issue here is whether it is permitted to cover up cold food on the Sabbath so that it will not heat up, or whether there is a worry that this might be seen as similar to covering up hot foods, which must be covered up before the Sabbath. Rabbi forbade this practice, but when he heard from Rabbi Ishmaʿel the son of Rabbi Yose that his father had permitted it, he changed his opinion. The Babylonian Amora Rav Pappa comments on this in the continuation of the passage:

Come and see how much they [Rabbi and Rabbi Yose] like each other! For if Rabbi Yose had been alive, he would have submitted and sat down before Rabbi, for Rabbi Ishmaʿel the son of Rabbi Yose had taken the place of his father, and he submitted and sat down before Rabbi. And in spite of this Rabbi said: An Elder [Rabbi Yose, father of Rabbi Ishmaʿel] has already ruled on this.

Rav Pappa is surprised at what Rabbi did, when he changed his opinion because of what Rabbi Ishmaʿel reported in his father's name. The Jerusalem Talmud further reports humble words of Rabbi Judah haNasi addressed to Rabbi Yose himself:

---

[16] BT Shabbat 51a.

When Rabbi wanted to question Rabbi Yose, he said: We miserable people must question Rabbi Yose, for the difference between our generation and his is like the difference between the Holy of Holies [in the Temple] and the most profane of places.[17]

In other words, when Rabbi wanted to question the statements of Rabbi Yose, he said: We miserable people must ask Rabbi Yose for his opinion. This manifestation of respect for the opinion of the other from someone who was entitled to respect himself, undoubtedly bolstered Rabbi's image in the eyes of the other rabbis, raised his qualifications for redacting the Mishnah and was a further element in its acceptability to everyone.

5. Rabbi's Methodology in the Organisation of the Mishnah

Rabbi Judah haNasi included in his Mishnah the Mishnahs of the pupils of Rabbi 'Aqiva, above all the Mishnah of Rabbi Meir. One of the controversies in modern research surrounds the question of what methodology Rabbi used in organising his Mishnah: did he simply arrange the material he found and set it in place, or did he change the content and sift out the various different opinions?

Albeck, one of the most important scholars of Mishnah, claims that: 'The editor of the Mishnah neither changed nor emasculated nor cut short the material he had in front

---

[17] JT Gittin vi, 48b, col. 1082.

of him, but set it in his Mishnah as he had received it.'[18] He demonstrates his claim on the basis of the fact that some of the collections of Halakhot in the Mishnah were not placed in the appropriate tractate dealing with similar subjects. To take a few examples: the inclusion of the *taqqanot* of Rabban Yoḥanan b. Zakkai all together in Mishnah Rosh haShanah,[19] even though only the first is related to Rosh haShanah; the inclusion of *mishnayyot* according to the names of those who said them, such as the statements of Admon and Hanan who were judges in Jerusalem;[20] the inclusion of *mishnayyot* according to their linguistic pattern, such as e. g. '[something] differs from … except,'[21] or 'all.'[22] According to Albeck, if Rabbi were to have changed anything in his Mishnah, he would have set each *mishnah* in its place in the appropriate tractate. Albeck goes further, to back up his claim, and points out that sometimes the same Halakha is to be found in different tractates, and the same *mishnayyot* are even sometimes found in different tractates and in a different form or with different contents. Therefore his conclusion is that Rabbi copied the *mishnayyot* received from the different Batei Midrash as they were written, without inserting his own opinions.

In contrast, other scholars of Talmudic literature, such as Epstein, Urbach and HaLivni, claim that the Mishnah

---

[18] Ch. Albeck, *Introduction to the Mishnah* (Jerusalem, 1959, Heb.), p. 102.

[19] M Rosh haShanah iv, 1–4.

[20] M Ketubbot xiii, 1–9.

[21] M Megillah i, 3–11.

[22] M Qiddushin i, 6–10.

is not uniform in its make-up. There are Halakhot where Rabbi did not change anything, as Albeck has demonstrated, but he did change and re-style other Halakhot. It is possible to demonstrate, for example, by comparison with the Tosefta, the collection which is parallel to the Mishnah, that Rabbi sometimes worded the Mishnah according to his own opinion without noting this explicitly, as can be demonstrated from the fact that it appears in the Tosefta under his name. Sometimes Rabbi notes the statement of a single rabbi as 'the rabbis say,' and by attributing the statement to a number of rabbis he gives it validity. Rabbi also cites Halakha in the Mishnah anonymously, without mentioning the name of a specific Tanna; and sometimes brings another Halakha on the same subject and blocks it with the opinion of another Tanna. It is also possible to demonstrate that in one or two other *mishnayyot* Rabbi has cut out parts of the source he had in front of him, or joined two sources together. In some of the cases where there were two opinions on a particular case, Rabbi changed the original textual version, especially if it was an opinion at variance with his own. For example, it is reasonable to assume that in the original text a rabbi with whom he disagreed said more than a single word, but in the Mishnah as we have it, his opinion is cut down to a single word, such as 'obliged,' 'permitted,' 'pure,' or 'impure.' Sometimes Rabbi also summarises the statement of someone he disagrees with, and cites it in other words, such as, e. g., 'Abba Shaul said: The opposite is the case.'[23] Abba Shaul clearly did not use the

---

[23] M Gittin v, 4.

words 'the opposite is the case' – it was the redactor of the Mishnah who put it in this way. However, in spite of what we have just said, it is often still possible to identify the various sources of Rabbi's Mishnah from their differences in style and the different ways of expressing things, sometimes even in a single tractate or a single chapter.

An additional problem which derives from the first problem of whether Rabbi did introduce changes into extant textual versions, is whether he organised the Mishnah when he redacted it as a legal codex or an anthology of Halakhot. As we have already noted, there was no such thing as a legal codex in the modern sense in antiquity, and Roman law also contained layers and differences of opinions. In Albeck's opinion, the Mishnah is a digest of the oral law. This derives, of course, from his claim that Rabbi did not change anything in the Mishnah. Epstein and Urbach, on the other hand, claim that Rabbi did indeed use the methodology of collecting Halakhot, but did not shrink from making new laws. Urbach defines the Mishnah as a canon of laws. In his opinion, by the very act of selecting and adding, Rabbi aimed at varying his Mishnah and giving representation in it to the different schools of Halakha. By this act the die was cast, and a canon created by which the other Tannaitic sources were evaluated and the final redaction came about, for after Rabbi's time almost no new material was added to the Mishnah. Rabbi's collection became *the* Mishnah, and other Tannaitic collections and halakhic material became external Baraitot.

To sum up, the question is not what Rabbi Judah ha-Nasi aimed to achieve, but what he actually achieved, and this is the shared basis of the Halakha. For a generation or two after Rabbi's death, further Tannaitic collections were produced, the Tosefta and the *midrashei halakhah,* but it is the Mishnah which is the foundation both of the Jerusalem and of the Babylonian Talmud.

The Mishnah which was finally redacted by Rabbi includes Halakhot only (apart from tractate Avot). It is true that there are passages of Aggadah in it, but these are very few, and some of them were produced in subsequent generations, such as, for example, the last *mishnah* in tractate Sotah.[24] The Mishnah is very rarely dependent on a biblical verse, and there are those who think that those *mishnayyot* which cite such verses are early ones which were already worded in the time of the Second Temple. In some of the cases where Rabbi changed the original version in the Mishnah, his aim was to prefer the statement of one Tanna over another. Similarly, he showed his wish to give authority to statements which he cited anonymously, i. e. without citing the name of the Tanna, or to note the statement of one or other Tanna as the view of the majority, in the form 'the rabbis say,' or 'the words of the rabbis.' In these cases, Rabbi was in fact determining what was the ruling of the Halakha. Further rules for deciding Halakha as found in the Talmud, such as: '[If we find] Rabbi Meir and Rabbi Judah – the Halakha goes by Rabbi Judah,'[25] do not arise from Rabbi's activities in editing and redacting the Mishnah, but belong to the rulings of the Amoraim of

---

[24] M Sotah ix, 15.
[25] JT Terumot iii, 42a, col. 228; BT Eruvin 46b etc.

the Talmud. However, Rabbi contributed to the possibility of fixing them, in that he cited statements in the original words of the speakers, and not in the language which is prevalent in the Talmud. For example, there are times when the Talmud cites a disagreement between Rabbi Meir and Rabbi Judah on a certain subject, and only writes that 'one said' as follows, and 'the other said' something different. In cases like this, where it is in fact impossible to know what was the opinion of Rabbi Meir and the opinion of Rabbi Judah, the rules which were laid down by the Amoraim themselves are of no help in fixing the Halakha.

Rabbi's prestige and authority were so great that on the final redaction of the Mishnah it was widely published, and its validity was accepted immediately, so that the period of the Tannaim came to an end. One of the reasons for the fact that the Mishnah was received without question is certainly rooted in the fact that Rabbi did not bring his personal opinion into it, but chose the opinion which had been accepted and agreed among the rabbis of the time. Thus we may explain the relatively few occasions when a statement of Rabbi himself appears in the Mishnah, and the fact that the Talmud notes that, on the occasions when the opinion of the Mishnah is opposed to the opinion of Rabbi: *matnitin delo' keRabbi*/ our Mishnah is not according to Rabbi['s opinion].[26] This arises from the fact that it would appear that Rabbi aimed to produce a Mishnah which would finally redact all the Mishnahs which had preceded him in the Ushah period, and which would include

---

[26] BT Eruvin 35a.

all the opinions fixed in all the Mishnahs, and not just his own opinion. Achieving this aim led to the primacy of the Mishnah redacted by Rabbi Judah haNasi, and eventually, as we have noted, to the end of the period of the Tannaim who had produced the Mishnah.

A further subject of controversy in modern research is whether Rabbi actually wrote down the Mishnah himself, or whether he left it as oral Torah. An exacting survey of the Mishnah by Ya'akov Sussmann leads us to prefer the possibility that Rabbi did not, in fact, write down the Mishnah, but that it remained as oral Torah.[27] In his opinion, the culture of the rabbis was an unmistakably oral culture, and they refrained from writing it down. In order to guard the text of the Mishnah and to present it to the Amoraim, the function of the Tannaim developed: this term, which signified the rabbis in the time of the Mishnah, took on another meaning in the period of the Talmud: from now on it represented the people who memorised and could hand on the oral tradition of the Mishnah, or parts of it. These Tannaim were usually young men who did not belong to the group of the rabbis, and were not necessarily intellectuals, but they had an excellent memory. The very existence of this function in the time of the Amoraim in Palestine and Babylonia demonstrates that the Mishnah was not written down by Rabbi, or even in the period of the Amoraim. It should be noted here that other cultures

---

[27] Y. Sussmann, 'Torah shebe'al peh, pshutah kemashm'ah – koḥo shel qotzo shel yod,' idem et al., *Mekhqarei Talmud,* vol. III,1 (Jerusalem, 2005), pp. 209–384.

in the ancient world also produced and handed on large bodies of literature orally.

The only Tannaitic work where there was exacting care to preserve its text was Rabbi's Mishnah. Whereas there is no trace of any written book of Halakha from the Amoraic period, by the period of the *ge'onim,* in the eighth century, it is clearly understood that there are extant books of Mishnah and Talmud in writing. The transition from an oral to a written culture thus took place in Babylonia in the period hidden between the time of the Amoraim and the *ge'onim,* that is, between the fifth and eighth centuries.

The unique status of the Mishnah is due to the dominant personality of Rabbi Judah haNasi; to the clement political and economic circumstances of the time when he was active; to Rabbi's wish to hand on the accepted and agreed opinion; to its conciseness, and to its nature as a decidedly literary creation, with an organised and unified framework. The Amoraim of Palestine summed up the status of the Mishnah – a 'pillar of iron.'[28]

6. The Language of the Mishnah and Rabbi's Attitude to Hebrew

In Rabbi's time there were three main languages in use in Palestine: Hebrew, Greek and Aramaic. It is impossible to know which language was most commonly used, although it is probably not far from the truth to assume that Hebrew

---

[28] Leviticus Rabbah xxi, 5 (ed. Margulies, p. 481).

was for the most part the language of the rabbis, Greek –
which was the international language of the time – was
used by the elite who wanted to get close to the Roman
authorities, while Aramaic was the language of the common people.

Rabbi was a great supporter of the Hebrew language,
and we find in a Baraita:

Rabbi said: Why *Sursi*/ the Aramaic language, in the Land of Israel?
[Speak] either the Holy tongue or the Greek language.[29]

In this source Rabbi thus brings his opinion that in the
Land of Israel one should speak one of two languages, He-
brew or Greek, for in his view Aramaic was unnecessary.
Greek had always been the language in which the Jewish
leaders had communicated with the Roman authorities,
and it was also the language of culture and literature in the
Hellenistic East. Greek had been studied in the house of
Rabban Gamliel of Yavneh, Rabbi's grandfather:

They allowed them, the house of Rabban Gamliel, to teach their
children Greek, because they were close to the [Roman] rulers.[30]

According to the evidence given by Rabban Shim'on b.
Gamliel, Rabbi's father and the son of Rabban Gamliel
of Yavneh:

Five hundred [people] learned Torah and five hundred learned
Greek wisdom.[31]

---

[29] BT Bava Qama 82b–83a.
[30] Tos. Sotah xv, 8 (ed. Lieberman, p. 242). The Erfurt MS has: 'because they needed the [Roman] rulers.'
[31] BT Sotah 49b; BT Bava Qama 83a.

In spite of the clearly exaggerated numbers here, it is interesting to see that this text notes equal numbers of people studying Torah and studying Greek philosophy. The Jerusalem Talmud tells us of permission to study Greek in the house of Rabbi himself:

They allowed three things in the house of Rabbi: They could look at themselves in a mirror; they could cut their hair in a *kome* style, and they could teach their children Greek, because they needed [it to communicate with] the [Roman] rulers.[32]

The innovation in the statement above of Rabbi Judah haNasi was the fact that he rejected Aramaic (Syriac) in favour of Greek. Rabbi also fixed the preference for Hebrew as Halakha:

The rabbis taught: Reciting the Shema prayer [should be] as it is written, according to Rabbi. But the rabbis say: [It can be recited] in any language.[33]

It is hardly surprising that Rabbi, who redacted the all-Hebrew Mishnah, should be the source of the demand to speak Hebrew, whether in everyday life or in the prayers. Following Rabbi's opinion, we hear from one of his leading pupils:

Rabbi Yoḥanan said: Anyone who prays in Aramaic – the angels in heaven do not help him, for the angels in heaven do not understand Aramaic.[34]

Here we find a practical 'reason' for praying in Hebrew: the angels in heaven, who bring human prayers to the

---

[32] JT Shabbat vi, 7d, col. 395.
[33] BT Berakhot 13a.
[34] BT Shabbat 12b.

Holy One blessed be He, do not know Aramaic. In Babylonia also they attempted to remove Aramaic from the prayers in favour of Hebrew. In the words of Rav Judah, the head of the Yeshivah at Pumbedita in the second generation of Babylonian Amoraim in the second half of the third century:

A man should never pray for anything in Aramaic.[35]

The language of the Mishnah is Hebrew, but it is a Hebrew which is different from the language of the Hebrew Bible in both grammar and vocabulary. There is also no sign in the Mishnah that it was translated from another language. Thus, as we have noted, it was Rabbi's especial love for the Hebrew language and his rejection of Aramaic which led to this. However, the Mishnah does introduce into its vocabulary various words which are influenced by Aramaic. It should also be remembered that not all the Hebrew language was preserved in the Bible, so that many of the words which are found in the Mishnah and not in the Bible, still originate from biblical Hebrew. Here and there in the Mishnah we also find words borrowed from Greek and Latin.

An interesting curiosity is the episode reported in the Jerusalem Talmud about Rabbi's maidservant, who was such an expert in Hebrew that the rabbis learned the explanation of certain words from the Halakha or Scripture which they had not known from her.[36]

---

[35] *Loc. cit.*
[36] For example, JT Megillah ii, 73a, cols. 758–759.

Rabbi's maidservant knew Hebrew so well that she could understand unusual words. From the conversation she had with her companion, the rabbis learned the meaning of the word *matatei* in Isaiah. In the parallel episode in the Babylonian Talmud, the rabbis did not understand the verse which says of Wisdom: *salseleha* [exhalt her = turn her = curl her] and she shall promote thee, in Proverbs 4.8, until they heard Rabbi's maidservant say to a man who was twirling his hair: How long are you going to continue to curl *(mesalsel)* your hair?[37] We can explain this interesting phenomenon in three possible ways. First of all, Rabbi must have insisted that the members of his household should all speak Hebrew, so that this maid also spoke good Hebrew. Secondly, the use of Hebrew as a spoken language may have been deep-rooted among the lower classes, who were naturally conservative and preserved the local traditions. The third possibility, in contrast to the second, is that at the time there were people from the upper classes who because of their circumstances were forced to become servants. It is reasonable to suppose that it would have been an exceptional honour to serve as a maid in Rabbi's house, and that a woman from a higher class, who knew Hebrew, was chosen for this honour.

Another example of the subject of languages can be seen in the statement of Rabbi Yonatan of Beit Guvrin, from the second generation of Palestinian Amoraim, who lived in the second half of the third century CE, where he speaks of four languages:

---

[37] BT Megillah 18a.

Rabbi Yonatan of Beit Guvrin said: There are four languages which are pleasant to use in the world, and these are they: Greek for song; Latin for battle; *Sursi*/Aramaic, for mourning; Hebrew for speaking.[38]

Beit Guvrin/Eleutheropolis, where Rabbi Yonatan was active, was one of the mixed cities inhabited by both Jews and non-Jews, and it is because of this that he has a fine understanding that there were not only three languages which were then in common use in Palestine, Greek, Hebrew and Aramaic, but also Latin. However, like Rabbi, he prefers Hebrew as the spoken language, whereas Greek is good, in his opinion, for *zemer*/song, or poetry. For example, it is said of Elisha b. Avuyah, Rabbi Meir's teacher who left Judaism at the time of the repressive legislation following the Bar Kokhva revolt, and is thus known as Aher, 'the Other,' that 'Greek song/poetry never left his mouth.'[39] In Rabbi Yonatan's opinion, Aramaic is suitable for use as mourning poetry, and from this it is clear that this was the language of everyday life, for at a time of sorrow and distress when there is no time to look for words and things break out naturally, it is natural to use one's mother-tongue. Funeral oration poetry in Aramaic became one of the commonest genres in Late Antiquity. And finally, Latin, in Rabbi Yonatan's opinion, is the language of the barracks, and suitable for use on the battlefield. Hebrew from this time, indeed, includes many borrowed words from Latin related to the army and government. However, according to a different

---

[38] JT Megillah i, 71b, col. 748. See on this, Y. Yahalom, *Poetry and Society in Jewish Galilee of Late Antiquity* (Tel Aviv, 1999, Heb.), pp. 48–51.

[39] BT Hagigah 15b.

explanation, the whole statement relates to different literary genres, and the 'battle' here relates to prayer.

A partial picture of the prevalence of the various languages in Palestine in the days of Rabbi can be seen from funerary and synagogue inscriptions which have survived from that time. These inscriptions include Hebrew, side by side with Greek and Aramaic. It is true that the language of inscriptions is not exactly the language of everyday speech, and certainly the languages used in the inscriptions cannot tell us anything about the percentages of speakers of each language, but they do give us evidence that these languages were indeed in actual use. For example, in the five ancient synagogues found up to now in Israel which have a mosaic with pictures of the zodiac, the names of the seasons, the year and the months are in Hebrew, although on the mosaic from Zippori/Sepphoris some of the names appear in Greek as well. Hebrew names also appear in the mosaics at Beit Alfa (at Kibbutz Ḥeftzibah), Ḥammat Tiberias, Naaran (near Jericho), and Ein Gedi (a list only, without pictures). Even though these synagogues post-date Rabbi, they are also further evidence both of the centrality of everything connected to the Jewish calendar, and of the importance of the Hebrew language as insisted on by Rabbi. In the fourth century, the church father Epiphanius, condemning the belief in the signs of the zodiac, notes that the Pharisees translated the names of these signs into Hebrew.

Chapter 8

The End of Rabbi Judah haNasi's Life

1. Rabbi's Will

Both Talmuds include what can be seen as the last will and testament of Rabbi Judah haNasi. In the Babylonian Talmud this is cited as part of a detailed legendary description of the death of Rabbi.[1] During this process, we are told that Rabbi called all the rabbis together and instructed them:

'My son Shimʿon should be *ḥakham;* my son Gamliel should be *nasi*ʾ; Ḥanina bar Ḥama should sit at the head.'

If this statement is authentic, it is clear that Rabbi Judah haNasi is renewing functions which had existed during part of the Ushah period, according to a tradition which is also found in the Babylonian Talmud. This tradition tells us that his father, Rabban Shimʿon b. Gamliel, was *nasi*ʾ, Rabbi Natan was the Av Beit Din, i.e., head of the Beit haVaʿad, and Rabbi Meir was the *ḥakham,* i.e. he held some sort of function in the leadership of the Beit haVaʿad whose nature is unclear to us.[2] It is clear that the division of functions in this manner would have cut down the authority of the patriarchate, even if two of the important functions were held by Rabbi's sons. In the parallel will in

---

[1] BT Ketubbot 103a–104a.
[2] BT Horayot 13b.

the Jerusalem Talmud, there is what appears at first sight to be a different version of Rabbi's instructions:

Rabbi used to appoint two officials. If they were suitable, they carried on, but if not, they were cancelled. When he was dying, he instructed his son, saying: Do not do it in this way, but appoint them all at the same time, and set Rabbi Ḥanina bar Ḥama at the head.[3]

According to the Jerusalem Talmud, the will was intended to change Rabbi's policy of appointments, for he instructed his son not to behave as he had – in other words, they should appoint all the office holders at the same time, instead of appointing only two a year, and they should appoint Rabbi Ḥanina bar Ḥama 'at the head.' The question is, what is the force of 'at the head' (literally: first)? Was he to be the head of all those appointed together, or was he to be appointed to the high office of the rabbi who sat 'at the head' of the Beit haVaʿad? If we examine the Talmudic uses of this term, it becomes clear that the Jerusalem Talmud generally adds a number to the details of the office holders, which alludes to their office and their place in the hierarchy of the leadership. For example, in the Jerusalem Talmud's version of the episode dealing with the unseating of Rabban Gamliel of Yavneh, in one place it says that when they put Rabban Gamliel back in his place:

They did not demote him [Rabbi Elʿazar b. Azariah who had temporarily taken his place] from his high place, but appointed him Av Beit Din, head of the Beit haVaʿad.[4]

---

[3] JT Taaniyot iv, 68a, col. 728. Cf Ecclesiastes Rabbah vii, 7.

[4] JT Berakhot iv, 7d, col. 36.

In another place it says:

Three people gave up their place in this world and received life in the World to Come, and these are they: Jonathan son of Saul, and El'azar b. Azariah and the elders of Beterah … and El'azar b. Azariah was the second.[5]

From this we understand that the word 'second' relates to the office of Av Beit Din, which was second in importance to the patriarch. In other words, it is very reasonable to assume that Rabbi Judah haNasi's instruction to appoint Rabbi Ḥanina bar Ḥama 'at the head' or 'first,' is there to note that Rabbi's son – who was intended to be the patriarch after him – should appoint Rabbi Ḥanina bar Ḥama as the first after himself. In other words, he should be appointed to the position of the head of the Beit haVaʿad.[6]

The order of appointment of the rabbis thus tells us of their status, as is clear from further sources. For example, when Rabbi ʿAqiva appointed Rabbi Meir and Rabbi Shimʿon, he took care to appoint Rabbi Meir first, and then Rabbi Shimʿon's face fell.[7] This was understandable, for Rabbi Meir held the office of *ḥakham,* which was third in the hierarchy in the Beit haVaʿad in the Ushah period. In the continuation of the tradition we are dealing with in the Jerusalem Talmud, there is also a struggle between the rabbis as to who will be appointed first. In other words,

[5] JT Pesaḥim vi, 33a, col. 530.

[6] G. Alon, *The Jews in Their Land in the Talmudic Age* (Jerusalem, 1984), pp. 726–730. For a survey of the scholarly literature and a different approach, see, M. Jacobs, *Die Institution des jüdischen Patriarchen* (Tübingen, 1995), pp. 70–77.

[7] JT Sanhedrin i, 11a, col. 1270.

the first to be appointed is the first in honour and status. To sum up, there is in fact no contradiction between the traditions in the Babylonian and Jerusalem Talmuds on the will of Rabbi Judah haNasi, and the Jerusalem Talmud certainly does not contradict the Babylonian Talmud on the office of *ḥakham,* which was given to Rabbi Shimʿon, son of Rabbi Judah haNasi.

It must be remembered that Rabbi Natan, who came from Babylonia, held the office of the Av Beit Din, in other words, he was second in importance to Rabban Shimʿon b. Gamliel, the head of the Beit haVaʿad in the Ushah period. Rabbi held unbounded authority without any deputies, but the rabbi who was first in importance after him was Rabbi Ḥiyya, who also originated from Babylonia. It is thus not surprising that Rabbi instructed that after his death, Rabbi Ḥanina bar Ḥama, who also originated in Babylonia, should function as the Av Beit Din. This policy of giving high offices to rabbis who had come to Palestine from Babylonia contributed a great deal to preserving good relationships with the large diaspora community in Babylonia when its power began to rise after the Bar Kokhva revolt – but also continued the hegemony of Palestine over Babylonia. As we have seen above, when Ḥananiah, son of Rabbi Joshua's brother, tried to fix the calendar independently in Babylonia, Rabbi Natan was one of the members of the deputation sent to him from Palestine in order to force him and the Jews of Babylonia to go back and use the calendar which had been fixed in Palestine.[8] The

---

[8] Thus in the Palestinian tradition: JT Sanhedrin above.

presumption behind this act was, almost certainly, that a messenger who originated in Babylonia and had reached a high position in Palestine would be effective with the Jews of Babylonia, as in fact did happen.

Following the will in the Babylonian Talmud, Rabbi hands over the 'order of the patriarchate' to his son Gamliel and instructs him:

My son, act with a high hand in your patriarchate, deal severely with your pupils.[9]

Here Rabbi advises his son to act in his patriarchate just as he had done – high-handedly towards the public, and strictly and severely with his pupils. Rabbi had indeed navigated in his relations with the rabbis between a punitive dictatorship, and equality and distribution of honours, but he had behaved with the utmost severity towards his pupils. To one pupil, who on the basis of reason set before him a Halakha on matters of purity and impurity, he responded:

Rabbi said to him: Bar Piqa still holds to his nonsense.[10]

When Levi, another pupil of Rabbi's, went further than the Mishnah which rules that there are fifteen women forbidden to a man because of incestuous relations, such as his sister, granddaughter and aunt,[11] and wanted to increase the number to sixteen, Rabbi related to his words with scorn:

It seems to me he has no brains in his head![12]

---

[9] BT Ketubbot 103b.
[10] JT Nazir ix, 57d, col. 1134.
[11] M Yevamot i, 1.
[12] BT Yevamot 9a.

2. The Process of Separating the Patriarchate
from the Beit haVaʿad

It is impossible to know whether the contents of Rabbi's will relating to the tripartite division of the leadership are authentic or anachronistic. The division of functions in Rabbi's time was different from that in the Ushah period, when there were three leaders within one leadership body. As noted above, after Rabbi's death the leadership was divided into two institutions – the patriarchate and the Beit haVaʿad, and it is possible that Rabbi already instructed that these should be separated in his will. There is evidence for this in the fact that Rabbi Ḥanina bar Ḥama apparently served as the Av Beit Din of the Beit haVaʿad in the first generation of Palestinian Amoraim, and in the way that the patriarchate was divided from the Beit haVaʿad and became an independent institution. Either way, the process of separation certainly began immediately after Rabbi's death.

The main factor which led to the separation originates in the way Rabbi managed his patriarchate during his period of office. As noted, Rabbi was close to the Roman authorities, and acted as the representative of the people to them; he ran his patriarchate with a high hand and at the same time was the head of the leadership of the rabbis – which was popular in nature – as well as Av Beit Din of the Beit haVaʿad. Not only did Rabbi pour into the vessel of the patriarchate more contents than it could comfortably hold, but these contents also included incompatible material. All the while that Rabbi was alive, he could hold the reins of leadership with all its different elements, and include aspects of authority in the patriarchate, as well as more popular aspects. This was due to his exceptional personality, his high status, his close knowledge of the Roman authorities and all his superior qualities. However, when he died, the bundle was untied, and whether he laid it down himself in his will or not, the patriarchate and the Beit haVaʿad came to a parting of the ways: the patriarchate continued to be a sort of monarchy which held the secular political rule – if we can really describe anything as 'secular' at the time – while the Beit haVaʿad acted as a spiritual and religious leadership. This division was similar in many respects to the division between the rule of the exilarchs and the spiritual and religious leadership of the Yeshivot which existed at the same time in Babylonia. It is possible to identify the first signs of the processes which brought about this separation long before Rabbi's time. From the time of Yavneh, when the rabbis took over the traditions of leadership, tensions were created between the tendency of every leadership to turn into a closed institution full of privileges, and between the inclination of the rabbis to preserve their popular characteristics, in order to be accessible to Jews from all the fringes of the people. Rabbi's authority tended towards the pole of an exclusive class, rich in privileges, and this is expressed in the fact that he exempted the rabbis from taxes, gave ordination to someone whose father was an important rabbi without checking the credentials of the son, and so on. While he was alive, his exceptional status allowed him to overcome his distance from the radical populism of the rabbis, but when he instructed his son to behave like himself, and certainly from the time of his death, the introversion of the patriarchate and the populist tendency of the rabbis who were members of the Beit haVaʿad became factors in the separation between the patriarchate and the leadership of the rabbis.

The final redaction of the Mishnah also contributed to the separation of the two institutions. From the moment it was closed, there was now a shared platform between the rabbis for continuing the halakhic debate, which was now possible in the Batei Midrash outside the centre. This led to the rise of local Batei Midrash such as Caesarea, Zippori (after the leadership institutions had moved to Tiberias) and Lod. The separation led to excessive independence of activity in Batei Midrash outside the centre, in contradistinction from Rabbi's centralising policies, which had been characterised by concentration of ordination in his hands only, the ban he placed on candidates for ordination to rule on actual Halakha, and the restriction of the right to teach pupils who were preparing themselves for ordination to recognised Batei Midrash only.

The clearest expression of the rise in power of the local Batei Midrash in the Talmudic literature is the use of terminology which designates groups of rabbis who were active in a particular place, sometimes around a central rabbi, where whole *halakhot* and *sugiyot,* chapters of Halakha and sometimes even *taqqanot* are cited in their name. For example: 'the elders of the South,' 'the rabbis of Caesarea,' 'the rabbis of Naweh,' and 'those of the house of Rabbi Yannai.' This terminology clearly expresses the strength and independence of these Batei Midrash in relation to the Beit haVaʿad. In the local Batei Midrash in the period before the separation, Halakhot were cited only in the name of a particular rabbi.

The separation was expressed by the fact that not only was ordination no longer the exclusive preserve of the patriarch, but that now even the heads of local Batei Midrash ordained their pupils. Not only did Rabbi Yoḥanan, who was the Av Beit Din in the second generation of Palestinian Amoraim, ordain his own pupils, but even Rabbi Joshua b. Levi, who was a *ḥasid* who functioned as the head of the Beit Midrash at Lod in the first generation of the Amoraim, 'ordained all his pupils.'[13]

3. The Death of Rabbi

There is a detailed description of the death of Rabbi in an Aggadah in the Babylonian Talmud:

On the day that Rabbi died the rabbis declared a fast and asked for mercy. They said: Anyone who says that Rabbi has died will be run through with a sword. Rabbi's maidservant went up onto the roof and said: Those above [in heaven] are asking for Rabbi and those below [the rabbis] are asking for Rabbi. May it be [God's] will that those below will win over those above. When she saw how many times [Rabbi] went to the toilet, and took off his Tefillin and put back his Tefillin, and suffered, she said: May it be [God's] will that those above will win over those below. But the rabbis did not cease to ask for mercy. She took a jug and threw it down from the roof to the ground [and because of the sudden noise] they stopped asking for mercy, and Rabbi died. The rabbis said to Bar Qappara: Go and check. He went, and found him dead. He tore his clothes and turned the tear to the back [so they would not see it]. He began to

---

[13] JT Hagigah i, 76c, col. 780.

speak: The angels and mortal men took hold of the Holy Ark, the angels won over the mortal men and the Holy Ark was taken captive! They said to him: Has he died? He said to them: You said it, I did not say it [for they had said that anyone who said Rabbi was dead would be put to the sword]. When Rabbi was dying, he lifted up his ten fingers and said: Lord of the World, it is clearly known to you that I laboured with my ten fingers on the Torah and did not enjoy even with my little finger. May it be thy will that I should rest in peace. A *bat qol*/heavenly voice, came out and said: *He shall enter in peace to them that rest in their graves* (Isaiah 57.2).[14]

According to various sources, Rabbi Judah haNasi suffered from a number of illnesses for many years before his death. He is said to have had kidney stones, blood effusions because of scurvy, gums which were swollen, blue and infected which gave him bad breath, new sores which would not heal and old scars which were liable to open again.[15] According to the source under discussion, Rabbi Judah haNasi's death came about after an acute gastro-intestinal illness, because of which he suffered from the need to remove his Tefillin on every one of the frequent occasions when he had to go to the toilet (in his time the rabbis used to wear Tefillin all day). In the continuation of the legendary source we dealt with above, we are told that the man in charge of the stables in Rabbi's house used to feed the horses every time that Rabbi went to the toilet, so that people would not hear his cries of pain, but even so his

---

[14] BT Ketubbot 104a.

[15] A. Shoshan, 'Maḥalato shel Rabbi Yehudah haNasi', *Korot* 7 (1978), pp. 521–524; E. Dvorjetski, 'The Medical History of Rabbi Judah the Patriarch: A Linguistic Analysis,' *Hebrew Studies* 43 (2002), pp. 39–56.

cries were louder than the joyous neighing of the horses, and were heard even by the sailors at sea.[16]

It is interesting to note the place of Rabbi's maidservant in the Talmudic traditions, particularly in the light of the almost total absence of mentions of his wife. We have already seen that the maid is noted as someone who is expert in Hebrew who can even teach the rabbis the meaning of rare words (see above, p. 212). This source stresses her sensitive personality – on the one hand she prays for Rabbi to stay alive; on the other hand when she sees the extent of his suffering she becomes the direct cause of his death: she surprises the rabbis and they stop their prayers for mercy, which allows Rabbi to die.

The tradition in the passage quoted here attributes a statement to Rabbi Judah haNasi on his death-bed, where he stresses that he did not enjoy the riches of this world even to the extent of his little finger, for he laboured with all ten of his fingers at studying Torah.[17] From these words it would seem that Rabbi wanted to stress that he did not enjoy the fruits of his great wealth and authority, for all his consciousness was directed to studying Torah.

Even though Rabbi Judah haNasi used aggressive force to run his patriarchate, he was revered and honoured at

---

[16] In the Jerusalem Talmud there is evidence about Rabbi when he went with the rabbis to the baths at Ḥammat Gader, and allowed them to carry small stones on the Sabbath which they had prepared before the Sabbath, and which they then used for cleaning themselves after evacuating faeces. It is possible that this reflects Rabbi's concerns about his gastro-intestinal illnesses, because of which he had to use the toilet often: JT Shabbat xviii, 16c, col. 443.

[17] BT Ketubbot 104a.

his death, both by the rabbis, even those who were critical of him during his life, and by the simple people.[18] The same Bar Qappara who had laughed at Rabbi's rich and ignorant son-in-law and was punished by being refused ordination, was present near Rabbi in his last moments, and was the first to discover his death, tore his clothes as a sign of mourning and brought the news to his colleagues. In the Babylonian Talmud, Bar Qappara compares Rabbi to the Holy Ark which the angels have captured, and in the parallel source in the Jerusalem Talmud he compares him to the (first) Tablets of the Law which were snatched by angels. His words also reflect the process of coming to terms with death, which is inevitable.

The common people also showed their appreciation of Rabbi at this time:

On the day of Rabbi's funeral oration,[19] a *bat qol* came out and said: 'Everyone who was present at the funeral oration for Rabbi will be entitled to eternal life in the World to Come.' There was a laundryman who had come to [honour Rabbi] every day. That day he did not come, and because he heard this he went up to the roof and fell to the ground and died. A *bat qol* came out and said: 'This laundryman is also entitled to eternal life in the World to Come.'[20]

The 'laundryman' in Aggadot like this is there to signify the simple man, who works hard for his living.[21] Laundry

---

[18] There is evidence of this in the source above and in JT Ketubbot xii, 35a, col. 1009.

[19] The term ʾ*ashkavah* can mean burial or as in the Munich MS, the great funeral oration at the end of twelve months of mourning.

[20] BT Ketubbot 103b. Cf JT Kilayim ix, 32b, col. 174; JT Ketubbot xii, 35a, col. 1009.

[21] On the tradition about the laundryman see, O. Meir, *Rabbi Yehudah haNasi*ʾ (Tel Aviv, 1999, Heb.), pp. 308–309.

was at the time men's work, and the substance used for it was urine, because of the ammonia in it. In this case, the laundryman took care to come to all the days of mourning for Rabbi Judah haNasi for twelve months. However, on the anniversary of his death he did not come, and understood that by this he had lost his chance of a place in the World to Come. In great sorrow he committed suicide, but a *bat qol* came out which promised a place in the World to Come for him too.

Here it should be mentioned that the ban on suicide in Judaism was instituted after Rabbi's time. In the time of the Second Temple and the period of the Mishnah, suicide was not seen as a sin. On the contrary, there were suicides whose action was pointed out as good. For example, the act of the Roman official who saved Rabban Gamliel after the destruction of the Temple (or Rabban Shimʿon b. Gamliel after the Bar Kokhva revolt) from the Romans: This official committed suicide in order to get a place in the World to Come, and a *bat qol* came out and proclaimed that he had got his place in the World to Come.[22] Similarly, the sources praise the act of the priests during the destruction of the First Temple, and later the Second Temple, when they threw the keys to the Temple up to heaven and then jumped into the flames which were consuming the Sanctuary.[23]

We have already noted how Rabbi Judah haNasi was given the status of royalty at his funeral: 'The day Rabbi

---

[22] BT Taʿanit 29a.
[23] BT *loc. cit.* Cf Avot deRabbi Natan B vii (ed. Schechter, pp. 21–22).

died holiness was cancelled.'[24] In other words, just as the priests did not have to worry about their purity status at a funeral of a king, and were allowed to take part in it, so the Halakha allowed them to become impure at the funeral of Rabbi Judah haNasi. The rabbis also acted similarly at the funeral of Rabbi Judah Nesiah, Rabbi's grandson:

> How come that a priest should defile himself in honour of the patriarch? When Rabbi Judah Nesiah died, Rabbi Yannai proclaimed and said: 'There is no priesthood today.'[25]

The Baraita notes the place where Rabbi was buried:

> It is taught: Rabbi was laid out in Zippori, and a place was prepared for him in Beit She'arim.[26]

In other words, even though Rabbi Judah haNasi died in the city of Zippori/Sepphoris, he chose to be buried on his property at Beit She'arim, which he probably received from the Roman authorities. It is interesting to note that although Rabbi Judah haNasi's burial place is explicitly mentioned in this Baraita, mediaeval Jewish travellers identified his tomb at Zippori. The only one to relate to this identification with any degree of doubt was Eshtori haFarhi (ca. 1280–1355), the first scholar of the topography of the Land of Israel. In his book *Kaftor vaFerah,* Eshtori haFarhi discusses Rabbi's activities at Zippori, and writes:

---

[24] BT Ketubbot 103b. The version in the Munich MS is: 'the priesthood was cancelled.' See S. Safrai, 'The Attitude of the Aggadah to the Halakha' (Heb.), *Dor le-Dor: From the End of Biblical Times up to the Redaction of the Talmud; Studies in Honor of Joshua Efron* (eds. A. Kasher & A. Oppenheimer; Jerusalem, 1995, Heb.), p. 226.

[25] JT Berakhot iii, 6a, col. 26.

[26] BT Ketubbot 103b.

And today his tomb is supposed to be *(ramuz)* in a cave with a slab of stone at its entrance.[27]

Rabbi's choice of burial at Beit Sheʿarim was decisive for the future of the settlement, for this site became a very desirable place to be buried, chosen by many Jews. Thus in the century or so after Rabbi's death, Beit Sheʿarim became the most notable Jewish necropolis in Palestine. They brought Jews here for burial from all over Palestine and the Diaspora: from Babylonia, Syria and even from Himyar, in the south of the Arabian Peninsula. Rabbi would thus seem to have contributed more to the economy of Beit Sheʿarim after his death than during his life. Burial at Beit Sheʿarim also carried on for hundreds of years after his death.[28]

The Jerusalem Talmud tells us about Rabbi's funeral procession from Zippori to Beit Sheʿarim:

Rabbi Naḥman in the name of Rabbi Mana: Miracles happened on that day. It was a Friday, and all the [people] of the settlements assembled [in Zippori] for his funeral orations, and they laid him in eighteen synagogues [or: in eighteen places of assembly], and they took him down to Beit Sheʿarim, and the day was prolonged for them so that every one of them could get to his house and fill his vessel with water and light his lamp [i. e. finish his preparations for the Sabbath].[29]

---

[27] Kaftor vaFeraḥ xi (ed. Luntz, p. 302).

[28] Z. Weiss, 'Burial Practices in Beth Sheʿarim and the Question of Dating the Patriarchal Necropolis,' *'Follow the Wise': Studies in Jewish History and Culture in Honor of Lee I. Levine* (eds. Z. Weiss, et al.; Winona Lake, IN, 2010), pp. 207–231.

[29] JT Kilayim ix, 32b, col. 174.

Apart from the detail that the day was miraculously prolonged so no-one should have to profane the Sabbath, the
description seems realistic. The Talmudic literature notes
many synagogues in Zippori, and it is reasonable that people would have come from all the neighbouring settlements
to hear the funeral orations on Rabbi Judah haNasi in these
eighteen synagogues. For example, it is said of Rabbi:

Our Rabbi used to sit and study Torah in front of the synagogue of
the Babylonians in Zippori.[30]

In spite of the explicit statements in both the Talmuds that
Rabbi was buried in Beit She'arim, his tomb has not yet
been discovered. There are those who think, because of the
tomb inscriptions on it, that the grave is to be found in
the grandiose burial complex uncovered there, which the
archaeological reports note as number 14.

In the Hebrew inscriptions found in this burial complex
we find the names of Rabbi Gamliel, Rabbi Shim'on, and
Rabbi Aniana or Anina (apparently Rabbi Ḥanina bar
Ḥama). These are the three leaders, of whom two were
his sons, between whom Rabbi Judah haNasi divided the
leadership in his will, according to the tradition we discussed above. In the back room is a single impressive tomb
without an inscription, and it is possible that this is the
tomb of Rabbi Judah haNasi. The lack of an inscription
could be explained by the fact that everybody at the time
would have known who was buried in this special tomb.
It is not impossible that this burial hall was used at first by
the family of the patriarch, and then later Rabbi Ḥanina

---

[30] Genesis Rabbah xxxiii (eds. Theodor & Albeck, p. 305).

bar Ḥama, who was given the function of Av Beit Din by Rabbi, was also buried there. It should be noted that the name of Rabbi Gamliel appears on the tomb inscription in Greek as well. This bilingualism certainly fits the presumption that this is the tomb of a patriarch, for as we have seen, the family of the patriarchs was 'allowed' to learn Greek in order to facilitate communication with the authorities.[31]

---

[31] For all this see e. g. E. Stern (ed.), *The New Encyclopedia of Archaeological Excavations in the Holy Land* (5 vols.; Jerusalem, 1993–2008), vol. 1, s. v. Beth Sheʿarim.

Epilogue

Rabbi Judah haNasi – a Harmony of Discords

Rabbi Judah haNasi brought to an end the process of re-fashioning Judaism which had been begun by Rabban Yoḥanan b. Zakkai following the destruction of the Second Temple, and which was centred on the transition from the Temple to the Beit Midrash. With his final redaction of the Mishnah, a firm foundation was created for the continuation of the development of the oral law in the Batei Midrash in Palestine, and the Yeshivot in Babylonia. It is an interesting question whether the successful ending of this process which set the study of Torah at the head of the scale of values of Judaism, also marked the end of the process of disengagement from the Temple and its ritual. It was already clear from the *taqqanot* of Rabban Yoḥanan b. Zakkai and Rabban Gamliel of Yavneh that it was impossible to fill the vacuum left by the destruction of the Temple without partial disengagement from the Temple. In this spirit, Rabban Yoḥanan b. Zakkai separated the mitzvah of taking the Lulav on all seven days of the festival of Sukkot from the Temple, and transferred it to every place. However, even he still tried to have his cake and eat it, as it were, for he stated that although the mitzvah of Lulav takes place anywhere, it is there as 'a memory of the Temple.'[1] Rabban Gamliel and the rabbis of his generation

---

[1] M Rosh haShanah iv, 3; M Sukkah iii, 12.

transferred the Passover Seder from the public ritual of sacrificing the Paschal lamb in the Temple and eating it in fellowships in Jerusalem, to the family ritual of the Seder which takes place anywhere and engages with the narrative of the Exodus from Egypt. Rabbi ʿAqiva, however, ruled that the people must finish the recitation of the Aggadah at the Seder with a blessing of redemption – not only the historic redemption from Egypt, but a foreshadowing of the future redemption as well:

We rejoice in the building of your city and are happy in your service, and will eat there of the festival offering and the Passover offering.[2]

It would seem that Rabbi Judah haNasi dared to go even further than his predecessors in the process of disengagement from the Temple. This is clear from his attempt to cancel the fast of the Ninth of Av, and the way he behaved in practice on the fast of the Seventeenth of Tammuz, when he went to bathe in public in the springs of Zippori. By this act Rabbi Judah haNasi aimed at giving validity to his *taqqanah* when it was clear from the start that there would be problems in accepting it. The continued consciousness of ruin, which had accompanied the rabbis since the destruction of the Second Temple and the fall of Beitar (which had been appropriated to the date which signified destruction, the Ninth of Av),[3] stood in contrast to the intimations of redemption which prevailed in the days of Rabbi. There can be no doubt that Rabbi Judah haNasi was aware that his time could not be considered as

---

[2] M Pesaḥim x, 6.
[3] M Taʿanit iv, 6.

a time of redemption, unless one of two things happened: the Temple was rebuilt or the consciousness of the destruction disappeared.

There is not a single hint in all the Talmudic literature that Rabbi Judah haNasi ever made a request to the Roman authorities to allow the building of the Third Temple in Jerusalem. Rabbi Shimʿon b. Elʿazar, Rabbi's friend and contemporary, is noted as saying:

If children say to you 'build the Temple,' do not listen to them.[4]

It is the young who are full of enthusiasm and militancy, whereas Rabbi himself preferred to promote the process of disengagement from the Temple and Jerusalem, and to cancel the fasts in memory of the destruction of the Temple, in spite of the fact that in his time Jews returned to live in the city, and there was a *qahalaʾ qadishaʾ di-b'Yerushalayim* there. However, as we have noted, this process was seen as excessively rash and reformatory by the rabbis of his generation, and Rabbi finally understood that he had no option but to retreat from his aim to make this *taqqanah* obligatory.

In this context we should mention a further Aggadah from the traditions of conversations between Rabbi and ʿAntoninus':

Antoninus asked Rabbi: What is it to build an altar? He said to him: Build it and hide its stones. What is it to prepare incense for it? He said to him: One of its ingredients is missing.[5]

---

[4] Tos. Avodah Zarah i, 19.
[5] JT Megillah i, 72b, col. 754.

The Aggadah is telling us that Antoninus wanted to construct an altar and burn incense on it to the God of Israel, but Rabbi said no to him. We might have thought that Rabbi would include his desire to build the Temple and his hopes of renewing the rites in his answer to Antoninus. In contrast, he notes in his answer the impossibility of building a functioning altar, as well as the ban on preparing incense according to the halakhic recipe without the Temple. We may note here also, that even though there is no halakhic ban on burning incense outside the Temple, Rabban Yoḥanan b. Zakkai had already chosen not to include incense in the ritual of the synagogue. Thus it is possible to conclude from the Talmudic literature that the transition from the Temple to Beit Midrash was in some way acceptable to Rabban Yoḥanan b. Zakkai and was also an important element in the policies of Rabbi Judah haNasi and his tendency to attribute signs of a kind of royalty and messianism to the leadership.

One of the characteristics of Rabbi's leadership was his flexibility, which was a result of his being a strong and self-assured leader. A further characteristic was his ability to act as a harmoniser of discords. As we have seen throughout, Rabbi ruled a number of far-reaching reformatory *taqqanot,* which at first glance looked as if they were replacing laws of the Torah, at least in part, but he went back on himself in two of the most important cases: the cancellation of the sabbatical year, and the cancellation of the days of mourning for the destruction of the Temple – the Seventeeth of Tammuz and the Ninth of Av. By retracting his cancellation of the sabbatical year, he gave up on this aspect of economic normalisation, while by retracting his cancellation of Tish'a beAv he gave up on an important stage in the process of disengagement from the Temple, and dimmed the halo of royalty and messianism which surrounded his leadership.

In the final redaction of the Mishnah we can see contrasts of a different sort: this breakthrough also acted as a sort of brake. The Mishnah became an authority on halakhic matters, and as a result the rabbis of that generation were still able to differ from rabbis of previous generations, but the rabbis of the generation after him were no longer able to differ from a Halakha which was found in the Mishnah or in a Baraita. The dynamics of the oral law, which had been a leading light for the Pharisees in their struggle with the Sadducees, thus disappeared, and the Amoraim – the rabbis of the Talmud – were forced to produce harmonisation between Tannaitic sources which differed from each other, and to make their own Halakhot only in the loopholes which remained open between the Halakhot of the Mishnah and the Baraitot. Because of this, the ability of the patriarchate and the rabbis of the Beit haVa'ad to rule *taqqanot* like those of Rabbi Judah haNasi was severely curtailed.

Rabbi's harmonising of discordant oppositions is also seen in his attempt to create a bridge to social classes which were as distant from himself and his world as east from west. As noted, among other things he married his daughter to Ben El'ashah, who belonged to the urban elite who were far from the ways of Torah. The man for whom the study of Torah was the centre of his world reached out to the ignorant *'ammei ha'aretz* who did not come to synagogue to listen to the reading of the Torah, the prayers, or the exegesis of the rabbis on the Sabbath. He was even prepared to open his stores of grain to them in a drought year. All this was in order to bolster up his leadership and to be the acknowledged leader, so that he could control the rich and the members of the city leadership institutions, and at the same time be revered by the *'ammei ha'aretz* and the simple people.

We can see a further contradiction between Rabbi as a man of Halakha, and his rapprochement with pagan culture and the Roman authorities: his household learned Greek, and he himself looked in the mirror like a woman and wore his hair in the *kome* style like non-Jews, so that we can assume his external appearance was more like one of the upper-class Romans than one of the rabbis. The rabbis understood that the patriarchate needed these external expressions in order to be recognised and respected by the Romans and to communicate with them, so that they allowed this to Rabbi, as they had to his grandfather, Rabban Gamliel of Yavneh, before him.

A Baraita from the end of tractate Sotah notes the contrast between Rabbi as a man of power, who aspired to be a kind of king, and Rabbi as a man of great meekness or modesty:

When Rabbi died modesty ended.[6]

---

[6] M Sotah ix, 15. On this *mishnah* as a later addition, see, e.g., Y.N. Epstein, *Mevo' leNusah haMishnah* (Jerusalem, 1964²), pp. 976–977.

But other sources, such as, for example, the one which tells us that Rabbi was not willing to give up his seat to anyone, contradict this Baraita completely. It is possible that the description of Rabbi as very modest is there to complete the comparison between him and the biblical figure of Moses, of whom it was said:

Now the man Moses was very meek, more so than all the men that were upon the face of the earth. (Numbers 12.3)

The comparison with Moses is made explicit in the following saying about Rabbi:

Rabbah the son of Rava, or some say Rabbi Hillel son of Rabbi Walas, said: From the days of Moses until the days of Rabbi we have not found Torah and greatness [together] in the same place.[7]

It is, however, possible that in attributing modesty to Rabbi there is a further significance, for as we have already noted:

When Rabbi was dying, he lifted up his ten fingers and said: Lord of the World, it is clearly known to you that I laboured with my ten fingers on the Torah and did not enjoy [any worldly benefits] even with a small finger.[8]

Whoever spoke or wrote these words – whether it was Rabbi Judah haNasi himself or whether it was one of the Babylonian rabbis – he clearly felt the contradictions in the personality of Rabbi, who was on the one hand a rich and powerful leader, while on the other aimed at being a popular leader as well, in charge of guarding the study of Torah and the observance of the mitzvot.

---

[7] BT Gittin 59a and parallels.
[8] BT Ketubbot 104a (tr. Soncino, adapted).

Because of his exceptional personality, Rabbi Judah ha-Nasi succeeded in bridging the contradictions we have just listed all the time he was alive. However, as we have already noted, after his death the self-governing leadership split between the patriarchate and the Beit haVaʿad. According to Rabbi's will in both the Jerusalem and Babylonian Talmuds (as discussed in Chapter 8), the impression is that he himself instructed that this separation should take place, for he apparently was aware that he had managed to raise the status of the patriarchate to a height which only his own character could sustain. He knew, in fact, that he had poured into the vessel of the patriarchate more contents than the vessel could contain.

The essence of Rabbi Judah haNasi as leader can be found in his own words, as quoted in Mishnah Avot:

Rabbi said: Which is the straight way that man should choose? כל שהיא תפארת לעושה/That which is an honour to him who does it, and gets honour from men.[9]

In other words, in Rabbi's opinion, a man should choose the way which does him credit, but is also approved of by others. There are also those who interpret the words כל שהיא תפארת לעושה as meaning that his way should be to glorify God, the Maker. This principle is clear from the way Rabbi Judah haNasi actually chose: as a man of Halakha, he did not shut himself up in the strait world of Halakha only, but devoted much effort to adapt the Halakha to changing circumstances. At the same time, he did not confine himself to activities among the Jews alone, but sought

---

[9] M Avot ii,1 (tr. Danby, adapted).

the company and help of the Romans. It is thus possible that when he said 'gets honour from men,' he meant all men, not just Jews.

As well as modesty, Rabbi Judah haNasi was credited with other good qualities. Rabbi Shimʿon b. Menasia, a contemporary of Rabbi, who was a member of the *qahalaʾ qadishaʾ de-b'Yerushalayim,* listed the qualities suited to the righteous, and Rabbi Yoḥanan, the greatest of the Palestinian Amoraim, who studied with Rabbi Judah haNasi, claimed that they were all present in Rabbi:

Rabbi Shimʿon b. Menasia says: Beauty and power and riches and wisdom and grey hairs and honour and children are becoming to the righteous and becoming to the world. … Rabbi Yoḥanan says: All the seven qualities which the rabbis specified for the righteous were present in Rabbi.[10]

In other words, in the eyes of Rabbi's generation, as in the eyes of the Amoraim after him, Rabbi Judah haNasi achieved a perfection of qualities in his personality and his behaviour. In the light of this, the rabbis transferred all the good qualities which were brought together in his personality – wisdom on the one hand, and power, riches and honour on the other, together with beauty, grey hairs and children – from the characteristics of ideal leadership to the characteristics of his real leadership.

---

[10] JT Sanhedrin xi, 30a, col. 1329; cf the Baraita at the end of M Avot (vi, 8); Tos. Sanhedrin xi, 8.

Figures

Figure 1

Figure 2

Figure 3

Figure 4

Figure 5

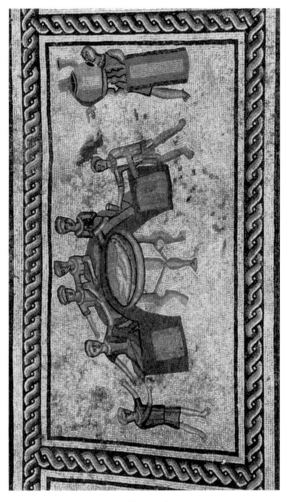

Figure 6

Figure 7

Figure 8

Figure 9

Figure 10

Figure 11

Figure 12

Figure 13

Figure 14

Figure 15

Figure 16

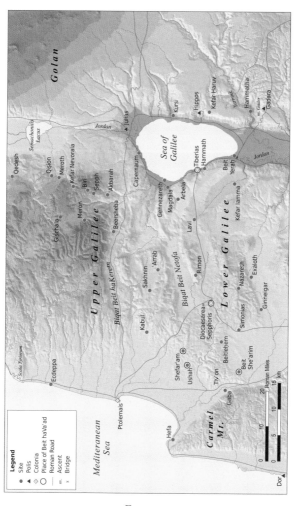

Figure 17

Legends

Sepphoris – the house of Dionysos

At the beginning of the third century a mosaic was installed in the triclinium of the house of Dionysos in Sepphoris, Lower Galilee. According to Zeev Weiss this is Rabbi's villa (see pp. 151–152).

Figure 1: A female acanthus head, the so-called Mona Lisa of the Galilee. Courtesy of Prof. Zeev Weiss. The Sepphoris Excavations, the Hebrew University of Jerusalem. Photo: Gabi Laron.

Figure 2: Dionysiac procession. Courtesy of Prof. Zeev Weiss. The Sepphoris Excavations, the Hebrew University of Jerusalem. Photo: Gabi Laron.

Figure 3: Nilotic scenes that replaced the Dionysiac. Courtesy of Prof. Zeev Weiss. The Sepphoris Excavations, the Hebrew University of Jerusalem. Photo: Gabi Laron.

Sepphoris – the house of Orpheus

Orpheus, the divine musician, is depicted in the largest panel of the mosaic, which is surrounded on three sides by white tesserae marking the area for the *klinai.*

Figure 4: General view of the mosaics in the Orpheus house. Courtesy of Prof. Zeev Weiss. The Sepphoris Excavations, the Hebrew University of Jerusalem. Photo: Gabi Laron.

Figure 5: The largest panel with the figure of Orpheus. Courtesy of Prof. Zeev Weiss. The Sepphoris Excavations, the Hebrew University of Jerusalem. Photo: Gabi Laron.

Figure 6: A banquet scene. Courtesy of Prof. Zeev Weiss. The Sepphoris Excavations, the Hebrew University of Jerusalem. Photo: Gabi Laron.

Figure 7: A servant taking care of the *miliarium*. Courtesy of Prof. Zeev Weiss. The Sepphoris Excavations, the Hebrew University of Jerusalem. Photo: Gabi Laron.

Sepphoris – synagogue

A synagogue dated to the early fifth century CE, which does not face Jerusalem. The most significant remnant of the synagogue is its mosaic floor. The largest band of the mosaic is the zodiac.

Figure 8: The zodiac sign of Scorpio (עקרב), which is accompanied by a youth and a star. Courtesy of Prof. Zeev Weiss. The Sepphoris Excavations, the Hebrew University of Jerusalem. Photo: Gabi Laron.

Figure 9: The sacred utensils – among them a *menorah*. Courtesy of Prof. Zeev Weiss. The Sepphoris Excavations, the Hebrew University of Jerusalem. Photo: Gabi Laron.

Naḥal Rephaim

A mosaic from Naḥal Rephaim, South-West of the Old City of Jerusalem, with two artichokes. They were at that time a very expensive luxury, with a long distance trade in them (see pp. 179–189)

Figure 10: A mosaic with *xenia* motifs. Courtesy of Shlomit Weksler Bdolaḥ, Israel Antiquities Authority. Photo Mariana Salzberger

Lod – The floor mosaic

The mosaic probably adorned the reception hall of a Roman villa. It can be dated to the end of the third or the beginning of the fourth century CE.

Figure 11: The square middle panel. B-54901 Mosaic Lod. Courtesy Israel Antiquities Authority. Photo Nicky Davidov.

Figure 12: Ship in the marine scene of the southern panel. B-54911 Mosaic Lod. Courtesy Israel Antiquities Authority. Photo Nicky Davidov.

The photographs of Figure 1 to Figure 12 have been reproduced with the kind permission of Prof. Rina Talgam, the Hebrew University Jerusalem, and are taken from R. Talgam, *Mosaics of Faith*, Jerusalem-Pennsylvania 2014.

Coins of cities

Figure 13: Caracalla coin of Sepphoris. Israel Museum Jerusalem no. 78.2974 (see pp. 48–58).

Figure 14: Caracalla coin of Sepphoris. Israel Museum Jerusalem no. 81.3642 (see pp, 48–58).

Figure 15: Elagabalus Coin of Tiberias. No. 78.2998 (see pp. 81–85).

Photo © The Israel Museum, Jerusalem by Vladimir Naikhin
I am grateful to Dr. Haim Gitler, Curator of Numismatics, and to Mr. Yaniv Schauer who supplied the photographs.

Maps

Figure 16: Syria-Palaestina/Judaea in the time of Rabbi Judah ha-Nasi.

Figure 17: Galilee in the Roman Period.

Selected Bibliography

Aberbach, M., 'Hezekiah King of Judah and Rabbi Judah the Patriarch: Messianic Aspects' (Heb.), *Tarbiz* (1984), pp. 353–371.

Albeck, Ch., *Untersuchungen über die Redaktion der Mischna*)Berlin, 1923(.

– 'Semikha and Minnui Beth Din' (Heb.), *Zion* 8 (1943), pp. 85–93.

– 'The Sanhedrin and Its President' (Heb.), *Zion* 8 (1943), pp. 165–178.

– *Introduction to the Mishnah* (Jerusalem, 1959, Heb.). German translation, *Einführung in die Mischna* (Berlin & New York, 1971).

Alon, G., *Toledot ha-Yehudim be-ʾEretz Yisraʾel bi-Tequfat ha-Mishnah ve-haTalmud,* vol. II (Tel Aviv, 1956). English translation, *The Jews in Their Land in the Talmudic Age* (Jerusalem, 1984).

– 'On Philo's Halakha,' idem, *Jews, Judaism and the Classical World* (Jerusalem, 1977), pp. 89–137.

– 'The *strategoi* in the Palestinian Cities during the Roman Epoch,' idem, *Jews, Judaism and the Classical World* (Jerusalem, 1977), pp. 458–475.

Avi-Yonah, M., *In the Days of Rome and Byzantium* (Jerusalem, 1970[4], Heb.). German translation, *Geschichte der Juden im Zeitalter des Talmud* (Berlin, 1962).

Bacher, W., 'Die Staatswagen des Patriarchen (קרונות של בית רבי),' *JQR* 15 (1903), pp. 100–101.

Baumgarten, A. L., 'Rabbi Judah I and His Opponents,' *JSJ* 12 (1981), pp. 161–170.

– 'The Politics of Reconciliation: The Education of R. Judah the Prince,' *Jewish and Christian Self-Definition,* vol. II (eds. E. P. Sanders, et al.; London, 1981), pp. 213–225, 382–391.

Bevan, A. A., *The Hymn of the Soul Contained in the Syriac Acts of St. Thomas* (Texts and Studies V, No. 3; Cambridge, 1897).

Bodek, A., *Marcus Aurelius Antoninus als Zeitgenosse und Freund des Rabbi Jehuda ha-Nasi* (Leipzig, 1868).

Brodi, R., 'The Epistle of Sherira Gaon,' *Rabbinic Texts and the History of Late-Roman Palestine* (eds. M. Goodman & P. Alexander; Oxford/New York, 2010), pp. 253–264.

Büchler, A., 'Der Patriarch R. Jehuda I., und die griechisch-römischen Städte Palästinas,' *JQR* 13 (1901), pp. 683–740. English translation, idem, *Studies in Jewish History* (London, 1956), pp. 179–244.

– 'Die Maultiere und die Wagen des Patriarchen Jehuda I.,' *MGWJ* 48 (n.s. 12) (1904), pp. 193–208.

– *The Political and Social Leaders of the Jewish Community of Sepphoris in the Second and Third Centuries* (London, 1909).

Cohen, S. A., *The Three Crowns: Structures of Communal Politics in Early Rabbinic Jewry* (Cambridge, 1980).

Cohen, S. J. D., 'The Conversion of Antoninus,' *The Talmud Yerushalmi in Graeco-Roman Culture,* vol. I (ed. P. Schäfer; Tübingen, 1998), pp. 141–171.

– 'Patriarchs and Scholarchs,' *PAAJR* 48 (1981), pp. 57–85.

– 'The Conversion of Antoninus,' *The Talmud Yerushalmi and Graeco-Roman Culture,* vol. I (ed. P. Schäfer; Tübingen, 1998), pp. 141–171.

Colin, J., *Les villes libres de l'Orient gréco-romain* (Brussels, 1965).

Cotton, H. M., & W. Eck, 'Ein Staatsmonopol und seine Folgen: Plinius, *Naturalis Historia* 12, 123 und der Preis für Balsam,' *Rheinisches Museum für Philologie* 140 (1997), pp. 153–161.

Danby, H. D., *The Mishnah: Translated from the Hebrew with Introduction and Brief Explanatory Notes* (London, 1933, repr. Oxford, 1988; Peabody, 2011).

Dinari, Y., '"Rabbi sent a *Mezuzah* to Artaban …" (JT Peah I, 15d. col. 82),' *Michtam le-David: Rabbi David Ochs Memorial Volume* (eds. Y. Gilat & E. Stern; Ramat-Gan, 1978), pp. 86–105.

Dvorjetski, E., 'The Medical History of Rabbi Judah the Patriarch: A Linguistic Analysis,' *Hebrew Studies* 43 (2002), pp. 39–56.

Ensslin, W., 'The Senate and the Army,' *CAH,* vol. XII (eds. S. A. Cook, et al.; Cambridge, 1939, repr. 1971), pp. 57–72.

Epstein, J. N., *Introduction to Tannaitic Literature* (Jerusalem, 1957, Heb.).

– *Introduction to the Text of the Mishna* (Jerusalem, 1964², Heb.).

Feliks, Y., *The Jerusalem Talmud: Tractate Sheviʿit* (Jerusalem, 1986, Heb.).

Friedman, A., *Jewish Marriage in Palestine,* vol. II (Tel Aviv, 1981).

Fürst, J., 'Antoninus und Rabbi,' *MWJ* 16 (1889), pp. 41–45; 17 (1890), pp. 92–93.

Gafni, I. M., *Land, Center and Diaspora: Jewish Constructs in Late Antiquity* (Sheffield, 1997).

– 'A Generation of Scholarship on ʾEretz Yisraʾel in the Talmudic Era: Achievement and Reconsideration' (Heb.), *Cathedra* 100 (2001), pp. 199–226.

– 'On Talmudic Historiography in the Epistle of Rav Sherira Gaʾon: Between Tradition and Creativity' (Heb.), *Zion* 73 (2008), pp. 271–296.

Gager, G., 'The Dialogue of Paganism with Judaism: Bar Cochba to Julian,' *HUCA* 44 (1973), pp. 89–118.

Gizewski, C., 'Duoviri, Duumviri,' *Der Neue Pauly,* vol. 3 (Stuttgart, et al., 1997), cols. 843–845.

Goldberg, A., 'Purpose and Method in Rabbi Judah Hannasi's Compilation of the Mishna' (Heb.), *Tarbiz* 28 (1958), pp. 260–269.

Goodblatt, D., 'The Origins of Roman Recognition of the Palestinian Patriarchate,' *Studies in the History of the Jewish People and the Land of Israel,* vol. 4 (Haifa, 1978, Heb.), pp. 89–102.

– *The Monarchic Principle: Studies in Jewish Self-Government in Antiquity* (Tübingen, 1994).

Goodman, M., *State and Society in Roman Galilee A. D. 132–212* (Totowa, NJ, 1983).

– 'The Roman State and the Jewish Patriarch in the Third Century,' *The Galilee in Late Antiquity* (ed. L. I. Levine; New York, 1992), pp. 127–139.

Gray, A. M., 'The Power Conferred by Distance from Power: Redaction and Meaning in b. A. Z. 10a–11a,' *Creation and Composition* (ed. J. L. Rubenstein; Tübingen, 2005), pp. 23–99.

Grenfell, B. P., et al., *Fayûm Towns and Their Papyri* (London, 1900).

Gulak, A., 'Siqariqon' (Heb.), *Tarbiz* 5 (1934), pp. 27–32.

– '*Boule* and *strategoi:* On the Roman Tax System in the Land of Israel' (Heb.), *Tarbiz* 11 (1940), pp. 119–122.

Guttmann, A., 'The Patriarch Judah I, His Birth and His Death: A Glimpse into the Chronology of the Talmudic Period,' *HUCA* 25 (1954), pp. 239–261.

Habas (Rubin), E., *The Patriarch in the Roman-Byzantine Era: The Making of a Dynasty* (Ph.D. Thesis, Tel Aviv University, 1991, Heb.).

– 'The Title of Shim'on ben Kosba' (Heb.), *Jerusalem and Eretz Israel: Arie Kindler Volume* (eds. J. Schwartz, et al.; Jerusalem, 2000, Heb./Engl.), pp. 133–146.

– 'Θρεπτοί in the Inscriptions of Palestine' (Heb.), *The Path of Peace: Studies in Honor of Israel Friedman Ben-Shalom* (eds. D. Gera & M. Ben-Zeev; Jerusalem, 2005, Heb.), pp. 487–498.

Herman, G., 'The Influence of the Patriarchs on the Mourning of the Ninth of *Av*' (Heb.), *Asufot* 8 (1994), pp. 137–148.

– 'Ahasuerus, the Former Stable Master of Belshazzar, and the Wicked Alexander of Macedon: Two Parallels between the Babylonian Talmud and Persian Sources,' *AJS Review* 29 (2005), pp. 288–297.

– 'Table Etiquette and Persian Culture in the Babylonian Talmud' (Heb.), *Zion* 77 (2012), pp. 149–188.

Herr, M. D., 'The Historical Significance of the Dialogues between Jewish Sages and Roman Dignitaries,' *Scripta Hierosolymitana* 22 (1971), pp. 123–150.

– 'The Conception of History among the Sages' (Heb.), *Proceedings of the Sixth World Congress of Jewish Studies,* vol. III (ed. A. Shinan; Jerusalem, 1973), pp. 129–142.

Hezser, C., *The Social Structure of the Rabbinic Movement in Roman Palestine* (Tübingen, 1997).

– *Jewish Slavery in Antiquity* (Oxford, 2005).

– *Jewish Travel in Antiquity* (Tübingen, 2011).

Hill, G. F., *Catalogue of the Greek Coins of Phoenicia* (A Catalogue of the Greek Coins in the British Museum 26; London, 1910).

- *Catalogue of the Greek Coins of Palestine (Galilee, Samaria, and Judaea)* (A Catalogue of the Greek Coins in the British Museum 27; London, 1914; repr. Bologna, 1988).

Hoffmann, D., 'Die Antoninus-Agadot im Talmud und Midrasch,' *MWJ* 5 (1878), pp. 94–99.

Irshai, O., 'Constantine and the Jews: The Prohibition against Entering Jerusalem – History and Hagiography' (Heb.), *Zion* 60 (1995), pp. 129–137.

Isaac, B., *The Limits of Empire: The Roman Army in the East* (Oxford, 1990).

- 'Roman Colonies in Judaea: The Foundation of Aelia Capitolina,' idem, *The Near East under Roman Rule: Selected Papers* (Leiden / New York / Cologne, 1998), pp. 87–108; Postscript, pp. 109–111.

- 'Judaea after AD 70,' idem, *The Near East under Roman Rule: Selected Papers* (Leiden / New York / Cologne, 1998), pp. 112–119; Postscript, pp. 120–121.

Isaac, B., & I. Roll, *Roman Roads in Judaea,* vol. I: *The Legio-Scythopolis Road* (BAR International Series 141; Oxford, 1982).

- 'Judaea in the Early Years of Hadrian's Reign,' *Latomus* 38 (1979), pp. 63–64 = B. Isaac, *The Near East under Roman Rule* (Leiden / New York / Cologne, 1998), pp. 87–111.

Jacobs, M., *Die Institution des jüdischen Patriarchen* (Tübingen, 1995).

Jones, A. H. M., *The Cities of the Eastern Roman Provinces* (Oxford, 1971²).

Katz, S., *Die Strafe im talmudischen Recht* (Berlin, 1936).

Kindler, A., & A. Stein, *A Bibliography of the City Coinage of Palestine: From the 2nd Century B. C. to the 3rd Century A. D.* (BAR International Series 374; Oxford, 1987).

Klein, S., 'The Estates of R. Judah Ha-Nasi and the Jewish Communities in the Trans-Jordanic Region,' *JQR* 2 (1911–12), pp. 545–556.

- 'Aus den Lehrhäusern Erez Israels im 2.–3. Jahrhundert,' *MGWJ* 78 (1934), pp. 164–171.

- *Sefer haYishuv,* vol. I (Jerusalem, 1939).

- *Eretz haGalil* (Jerusalem, 1967²).

Krauss, S., *Griechische und lateinische Lehnwörter im Talmud, Midrasch und Targum: Mit Bemerkungen von Immanuel Löw; preisgekrönte Lösung der Lattes'schen Preisfrage,* vol. II (Berlin, 1899; repr. Hildesheim, et al., 1987).

– *Antoninus und Rabbi* (Vienna, 1910).

– *Synagogale Altertümer* (Vienna, 1922; repr. Hildesheim, 1966).

Kushnir-Stein, A., 'Coins of Tiberias with Asclepius and Hygieia and the Question of the City's Colonial Status,' *Israel Numismatic Research* 4 (2009), pp. 94–108.

Lavi, M., 'The Talmudic Narrative Mosaic: Teaching Torah, Greatness and Redemption: The Narratives of Rabbi and Rabbi Ḥiyya as Examples' (Heb.), *Jewish Studies: An Internet Journal* 8 (2009), pp. 51–98.

Lévi, I., 'L'origine Davidique de Hillel,' *REJ* 31 (1895), pp. 202–211; 33 (1896), pp. 143–144.

Levine, D., *Communal Fasts and Rabbinic Sermons: Theory and Practice in the Talmudic Period* (Tel Aviv, 2001, Heb.).

Levine, L. I., 'The Period of Rabbi Yehudah haNasi'' (Heb.), *Eretz Israel from the Destruction of the Second Temple to the Muslim Conquest* (Jerusalem, 1982, Heb.), pp. 94–118.

– *The Rabbinic Class in Palestine during the Talmudic Period* (Jerusalem, 1985, Heb.).

– 'The Finds from Beth-Shearim and Their Importance for the Study of the Talmudic Period' (Heb.), *Eretz-Israel* 18 (Jerusalem, 1985), pp. 277–281.

– 'The Jewish Patriarch (Nasi) in Third Century Palestine,' *ANRW* II.19.2 (Berlin & New York, 1979), pp. 649–688.

– *The Rabbinic Class of Roman Palestine in Late Antiquity* (Jerusalem & New York, 1989).

– 'The Status of the Patriarch in the Third and Fourth Centuries: Sources and Methodology,' *JJS* 47 (1996), pp. 1–32.

Lieberman, S., *The Talmud of Qisrin* (Supplement to *Tarbiz* II 4; Jerusalem, 1931, Heb.).

– *Greek in Jewish Palestine* (New York, 1942).

– *Hellenism in Jewish Palestine* (New York, 1950).

– *Tosefta Ki-fshutah: A Comprehensive Commentary on the Tosefta* (10 vols.; New York, 1955–88).

Linder, A., *The Jews in Roman Imperial Legislation* (Detroit, MI & Jerusalem, 1987).

Liver, J., *The House of David* (Jerusalem, 1959, Heb.).

– 'Nasi'' (Heb.), *Encyclopaedia Biblica,* vol. V (Jerusalem, 1968, Heb.), cols. 978–983.

Mantel, H., *Studies in the History of the Sanhedrin* (Cambridge, MA, 1961).

Margulies, M., 'To the Biography of Rabbi Yehudah haNasi'' (Heb.), *Sinai* 39 (1956), pp. 104–105, 153–154, 240–241, 282–283, 343–345; 40 (1957), pp. 38–41.

Marshall, A. J., 'Governors on the Move,' *Phoenix* 20 (1966), pp. 231–246.

Mazar, B., *Beth She'arim,* vol. I (Jerusalem, 1973).

Meir, O., *Rabbi Yehudah haNasi'* (Tel Aviv, 1999, Heb.).

Meshorer, Y., *City-Coins of Eretz-Israel and the Decapolis in the Roman Period* (Jerusalem, 1985).

– 'The Coins of Sepphoris as Historical Source' (Heb.), *Zion* 53 (1988), pp. 185–200.

Meyers, C., 'The Dionysos Mosaic,' *Sepphoris in Galilee: Cross-currents of Culture* (eds. R. M. Nagy, et al.; Winona Lake, IN, 1996), pp. 111–115.

Millar, F., 'The Roman *Coloniae* of the Near East: A Study of Cultural Relations,' *Roman Eastern Policy and Other Studies in Roman History* (eds. H. Solin & M. Kajava; Helsinki, 1990), pp. 7–58.

– *The Emperor in the Roman World* (London, 1992²).

Miller, S. N., 'The Army and the Imperial House,' *CAH,* vol. XII (eds. S. A. Cook, et al.; Cambridge, 1939, repr. 1971), pp. 1–56.

Miller, S. S., *Studies in the History and Traditions of Sepphoris* (Leiden, 1984).

Neusner, J., 'The Jews East of the Euphrates and the Roman Empire, 1ˢᵗ–3ʳᵈ Centuries AD,' *ANRW* II 9.1 (Berlin & New York, 1976), pp. 59–64.

– *Judaism: The Evidence of the Mishnah* (Tel Aviv, 1986, Heb.).

– 'Evaluating the Attributions of Sayings to Named Sages in Rabbinic Literature,' *JSJ* 26 (1995), pp. 93–111.

Oppenheimer, A., 'The Separation of First Tithes during the Second Temple Period' (Heb.), *Benjamin de Vries Memorial Volume* (ed. E. Z. Melamed; Jerusalem, 1968, Heb.), pp. 70–83.

– *The 'Am ha-Aretz: A Study in the Social History of the Jewish People in the Hellenistic-Roman Period* (Leiden, 1977).

– 'The Separation of the First Tithe after the Destruction of the Second Temple' (Heb.), *Sinai* 83 (1978), pp. 267–287.

– 'Links between Mesene and 'Eretz Yisra'el' (Heb.), *Zion* 47 (1982), pp. 335–341. German translation, 'Beziehungen zwischen Messene und Palästina,' idem, *Between Rome and Babylon* (Tübingen, 2005), pp. 409–416.

– 'Jewish Lydda in the Roman Era,' *HUCA* 59 (1988), pp. 115–136.

– *Galilee in the Mishnaic Period* (Jerusalem, 1991, Heb.).

– 'Roman Rule and the Cities of the Galilee in Talmudic Literature,' *The Galilee in Late Antiquity* (ed. L. I. Levine; New York, 1992), pp. 115–125.

– 'Messianismus in römischer Zeit: Zur Pluralität eines Begriffes bei Juden und Christen,' *Jahrbuch des Historischen Kollegs 1997* (ed. E. Müller-Luckner; Munich, 1998), pp. 53–74 = idem, *Between Rome and Babylon: Studies in Jewish Leadership and Society* (Tübingen, 2005), pp. 263–282.

– 'Gedalyahu Alon Fifty Years On' (Heb.), *Zion* 69 (2004), pp. 459–486.

– 'Urbanisation and City Territories in Roman Palestine' (Heb.), *The Jews in the Hellenistic-Roman World: Studies in Memory of Menahem Stern* (eds. I. M. Gafni, et al.; Jerusalem, 1996, Heb.), pp. 209–226. English translation, idem, *Between Rome and Babylon: Studies in Jewish Leadership and Society* (Tübingen, 2005), pp. 30–46.

– 'Das Verhältnis der Stadt Akko zum Land Israel und zu Galiläa,' idem, *Between Rome and Babylon: Studies in Jewish Leadership and Society* (Tübingen, 2005), pp. 83–92.

– 'Rabban Gamaliel of Yavneh and His Circuits of Eretz Israel,' idem, *Between Rome and Babylon: Studies in Jewish Leadership and Society* (Tübingen, 2005), pp. 145–155.

– 'Politics and Administration,' *Rabbinic Texts and the History of Late Roman Palestine* (eds. M. Goodman & P. Alexander; Proceedings of the British Academy 165; Oxford, 2010), pp. 377–388.

Oppenheimer, A., in collaboration with B. Isaac & M. Lecker, *Babylonia Judaica in the Talmudic Period* (Beihefte zum Tübinger Atlas des Vorderen Orients B/47; Wiesbaden, 1983).

Piccirillo, M., 'The Madaba Mosaic Map,' idem, *The Mosaics of Jordan* (Amman, 1993), pp. 81–95.

Piccirillo, M., & E. Alliata (eds.), *The Madaba Map Centenary 1897–1997: Travelling through the Byzantine Ummayad Period* (Jerusalem, 1999).

Raiskin, S., 'The Bundle Has Fallen Apart (נתפרדה החבילה): Which Bundle?' (Heb., with English summary), *Sidra* 23 (2008), pp. 133–135.

Robert, L., *Les gladiateurs dans l'Orient grec* (Limoges, 1940).

Rosenberger, M., *City Coins of Palestine,* vol. II (Jerusalem, 1975); vol. III (Jerusalem, 1977).

Rosental, E. S., 'Rav, the Son of Rabbi Ḥiyya's Brother, also the Son of His Sister? A Chapter in the History of the Text of the Bavli' (Heb.), *Henoch Yalon Jubilee Volume* (ed. S. Lieberman, et al.; Jerusalem, 1963, Heb.), pp. 281–337.

Rostovtzeff, M., 'Les inscriptions caravanières de Palmyre,' *Mélanges Gustave Glotz,* vol. II (Paris, 1932), pp. 792–811.

Roth-Gerson, L., *The Greek Inscriptions from the Synagogues in Eretz-Israel* (Jerusalem, 1987, Heb.).

Safrai, S., *'Siqariqon'* (Heb.), *Zion* 17 (1952), pp. 56–64 = idem, *In Times of Temple and Mishnah: Studies in Jewish History* (Jerusalem, 1994, Heb.), pp. 259–267.

– 'The Holy Assembly of Jerusalem' (Heb.), *Zion* 22 (1957), pp. 183–194 = idem, *In Times of Temple and Mishnah: Studies in Jewish History* (Jerusalem, 1994, Heb.), pp. 171–181.

– 'The Places Where They Sanctified the Months and Intercalated the Year in the Land of Israel after the Destruction of the Temple' (Heb.), *Tarbiz* 35 (1965), pp. 27–38 = idem, *In Times of Temple and Mishnah: Studies in Jewish History* (Jerusalem, 1994, Heb.), pp. 247–258.

- 'Teaching of Pietists in Mishnaic Literature,' *JJS* 16 (1965), pp. 15–33.
- 'The *Mitzvah* of the Sabbatical Year after the Destruction of the Second Temple' (Heb.), *Tarbiz* 35 (1966), pp. 26–46; 36 (1967), pp. 304–328 = idem, *In Times of Temple and Mishnah: Studies in Jewish History* (Jerusalem, 1994, Heb.), pp. 421–466.
- 'The Holy Congregation in Jerusalem,' *Scripta Hierosolymitana* 23 (1972), pp. 62–78.
- 'The *Nesi'ut* in the Second and Third Centuries and Its Chronological Problems' (Heb.), *Proceedings of the Sixth World Congress of Jewish Studies,* vol. II (ed. A. Shinan; Jerusalem, 1975), pp. 51–57 = idem, *In Times of Temple and Mishnah* (Jerusalem, 1994, Heb.), pp. 620–626.
- 'The Pious *(Ḥassidim)* and the Men of Deeds' (Heb.), *Zion* 50 (1985), pp. 133–154 = idem, *In Times of Temple and Mishnah: Studies in Jewish History* (Jerusalem, 1994, Heb.), pp. 518–539.
- 'The Attitude of the Aggadah to the Halakha', *Dor le-Dor: From the End of Biblical Times up to the Redaction of the Talmud; Studies in Honor of Joshua Efron* (eds. A. Kasher & A. Oppenheimer; Jerusalem, 1995, Heb.), pp. 215–234.
- Schäfer, P., *Geschichte der Juden in der Antike* (Stuttgart, 1983). French translation, *Histoire des juifs dans l'antiquité* (Paris, 1989); English translation, *The History of the Jews in Antiquity* (Luxemburg, 1995).
- Schlumberger, D., 'Les gentilices romains des Palmyréniens,' *Bulletin d'Études Orientales* 9 (1942–43), pp. 53–82.
- Schlüter, M., *Auf welche Weise wurde die Mishna geschrieben? Das Antwortschreiben des Rav Sherira Gaon; mit einem Faksimile der Handschrift Berlin Qu. 685 (Or. 160) und des Erstdrucks Konstantinopel 1566* (Tübingen, 1993).
- Schremer, A., *Male and Female He Created Them* (Jerusalem, 2003, Heb.).
- Schürer, E., *The History of the Jewish People in the Age of Jesus Christ* (revised and edited by G. Vermes et al.; 3 vols., Edinburgh, 1973–87).
- Schwabe, M., & B. Lifshitz, *Beth She'arim,* vol. II (Jerusalem, 1974).

Schwartz, J., 'The Tension between the Sages of Southern Judaea and the Sages of the Galilee in the Mishnah and Talmud Period (after the Bar-Kochba Revolt)' (Heb.), *Sinai* 93 (1983), pp. 102–109.

– *Jewish Settlement in Judaea after the Bar-Kochba War until the Arab Conquest* (Jerusalem, 1986, Heb.).

Schwartz, S., *Imperialism and Jewish Society 200 B.C.E. to 640 C.E.* (Princeton, 2001).

– 'Political, Social, and Economic Life in the Land of Israel, 66–c. 235,' *The Cambridge History of Judaism*, vol. 4: *The Late Roman-Rabbinic Period* (Cambridge, 2006), pp. 23–52.

Shahar, Y., 'Rabbi ʿAqiba and the Destruction of the Temple: The Establishment of the Fast Days' (Heb.), *Zion* 68 (2003), pp. 159–165.

Shapira, H., '"Nasiʾ" and "Dynasty": A Response' (Heb.), *Zion* 70 (2005), pp. 105–107.

Shoshan, A., 'Maḥalato shel Rabbi Yehudah haNasiʾ,' *Korot* 7 (1978), pp. 521–524.

Sivertsev, A., *Private Households and Public Politics in 3rd–5th Century Jewish Palestine* (Tübingen, 2002).

Smallwood, M., *The Jews under Roman Rule from Pompey to Diocletian* (Leiden, 1981^2).

Sokoloff, M., *A Dictionary of Jewish Palestinian Aramaic of the Byzantine Period* (Ramat Gan, 1990).

– *A Dictionary of Jewish Babylonian Aramaic of the Talmudic and Geonic Periods* (Ramat Gan, 2002).

Sperber, D., 'Kāra-bān' (Heb.), *LEŠONENU* 34 (1970), pp. 61–65 = idem, *Greek and Latin in the Mishna, Talmud and Midrashic Literature* (Jerusalem, 1982), pp. xl–xliv.

Spijkerman, A., 'The Coins of Eleutheropolis Iudaeae,' *Liber Annuus: Studium Biblicum Franciscanum* 22 (1972), pp. 369–374.

Squarciapino, M. F., 'The Synagogue at Ostia,' *Archaeology* 16 (1963), pp. 194–203.

Stein, A., *Studies in Greek and Latin Coin Inscriptions on the Palestinian Coinage* (Ph.D. Thesis, Tel Aviv University, 1990).

Stepansky, Y., 'Archaeological Discoveries in Mughar' (Heb.), *Cathedra* 97 (2000), pp. 169–171.

Stern, E. (ed.), *The New Encyclopedia of Archaeological Excavations in the Holy Land* (5 vols.; Jerusalem, 1993–2008).

Stern, M., *Greek and Latin Authors on Jews and Judaism,* vol. II (Jerusalem, 1980).

Stern, S., *Calendar and Community: A History of the Jewish Calendar, Second Century BCE–Tenth Century CE* (Oxford, 2001).

– 'Rabbi and the Origins of the Patriarchate,' *JJS* 54 (2003), pp. 193–215.

Strobel, K., 'Jüdisches Patriarchat, Rabbinentum und Priesterdynastie von Emesa: Historische Phänomene innerhalb des Imperium Romanum der Kaiserzeit,' *Ktema* 14 (1989), pp. 39–77.

– 'Aspekte des politischen und sozialen Scheinbildes der rabbinischen Tradition: Das spätere 2. und das 3. Jh. n. Chr. mit einem Anhang zur Münzprägung von Diocaesarea-Sepphoris in severischer Zeit,' *Klio* 72 (1990), pp. 478–497; Postscriptum, pp. 640–641.

Sussmann, Y., 'An Halakhic Inscription from the Bet She'an Valley' (Heb.), *Tarbiz* 43 (1974), pp. 88–158.

– 'Baraita di-Tehumei Eretz Yisrael,' *Tarbiz* 45 (1976), pp. 213–257.

– 'Torah shebeʿal peh, peshutah kemashmʿah – koḥo shel qotzo shel yod,' *Mekhqarei Talmud,* vol. III,1 (eds. idem, et al.; Jerusalem, 2005), pp. 209–384.

Syme, R., *Ammianus and the Historia Augusta* (Oxford, 1968).

Talgam, R., & Z. Weiss, *The Mosaics of the House of Dionysos at Sepphoris* (Jerusalem, 2004).

Tepper, Yigal & Yotam, *Beth Sheʿarim: The Village and Nearby Burials* (Yagur, 2004, Heb.).

Tsafrir, Y., et al., *Tabula Imperii Romani* (Jerusalem, 1994).

Tur-Sinai, N. H., *The Language and the Book,* vol. III (Jerusalem, 1955, Heb.).

Urbach, E. E., *The Sages: Their Concepts and Beliefs* (Jerusalem, 1975).

– 'Class-status and Leadership in the World of the Palestinian Sages,' *Proceedings of the Israel Academy of Sciences and Humanities* 2,4 (1966), pp. 1–37.

van der Vliet, N., 'Monnaies inédites ou très rares du médaillier de Sainte Anne de Jérusalem,' *Revue biblique* 57 (1950), pp. 116–117.

Veltri, G., 'Magic, Sex and Politics: The Media Power of Theatre Amusements in the Mirror of Rabbinic Literature,' *"The Words of a Wise Man's Mouth are Gracious" (Qoh 10,12): Festschrift for Günter Stemberger on the Occasion of His 65th Birthday* (ed. M. Perani; Berlin & New York, 2005), pp. 243–256.

Wallach, L., 'The Colloquy of Marcus Aurelius with the Patriarch Judah I,' *JQR* 31 (1940–41), pp. 259–286.

Weingarten, S., 'Wild Foods in the Talmud: The Influence of Religious Restrictions on Consumption,' *Wild Food: Proceedings of the Oxford Symposium on Food and Cookery 2004* (ed. R. Hosking; Totnes, 2006), pp. 323–333.

Weiss, Z., 'Between Paganism and Judaism: Toward an Identification of the "Dionysiac Building": Residents at Roman Sepphoris' (Heb.), *Cathedra* 99 (2001), pp. 7–26.

– 'Burial Practices in Beth She'arim and the Question of Dating the Patriarchal Necropolis,' *'Follow the Wise': Studies in Jewish History and Culture in Honor of Lee I. Levine* (eds. Z. Weiss, et al.; Winona Lake, IN, 2010), pp. 207–231.

Wroth, W., *Catalogue of the Greek Coins of Galatia, Cappadocia, and Syria* (A Catalogue of the Greek Coins in the British Museum 20; London, 1899).

Yahalom, Y., *Poetry and Society in Jewish Galilee of Late Antiquity* (Tel Aviv, 1999, Heb.).

Zucker, H., *Studien zur jüdischen Selbstverwaltung im Altertum*) Berlin, 1936).

Index of Sources

Biblical References

General Index